1 e4 c5 2 ♘c3 ♘c6

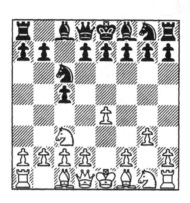

The Closed Sicilian

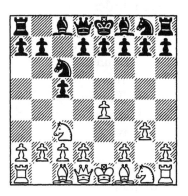

CHESS PRESS OPENING GUIDES

Other titles in this series include:

1 901259 05 6	Caro-Kann Advance	Byron Jacobs
1 901259 03 X	Dutch Leningrad	Neil McDonald
1 901259 10 2	French Advance	Tony Kosten
1 901259 01 3	Sicilian Taimanov	James Plaskett
1 901259 02 1	Scandinavian	John Emms
1 901259 09 9	Semi-Slav	Matthew Sadler
1 901259 00 5	Slav	Matthew Sadler
1 901259 04 8	Spanish Exchange	Andrew Kinsman
1 901259 08 0	Trompowsky	Joe Gallagher

Chess Press Opening Guides

The Closed Sicilian

Daniel King

The Chess Press, Brighton

First published in 1997 by Chess Press, a division of First Rank Publishing

British Library Cataloguing-in-Publication Data
A catalogue record for this book is available from the British Library.

ISBN 1 901259 06 4

Distributed in North America by The Globe Pequot Press, P.O Box 480, 246 Goose Lane, Guilford, CT 06437-0480.

All other sales enquiries should be directed to Gloucester Publishers plc, Northburgh House, 10 Northburgh Street, London, EC1V 0AT
tel: 020 7253 7887 fax: 020 7490 3708
email: info@everymanchess.com
website: www.everymanchess.com

Everyman is the registered trade mark of Random House Inc. and is used in this work under license from Random House Inc.

Cover design by Ray Shell Design.
Production by Navigator Guides.

Printed by Lightning Source

CONTENTS

1 e4 c5 2 ♘c3 ♘c6 3 g3

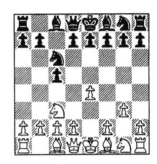

BIBLIOGRAPHY

Books

Encyclopaedia of Chess Openings vol.B, Sahovski Informator 1984
Beating the Anti-Sicilians, Gallagher (Batsford, 1994)
Winning with the Closed Sicilian, Lane (Batsford, 1992)

Periodicals

Informator
ChessBase MegaBase CD-ROM
New In Chess Yearbook
British Chess Magazine
Chess Monthly

INTRODUCTION

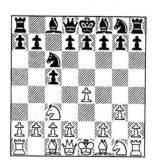

Having spent alarmingly large chunks of my life studying the white side of the Open Sicilian, I find myself asking, why did I bother? Was I really so vain as to think I could refute the Dragon, or the Najdorf, or that funny line with ...e7-e6 that I can never remember the name of? (Is it a Kan, or a Taimanov, and should I avoid a transposition to a Scheveningen?) There are certain players who long ago took the attitude that life is too short for all that business, and I should have joined their ranks long before now. Vassily Smyslov, Boris Spassky, Vlastimil Hort and Oleg Romanishin are just a few of the great players who have mastered the Closed Sicilian. They are natural players who have developed a 'feel' for the positions that arise rather than staking their reputations on hours and hours of home preparation.

The great advantage of the 'Closed' is that it is possible to put your own stamp on the opening – as all the above players have done. There isn't one approved method, and it's not going to be refuted overnight. What is important is an understanding of the ideas. Let's run through the first few moves and look at the reasoning behind them:

1 e4 c5 2 ♘c3

This move is important. Before White fianchettoes his king's bishop, it's crucial that ...d7-d5 is prevented, otherwise Black can cut across his plans. For instance, 2 g3 would allow 2...d5, which is still fine for White, as we shall see in Chapter 9, but it prevents the Closed Sicilian formation that we are heading for.

2...♘c6

Systems with ...e7-e6 followed by ...d7-d5 on the next move are discussed in Chapter 8.

3 g3 g6 4 ♗g2 ♗g7 5 d3

I'm taking this position as my fundamental starting point. White fianchettoes his bishop which increases the influence over d5, and in general bolsters White's centre. When White decides to attack, the reason he can get away with it is that his pawn centre, although not dominant, is a tough one to crack. It is difficult for Black to get a counterpunch through the pawn wall c2-d3-e4. As we shall see, from this point White can play the opening in many different ways. After ...

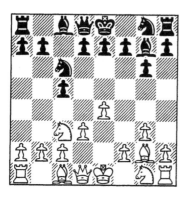

5...d6

... the most frequently seen move is still ...

6 f4

... aiming for a kingside attack. A few years back Black generally played ...

6...♘f6

However, there is a disadvantage to this natural developing move – it encourages White to play the natural f4-f5 ...

White's f4-f5

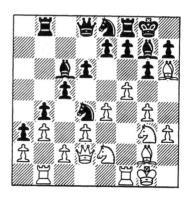

Moving the pawn from f4 to f5 opens the diagonal of the bishop to h6 as well as the f-file for the rook on f1. White might follow up by pushing his h-pawn a couple of squares to soften up Black's king position, or perhaps by doubling rooks on the f-file, and so on. The pawn on e4, supported by a healthy pawn chain and the bishop on g2, ensures that there is a strong barrier between Black's pieces and White's king. In view of the impressive power of White's attack with f4-f5, Black players started to prefer to adopt a different defensive formation ...

Black's ...f7-f5

After the standard Closed Sicilian opening sequence 1 e4 c5 2 ♘c3 ♘c6 3 g3 g6 4 ♗g2 ♗g7 5 d3 d6 6 f4, they usually played ...

6...e6!

see following diagram

... so that after ...

7 ♘f3 ♘ge7 8 0-0 0-0 9 g4

... (already threatening to push and cramp Black)

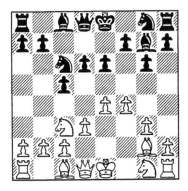

Black can immediately blockade with ...

9...f5!

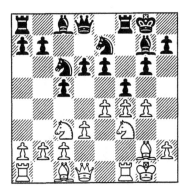

When White captures with g4xf5 Black generally recaptures with ...e6xf5, maintaining a strong king position (see Game 34). Here the fixed situation of White's pawn on f4 makes an enormous difference to the position. It means that the bishop on c1 is trapped in and unable to take part in the attack; the f-file is closed; and White's pawn centre has been stopped in its tracks. If White captures on f5 for a second time, Black recaptures with a piece, and the blockade continues. It isn't clear how White can develop his attack from here.

White's e4-e5 sacrifice

In view of the strength of Black's ...f7-f5 blockade, White was forced to find different ways to prepare the attack. The most notable in recent years has been the introduction of a pseudo-pawn sacrifice on e5 with (1 e4 c5 2 ♘c3 ♘c6 3 g3 g6 4 ♗g2 ♗g7 5 d3 d6 6 f4 e6 7 ♘f3 ♘ge7 8 0-0 0-0)

9 ♗e3 ♘d4 10 e5!?

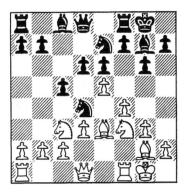

... blowing open the diagonals for White's bishops and giving the knight a square on e4. As this variation has been at the forefront of Closed Sicilian theory over the past few years, I have examined it in some detail in Chapter 1. Chapters 2 and 3 also deal with the main line after 8 0-0 0-0, examining various alternatives to the pawn sacrifice line for both White and Black are also concerned with 6 f4. Chapter 4 is concerned with the dynamic 6 f4 e5!?, while in Chapters 5-7 I examine more subtle strategies for White, whereby he usually delays playing his f-pawn forward for some time, so that the c1-h6 diagonal remains open. If White can possibly exchange the dark-squared bishops, then he almost certainly should do so ...

Exchanging dark-squared bishops

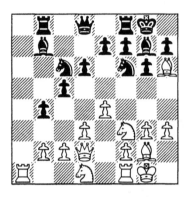

Even if it appears that there is little chance of an immediate attack, it is remarkable how often Black's king does eventually suffer. The exchange of bishops also weakens Black's hold over the centre and queenside.

Pushing the b-pawn

This last position brings me on to one of Black's main sources of counterplay: advancing the b-pawn.

Here we have a typical Closed Sicilian position. The b-pawn has forced the knight from c3, opening up the long diagonal for the king's bishop. At the moment White's rook is tied to defending the pawn – hardly an effi-cient use of fire-power – but if the white pawn moves to b3, then Black has complete control over the diagonal: the rook can penetrate down the a-file, and the knight can safely settle on d4. However, there can be drawbacks to the advance of the b-pawn. Black must take care that he isn't upset by e4-e5 from White, undermining the pawn on c5 (see Game 77).

Positional trick

White has more positive ways of meeting the advance of the b-pawn than simply moving the knight out of the way. Here's a nice positional trick:

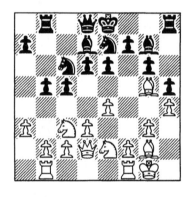

White has already played a2-a3 and ♖b1 in readiness for the oncoming black b-pawn. Black does not want to advance immediately, since after 11...b4 12 axb4 cxb4 13 ♘a4 he loses central control due to the side-step of his c-pawn. But if Black plays 11...a5, White responds with 12 a4!, to meet 12...b4 with 13 ♘b5 and 12...bxa4 with 13 ♘xa4, when Black's pawn front has been broken.

White's b2-b4

Alternatively, it is possible to block

the black b-pawn with b2-b4.

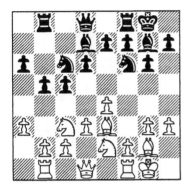

Although generally this move is strategically desirable – a wing pawn knocks out a centre pawn – White has to be careful that the horse on c3 isn't nobbled by a tactic on the long diagonal or c-file.

Summary

So there we have some of the main strategic ideas in the Closed Sicilian. When we get stuck into the different chapters, I shall be examining these strategies in greater detail. Patterns quickly emerge. Even if you are only interested in one particular line, it's good to play through as many games as possible, if you have time, as the same ideas can often be transferred from one kind of position to another.

In this book I have chosen to concentrate on new ideas for both sides, rather than repeating numerous old and well-known games.

And finally, I have always found one of the best ways to learn an opening is to study the games of a particular expert to see how he interprets the system. The obvious candidate to follow in the Closed Sicilian is Boris Spassky. Throughout his career he has contributed so many new ideas; even when he is at his most peaceful, there is a thoughtfulness about his play which is revealing. For this book I have selected as many of his games as possible, even when not directly relevant from a theoretical point of view.

Enjoy playing the Closed Sicilian, and don't forget: there is much more to this opening than just pushing the f-pawn down the board!

CHAPTER ONE

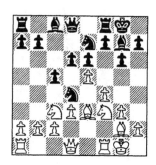

Main Line: 9 ♗e3 ♘d4
10 e5 Pawn Sacrifice

1 e4 c5 2 ♘c3 ♘c6 3 g3 g6 4 ♗g2 ♗g7 5 d3 d6 6 f4 e6 7 ♘f3 ♘ge7 8 0-0 0-0 9 ♗e3 ♘d4 10 e5

The most exciting development in the Closed Sicilian in recent years has been the introduction of the e4-e5 pawn sacrifice – and that's why I'm devoting a large chunk of space to this chapter. Players such as Spassky and Balashov enjoyed considerable success with this pseudo-sacrifice, which immediately plunges the game into great complications. From White's point of view, the appeal of the variation is that there are many ways for Black to go wrong: just by playing 'normal' moves he can find himself in an inferior position. Take a look at this game, in which Black fails to appreciate the dangers and gets blown off the board.

> ### Game 1
> ### A.Martin-Britton
> *Barnsdale Young Masters 1989*

1 e4 c5 2 ♘c3 d6 3 f4 g6 4 ♘f3 ♗g7 5 g3 ♘c6 6 ♗g2 e6 7 0-0 ♘ge7 8 d3 0-0 9 ♗e3 ♘d4 10 e5!?

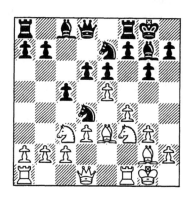

This is the move that shocked Black players at the end of the eighties. The pawn push has several objectives in mind:

a) The diagonals of the bishops are opened up across the board.

b) The support for Black's pawn on c5 is undermined.

c) White's knight can hop into the fantastic square on e4.

d) The f-file is often opened, giving White attacking chances on the kingside.

Heard enough? If you are not convinced of the potential dangers, play on:

10...♘ef5

Black's various other possibilities here are discussed in Games 9-18.

11 ♗f2 ♘xf3+

The most critical move. 11...♖b8 is considered in Game 7 and 11...d5 in Game 8.

12 ♕xf3 ♘d4

12...♗d7 is also playable – see Game 6.

13 ♕d1 ♖b8?

This move looks natural enough but, as we shall see, it is far too slow. Having got this far, Black should capture twice on e5 – see Games 2-4, since 13...dxe5 14 fxe5 ♖b8 15 ♘e4 (Game 5) and 13...d5 14 ♘a4 b6 15 b4 (Game 8, by transposition) are also promising for White.

14 ♘e4!

A typical move for this variation: the knight looks at the sensitive squares on c5, d6, and f6.

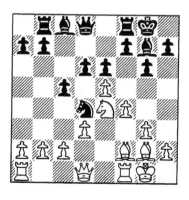

14...dxe5 15 c3 ♘f5 16 ♗xc5

The rook on f8 and the pawn on a7 are both under attack: White has a winning position. (The best practical course for Black might have been to give up the exchange with 16...exf4.)

16...♖e8 17 fxe5 b6

After 17...♗xe5 18 ♗xa7 ♖a8 19 ♗f2 White is a pawn up for nothing.

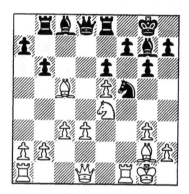

18 ♗d6 ♖b7 19 ♕e2 ♖d7 20 d4 ♗b7 21 ♗a3 ♕c8 22 g4 ♗a6 23 ♕f2 ♗xf1 24 ♖xf1 ♘e7 1-0

... and Black resigned before White could decide whether to play ♘d6 or ♕xf7+ first.

Black puts up a better defence in the next game, but White's strategy still works perfectly.

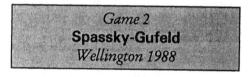

1 e4 c5 2 ♘c3 ♘c6 3 g3 g6 4 ♗g2 ♗g7 5 d3 d6 6 f4 e6 7 ♘f3 ♘ge7 8 0-0 0-0 9 ♗e3 ♘d4 10 ♗f2

The move order that Spassky employs here to get to the sacrifice is slightly unusual, and has no great advantage over the more commonly played 10 e5. Indeed, it just gives Black more options. For instance, here Black could play 10...e5, exploiting White's slow manoeuvres with the bishop. (See Chapter 2 if you would like to look at the tamer 10 ♗f2 in more detail.) Anyway, in this game we quickly transpose to a familiar position from the sacrifice.

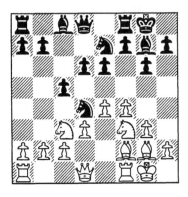

10...♘xf3+ 11 ♗xf3 ♘c6 12 ♗g2 ♘d4 13 e5!? dxe5

Compare this with the last game, where Black played the miserable 13...♖b8 at this point.

14 fxe5 ♗xe5!

In this particular position, the capture is by far the best move. For a time, this move was actually the most popular way for Black to counter the whole 10 e5 variation. The dubious 14...♖b8 is considered in Game 5.

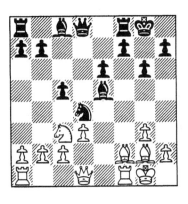

15 ♘e4

With this move White forces his opponent to return the pawn. Although Black's pieces look active, in fact, they must retreat, though that isn't his main problem. The real question is, how can Black develop the bishop on c8 when White's bishop on g2 cuts across the whole board?

15...f5

If Black doesn't force the knight to capture on c5, then after c2-c3 White will capture on c5 with the *bishop* which, as we saw in the first game, is actually far more dangerous. For example, 15...♕c7 16 c3 ♘c6 17 ♗xc5 ♖d8 18 d4 (18 ♗e3!?) 18...b6 19 ♗a3 ♗b7 20 ♕f3 puts Black on the defensive.

However, 15...c4?! is a crafty idea, trying to disrupt White's pawn structure, but it didn't pay off in Liemann-Wolf, Germany 1991, since 16 c3! ♘c6 (16...♘f5 is probably better, when J.L.Roos-Rotstein, French Team Championship 1996, continued 17 ♗c5 ♖e8 18 d4 ♗g7 with compensation for the pawn, but probably no more; 17 dxc4 would have been a better way to exploit the stray position of Black's knight on the kingside) 17 ♗c5 is strong, with the idea of 17...♖e8 18 d4 ♗g7 19 ♘d6.

16 ♘xc5 ♕d6

16...♕c7 is the major alternative – see Balashov-Karpman (Game 4). In the game Upmark-Borge, Stockholm 1996, Black attempted to randomise the situation with 16...f4, but this is rather dangerous as it neglects his development and could thus easily rebound.

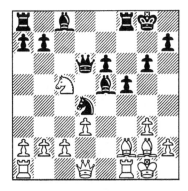

17 b4

The best move. White has to be a little careful here. For instance, 17 ♘a4 would have been strongly met by 17...f4, breaking through to White's king, while 17 ♘b3?! was refuted by 17...♘xb3 18 axb3 ♗xb2 19 ♖a5 ♗c3 20 ♖a4 b5 21 ♖xa7 ♖xa7 22 ♗xa7 e5 23 ♕f3 ♗e6 24 ♔h1 b4 with a clear advantage for Black in Miles-Marin, Manila 1990. Finally, 17 ♘xb7? would have been a dreadful mistake, handing over the initiative to Black after 17...♗xb7 18 ♗xb7 ♖ab8 19 ♗g2 ♖xb2. Here Black has solved his major problem, how to develop the bishop on c8, and his rook has thrown itself into the attack; far from being driven back, the knight on d4 looks like a fixture on d4, unless White wishes to exchange it, but in that case he would definitely stand worse.

17...♖b8?!

Once again, this seemingly natural move is a mistake. 17...♘c6 is stronger, as we shall see in Game 3, where move order differences mean that the same position is reached after 18 moves instead of 17!

18 c3 ♘b5 19 d4 ♗f6

19...♘xc3? loses material to 20 dxe5 ♕xd1 21 ♖axd1 ♘xd1 22 ♖xd1.

20 ♕b3

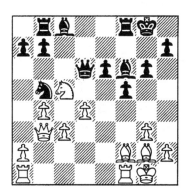

The picture becomes a little clearer. By knocking out the pawn on c5, White has gained greater control of the centre.

20...b6 21 ♘d3 ♗b7

Exchanging the bishops looks natural – Black hopes that White's kingside will be weakened – but take a look at the backward pawn on e6: target.

22 ♗xb7 ♖xb7 23 a4 ♘c7 24 ♖fe1 ♘d5 25 c4 ♘e7

If 25...♘c7 then 26 ♘e5 followed by b4-b5 and ♘c6, with a complete stranglehold over Black's position.

26 ♘f4

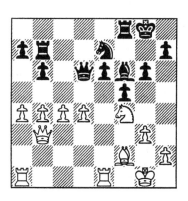

A clever piece of calculation from Spassky.

26...♘c6

26...♗xd4? 27 ♘xe6! ♗xf2+ 28 ♔xf2 ♖f6 (or 28...♖e8 29 ♖ad1 ♕b8 30 c5 and Black's king is caught in the crossfire) 29 ♖ad1 ♕c6 30 ♖d8+ ♔f7 31 ♖f8 mate.

27 ♖xe6 ♕xb4 28 ♕d3 ♘e7 29 ♗e1 ♕b2 30 ♗c3 ♕b3

Spassky wouldn't allow Black's queen into his position unless he had something lined up on the kingside. Although 15...f5 was necessary, this game is a good illustration of the potential drawbacks of this move: it opens up Black's king position.

31 ♖xf6! ♖xf6 32 d5 ♔f7

Or 32...♖f8 33 ♕d4 with the familiar battery.

33 ♘e6

As usual, Spassky plays the attack incisively. There are two principal threats: ♘d8+ and ♘g5+.

33...♖xe6 34 dxe6+ ♔xe6

The king doesn't last long here.

35 ♖e1+ ♔f7 36 ♕d4 ♕xa4 37 ♕g7+ ♔e8 38 ♗f6 ♔d8 39 ♕f8+ ♕e8 40 ♖d1+ ♖d7 41 ♗xe7+ c7 42 ♕xe8 1-0

In the next game Spassky's opponent was far better prepared. Hjartarson provides us with one of the most reliable methods of dealing with the 10 e5 pawn 'sacrifice'.

1 e4 c5 2 ♘c3 ♘c6 3 g3 g6 4 ♗g2

♗g7 5 d3 d6 6 f4 e6 7 ♘f3 ♘ge7 8 0-0 0-0 9 ♗e3 ♘d4 10 ♗f2

Once again, Spassky uses this quiet move as a means of entering the pawn sacrifice. Fair enough, but it is important to remember that Black is not obliged to go into the pawn sacrifice lines. At this point he has several reasonable alternatives – see Chapter 2.

10...♘ec6 11 ♘xd4 ♘xd4 12 e5 dxe5 13 fxe5 ♗xe5 14 ♘e4 f5 15 ♘xc5 ♕d6 16 b4 ♘c6!

This is better than Gufeld's 16...♖b8 (see the previous game). Other moves are also not as strong. For example, 16...♗g7 17 a4 (17 c3 ♘b5) 17...e5 18 c3 ♘c6 19 a5 gives White a strong queenside initiative, while the greedy 16...♘b5?!, attempting to take the rook in the corner, has potentially fatal consequences after 17 a4! and:

a) 17...♘c3 18 ♕d2 ♘e4 19 ♘xe4 fxe4 20 ♗xe4 (20 d4 ♖xf2) 20...♗xa1 21 ♖xa1 with tremendous compensation for the exchange.

b) 17...♗xa1 18 ♕xa1 ♘c7 19 ♘xb7 ♗xb7 20 ♗xb7 ♕xb4 21 ♗xa8 ♖xa8 22 ♕e5 threatening ♗d4. In both cases White develops tremendous pressure on the long diagonal.

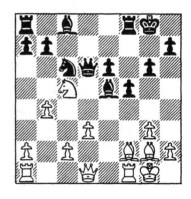

17 ♖b1 ♗d4!

Hjartarson finds a series of accurate moves to hold the balance, but there are still plenty of pitfalls along the way. The obvious moves aren't as effective. For instance:

a) 17...b6?! 18 ♘b3 ♗b7 19 d4 and White controls the centre.

b) 17...♖b8 18 ♕e1 (not 18 b5 ♘d4 19 ♘a4 f4!) 18...♗g7 19 ♘b3 b6 20 c4 with the initiative in Radulovski-Georgiev, Stara Zagora 1991.

18 ♕d2 ♗xf2+

This is a reliable move, but it is also possible to play 18...a5!?, bringing the rook on a8 into play: 19 ♗xc6 (this gives White some security on the queenside, but giving up the bishop can easily rebound as the kingside is weakened; note that 19 a3 axb4 20 axb4 ♖a2 is also irritating for White) 19...♗xf2+ (19...bxc6 20 c3 ♗xf2+ 21 ♕xf2 axb4 22 cxb4 e5 is balanced) 20 ♕xf2 bxc6 and ...e6-e5 when Black is fine. However, 18...♖b8 didn't fare so well in Djurhuus-Mednis, Stavanger 1989: 19 ♗xd4 ♘xd4 20 c3 ♘b5 21 d4 b6 22 ♘d3 ♗b7 23 ♗xb7 ♖xb7 24 a4 ♘c7 25 a5 b5 26 ♘c5 ♖bb8 27 ♖be1 with a big clamp.

19 ♕xf2 ♖b8 20 a3 b6 21 ♘b3 ♗b7

21...e5 has been suggested instead, although Black's centre appears to be a little loose after 22 ♖be1.

22 d4

---

see following diagram

22...♘d8!

This is a careful manoeuvre. Black brings the knight over to the kingside, where it covers some crucial squares. After 22...e5?! 23 d5 ♘e7 24 c4 the

white pawns are rolling.

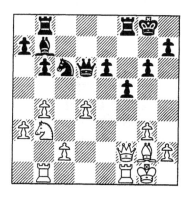

23 c4 ♘f7 24 ♗xb7 ♖xb7 25 ♕e3 e5

This move is essential if Black is to free his position. Compare with Djurhuus-Mednis above, or Spassky-Gufeld for that matter.

26 dxe5 ½-½

Spassky plays it safe and simplifies, accompanying his move with a draw offer. His judgement proves to be correct, as there isn't much in the position after 26...♕xe5 27 ♕xe5 ♘xe5. If instead 26 d5 then 26...b5 breaks up the queenside pawns. Hjartarson's treatment of the opening was reliable, though he had to play accurately to equalise.

In the next game we consider the alternative 16...♕c7.

1 e4 c5 2 ♘c3 ♘c6 3 g3 g6 4 ♗g2 ♗g7 5 d3 d6 6 f4 e6 7 ♘f3 ♘ge7 8 0-0 0-0 9 ♗e3 ♘d4 10 e5 ♘ef5 11 ♗f2 ♘xf3+ 12 ♕xf3 ♘d4 13 ♕d1 dxe5 14 fxe5 ♗xe5 15 ♘e4 f5 16 ♘xc5

This position ought to be familiar by now! Now something different:

16...♕c7

Perhaps not quite as good as 16...♕d6 but playable, as we shall see.

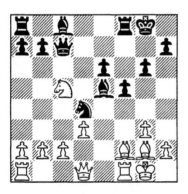

17 b4 ♗g7

This time 17...♘c6?! is somewhat lame: 18 d4 ♗g7 19 c3 a5 20 b5 ♘e7 21 ♕b3 and White dominated in Lyrberg-Nykopp, Helsinki 1992, while 17...♘b5?! is just greedy after 18 a4 ♗xa1 19 ♕xa1 ♘d6 20 ♖e1 with a fierce attack on the long diagonal in Knutgen-Lendwai, Oberwart 1996. However, 17...f4!? is an interesting attempt to unsettle White on the kingside before he establishes control in the centre and on the queenside. For example,

a) 18 c3 and now:

a1) 18...f3 19 ♗xd4 ♗xd4+ 20 cxd4 fxg2 21 ♖xf8+ ♔xf8 22 ♕f3+ ♕f7 23 ♕xg2 and White is on top.

a2) 18...♘b5 19 d4 fxg3 20 hxg3 ♗g7 21 ♕d3 and White has established his familiar central control.

a3) 18...♘f5!? 19 g4 f3 20 ♗xf3 (or 20 ♕xf3 ♘h4) 20...♗xh2+ 21 ♔g2 ♘g7 22 ♕e2 ♖b8 with an unclear position.

b) 18 gxf4?! rather plays into Black's hands, although even this was unclear in the following game: 18...♖xf4 19 c3 ♘f5 20 d4 ♖xf2 21 ♖xf2 ♗xh2+ 22 ♔h1 ♗g3 23 ♖f3 ♕e7 24 ♕d3 ♕h4+ 25 ♔g1 ♗h2+ 26 ♔f1 ♘g3+ 27 ♔e1 b6 28 ♖xg3 ♗xg3+ 29 ♔e2 and the complications weren't over yet in Salaun-Pedersen, Cannes 1995.

...f5-f4 is always worth looking out for in these lines. At a stroke Black has the potential to damage White's kingside. We will see more of this motif later (Game 10, for instance).

18 c3 ♘b5 19 ♕b3!

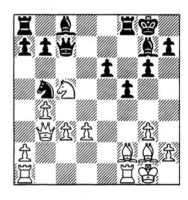

Instead, 19 d4 gives Black fairly easy equality: 19...♘xc3 20 ♕e1 ♘e4 21

♘xe4 fxe4 22 ♕xe4 ♕d6 23 ♗e3 ♗d7!
(preferring to give up a pawn tempo-
rarily to complete his development
rather than take a pawn with vague
consequences) 24 ♕xb7 ♗xd4 25
♗xd4 ♕xd4+ 26 ♔h1 ♖ab8 with equal
chances in Bastian-Kavalek, German
Bundesliga 1986.
**19...♘xc3 20 ♖ae1 ♕f7 21 ♘xe6
♗xe6 22 ♖xe6**
White has a slight advantage due to
the powerful bishops raking across the
queenside, but Black is aware of the
danger and seeks to liquidate as many
pawns as possible.
**22...a5! 23 bxa5 ♖xa5 24 ♖e7 ♕xb3
25 axb3 ♖f7 26 ♖fe1 ♖b5 27 ♖e8+
♖f8 28 ♖8e7 ♖f7 29 e8+ ♖f8 30
♖8e7 ½-½**
With accurate play Black was able
to maintain the balance, but White
was always pressing.

Black's play in the next game is
provacative, to say the least.

**1 e4 c5 2 ♘c3 ♘c6 3 g3 g6 4 ♗g2
♗g7 5 d3 d6 6 f4 e6 7 ♘f3 ♘ge7 8
0-0 0-0 9 ♗e3 ♘d4 10 e5 ♘ef5 11
♗f2 ♘xf3+ 12 ♕xf3 ♘d4 13 ♕d1
dxe5 14 fxe5 ♖b8?!**
It is very risky to leave the white
pawn on e5. The more standard
14...♗xe5 was considered in Games 1–
4.

---
see following diagram
---

15 ♘e4! b6 16 ♘f6+! ♔h8

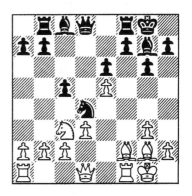

Or 16...♗xf6 17 exf6 and now:
a) 17...♕xf6 18 c3 ♘f5 19 g4 ♘d6 20
♗xc5 (or 20 ♗d4!? ♕g5 21 ♗f6 with
attacking chances for the pawn)
20...♕e7 21 ♗e3 and White can look
forward to an attack on the dark
squares.
b) 17...h5 18 g4 with a strong kingside attack.
**17 c3 ♘f5 18 g4 ♘e7 19 ♕f3 ♘d5
20 g5**

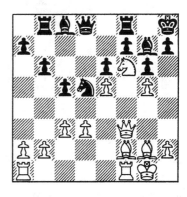

White has a ferocious attack but,
somehow, he doesn't quite manage to
clinch victory.
**20...♗xf6 21 gxf6 ♗b7 22 ♕g3 ♘c7
23 ♗xb7 ♖xb7 24 ♖ae1 ♕d5 25
♕g5 ♕xd3 26 ♖e3 ♕f5 27 ♕h6 ♖g8
28 ♖h3 g5 29 ♗xc5 ♕g6 30 ♗f8**

♕xh6 31 ♗xh6 ♘d5 32 ♖g3 ♖g6 33 ♗xg5 b5 34 ♖d1 h6 35 ♗c1 ♔h7 36 ♔f2 ♖c7 37 ♖dg1 b4 ½-½

In the final position White has thrown away the greater part of his advantage.

The next game shows an interesting alternative approach for Black on move 12.

1 e4 c5 2 ♘c3 ♘c6 3 g3 g6 4 ♗g2 ♗g7 5 d3 e6 6 f4 ♘ge7 7 ♘f3 0-0 8 0-0 d6 9 ♗e3 ♘d4 10 e5 ♘ef5 11 ♗f2 ♘xf3+ 12 ♕xf3 ♗d7

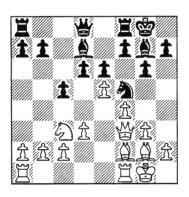

This has a similar motivation to 10...♗d7 (Games 16 and 17) – solving the problem of this light-squared bishop, and enjoyed some popularity after this convincing Black victory in 1990. White has a choice in this position: he can lead the game into well-known channels or plunge into complications.

13 ♕xb7

Kindermann takes the plunge, but

there is nothing wrong with 13 ♘e4!?, which should transpose to Game 16 after 13...♗c6! However, 13 exd6?! ♗c6 14 ♘e4 ♘xd6 15 ♗xc5 ♘xe4 16 dxe4 ♗d4+ is better for Black.

13...♖b8 14 ♕xa7 ♖xb2 15 ♖ac1

15 ♘e4!? has been suggested, but it doesn't appeal to me. After 15...♖xc2 16 g4 ♘d4 17 ♗xd4 cxd4 18 ♘xd6 g5! (undermining the pawn on e5) a messy position is reached, but personally that rook on the seventh rank would terrify me.

15...dxe5

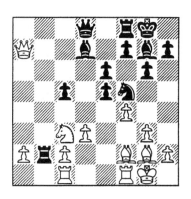

16 fxe5

If we are looking for improvements, then this might be the place. After 16 ♕a3 (I like the idea of expelling the rook before it can do any damage on the seventh) 16...♖b8 (16...♕b8 17 ♖b1 hands the initiative over to White) 17 ♗xc5 exf4 18 ♖xf4 the position is quite unclear. White is a pawn ahead, but his forces are rather scattered compared to Black's very compact position (Novicky-Zezulkin, USSR 1991).

16...♗xe5 17 ♘e4

After 17 ♕xc5 ♗d6 18 ♕c4 ♖b4 Black's active pieces promise good compensation for the pawn.

17...♗c6 18 ♕xc5 ♗xe4 19 dxe4?!

19 ♗xe4 ♗d4 20 ♗xd4 ♘xd4 is unclear according to Spasov, but I still prefer Black: his pieces are active, his king is safe and White's army is scattered – very much as in the remainder of the game.

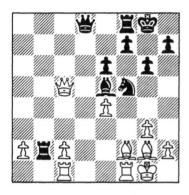

19...♗d4 20 ♕a3 ♘h6 21 ♗f3 ♕b6 22 ♗xd4 ♕xd4+ 23 ♔h1 ♖c8 24 ♖fd1 ♕e5 25 ♕a4 ♕c3 26 ♖f1 ♕d2 27 ♖fd1 ♕e3 28 ♖f1 ♕d2 29 ♖fd1 ♕c3 30 ♖f1 ♔g7 31 ♕a7 ♖c7 32 ♕a4 ♘g8 33 ♗g2 ♘f6 34 ♗f3 ♘d7 35 ♗g2 ♘e5 36 ♖f2 ♘d3 37 ♖f3 ♕d2 38 ♖cf1 ♘e5 39 ♖3f2 ♕c3 40 ♖d1 h5 41 ♖fd2 ♘g4 42 ♖e2 ♖cb7 0-1

There is no sensible defence to ...♖b1.

It is perhaps just a matter of taste, but I would prefer not to go on such a wild goose chase with my queen. Too often in these positions the queen loses connection with the rest of her army. As I mentioned above, White has a satisfactory alternative in 13 ♘e4, which should transpose to Lane-Sadler (Game 16).

Game 7
Idelstein-Brunner
Budapest Spring Open 1989

1 e4 c5 2 ♘c3 d6 3 g3 ♘c6 4 ♗g2 g6 5 d3 ♗g7 6 f4 e6 7 ♘f3 ♘ge7 8 0-0 0-0 9 ♗e3 ♘d4 10 e5 ♘ef5 11 ♗f2 ♖b8!?

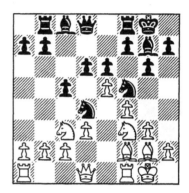

An interesting alternative to the normal 11...♘xf3+. With this move Black prepares to support the c-pawn with ...b7-b6. 11...d5 is considered in the next game.

12 ♘e4 b6

12...♘xf3+ ought to transpose to the game, and might actually be a more accurate move order, e.g. 13 ♕xf3 dxe5? (it's the same old story: if Black captures too early then he pays for it. Instead, 13...b6! transposes to the main game after 14 g4 ♗b7, although White is certainly not obliged to play 14 g4) 14 ♗xc5 ♖e8 15 fxe5 ♗xe5 16 g4 ♘h6 17 ♗e3 ♗d4 18 ♔h1 ♗xe3 19 ♕xe3 ♔g7 20 ♘f6 ♖h8 21 ♕e5 ♖a8 22 ♘h5+ 1-0 Van der Veen-Burkhardt, Dortmund 1989. A stark illustration of what can befall the unwary.

13 g4

Why not 13 ♘xd4!? (this is why I think it is better for Black to capture on f3 first before playing ...b7-b6) 13...cxd4 14 g4 (with the simple idea of capturing on d6) 14...♘e3 (not 14...♘h4 15 ♗xh4 ♕xh4 16 ♘xd6 but 14...dxe5!? could be Black's best, giving up a piece for lots of pawns: 15 gxf5 exf5 16 ♘d2 exf4 17 ♕f3 and it's anyone's game) 15 ♗xe3 dxe3 16 ♘xd6 f6 17 d4 and White is clearly on top.

13...♘xf3+ 14 ♕xf3 ♗b7

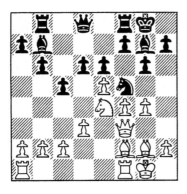

This is the point of Black's play. Only in this way can he hold his position together. If 15 gxf5?! exf5 16 exd6 fxe4 17 dxe4 ♕xd6 18 ♖ad1 ♕c6 followed by ...♖fe8 or ...f7-f5 with tremendous pressure on White's centre.

15 ♕h3

It might have been more sensible to play 15 ♕e2 (but not 15 gxf5?! exf5 16 exd6 fxe4 17 dxe4 ♕xd6 18 ♖ad1 ♕c6 followed by ...♖fe8 or ...f7-f5 with tremendous pressure on White's centre) 15...♗xe4 16 dxe4 ♘d4 17 ♗xd4 cxd4 18 exd6 ♕xd6 19 e5 with chances for both sides. White could play the bishop to e4 to secure the pawn on c2,

and then advance on the kingside.

15...♗xe4 16 dxe4 ♘d4 17 ♗h4 f6

Not 17...♘e2+? 18 ♔h1 ♘xf4 19 ♗xd8 ♘xh3 20 ♗e7 ♗xe5 21 ♗xf8 ♔xf8 22 ♗xh3 winning for White (count the rooks) in Thorhallsson-Petursson, Reykjavik 1989.

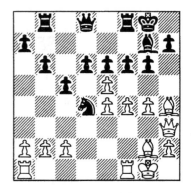

18 c3 ♘e2+ 19 ♔h1 dxe5 20 fxe5 g5 21 exf6 ♗xf6 22 e5 ♗g7 23 ♖xf8+ ♗xf8 24 ♕e3 gxh4 25 ♕xe2 ♕g5

In view of the weakness of the pawn on e5, Black is slightly better, but White goes down with unnecessary haste.

26 ♖d1 ♗g7 27 ♖d7 ♖f8 28 ♕d2 ♕xg4 29 ♖xa7 h3 0-1

Game 8
Le Blancq-Raymaekers
Guernsey Open 1988

1 e4 c5 2 ♘c3 e6 3 g3 ♘c6 4 ♗g2 d6 5 f4 ♘ge7 6 ♘f3 g6 7 0-0 ♗g7 8 d3 0-0 9 ♗e3 ♘d4 10 e5 ♘ef5 11 ♗f2 d5

This safe but uninspired move has been played on a few occasions, usually by Black players seeking to avoid the more critical lines. However, it doesn't really test White's idea.

but at least he has active pieces.

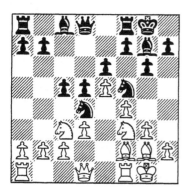

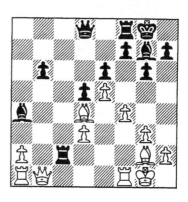

12 ♘xd4 ♘xd4

This position can also be reached, with one move extra played by both sides, via the move order 11...♘xf3+ 12 ♕xf3 ♘d4 13 ♕d1 d5.

13 ♘a4 b6 14 b4!

Testing Black's idea. 14 c3 is also possible: 14...♘c6 15 d4 cxd4 16 cxd4 ♗a6 17 ♖e1 ♘b4 18 ♖e3 and now Black will try to drum up play on the queenside, while White will play for a kingside attack with g3-g4 and f4-f5.

If Black is to avoid losing a pawn for nothing, then he must go in for the following:

14...♗d7 15 bxc5

Until now, everyone has gone for the pawn on c5, so it was surprising that a materialistic computer declined with 15 c4, and this may be even better as White keeps all the pressure on Black's centre. The game AARD-WOLF-Stefansson, chess.net 1996, continued 15...dxc4 16 bxc5 ♗xa4 17 ♕xa4 bxc5 18 dxc4, when White's bishops are mightily impressive.

15...♗xa4 16 ♗xd4 ♖c8 17 cxb6 ♖xc2 18 ♕b1 axb6

Black is going to be a pawn down,

19 ♗xb6!

After 19 ♕xb6 ♕xb6 20 ♗xb6 ♖b8, followed by activating the bishop on g7 by ...♗f8, Black had sufficient compensation for the pawn in Abramovic-Birmingham, Paris 1988.

19...♕d7 20 ♖f2 ♖fc8 21 ♖xc2 ♗xc2 22 ♕b4 ♗xd3

Sensibly, White returns the pawn to mobilise his pieces:

23 a4 ♗f8 24 ♕d4 ♗a6 25 a5 ♕b7 26 h4 h5 27 ♕e3 ♖c2 28 ♖c1 ♖xc1+ 29 ♕xc1 ♗c4?? 30 ♕xc4 1-0

For a while after the 10 e5 variation became fashionable, 10...♕b6 was hailed as the correct antidote, based on the game Spassky-Horvath (see below) in which the former World Champion failed to achieve any advantage. But then White players struck back:

Game 9
Balashov-Pigusov
USSR Team Ch., Podolsk 1990

1 e4 c5 2 ♘c3 ♘c6 3 g3 g6 4 ♗g2 ♗g7 5 d3 d6 6 f4 e6 7 ♘f3 ♘ge7 8 0-0 0-0 9 ♗e3 ♘d4 10 e5 ♕b6

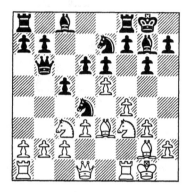

11 罝b1!

This is more testing than 11 ♘e4!? ♘ef5 12 ♗f2 ♕xb2 13 ♘xd4 cxd4 14 g4 ♘e3 15 ♗xe3 dxe3 16 ♘xd6 f6 17 ♕e2 fxe5 18 ♘c4 ♕d4 19 fxe5 罝f2 20 ♕xe3 罝xf1+ 21 罝xf1 ♗xe5 22 ♕xd4 ♗xd4+ 23 ♔h1 罝b8 24 罝b1 ½-½ Spassky-Horvath, European Club Cup, Rotterdam 1988. (White can eliminate one of the bishops after 24...b6 25 ♘a5, followed by ♘c6, for example, leaving the position dead level.) White was in no danger in this game, but it is difficult to find improvements after 11 ♘e4 – for both sides.

11...♘ef5 12 ♗f2 ♘xf3+ 13 ♕xf3 dxe5

13...♘d4 14 ♕d1 fxe5 15 fxe5 ♗xe5 16 ♘e4 simply transposes to the text as it is again dangerous for Black to leave the pawn on e5. For example, if instead of 15...♗xe5, 15...♗d7 then 16 ♘e4 ♗a4 (or 16...♗c6 17 b4!?) 17 b3 ♗c6 18 b4!? led to favourable complications for White in Balashov-Magerramov, Palma de Mallorca 1989.

14 fxe5

White cannot justify playing the knight out to the edge: 14 ♘a4? ♕c7

15 fxe5 ♗xe5 16 ♗xc5 ♗d7 17 ♗xf8 罝xf8 18 ♘c3 ♗d4+ 19 ♔h1 ♘e3 20 ♕e4 ♕b6 21 罝f4 e5 22 ♘e2 ♗c6 23 ♘xd4 ♗xe4 24 罝xe4 exd4 25 ♗f3 罝c8 26 罝e7 ♕f6 0-1 Bastian-Müller, German Bundesliga 1988.

14...♗xe5 15 ♘e4

A real pawn sacrifice this time. Doesn't the knight look better in the middle of the board?

15...♘d4

The amusing 15...♗d7? 16 ♗xc5 ♗d4+ 17 ♔h1! winning, occurred in Balashov-Kiselev, Moscow 1989.

16 ♕d1 f5 17 ♘d2 ♕c7 18 c3 ♘b5 19 ♕e2

Threatening d3-d4, which is actually surprisingly awkward to meet.

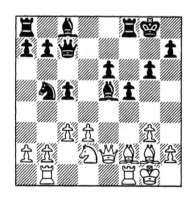

19...a6

Balashov deals with this move convincingly, but 19...♗f6 is a possible improvement – see the next game.

20 a4 ♘a7

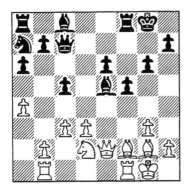

This is the drawback of 19...a6: Black's knight is miserably placed.

21 ♘c4 ♗f6 22 b4! cxb4 23 ♘b6 ♖b8 24 ♘xc8 ♘xc8 25 ♕xe6+ ♔g7 26 cxb4

26 ♖xb4 is also strong: 26...♕xc3 27 ♖xb7+ ♖xb7 28 ♗xb7, when the bishops dominate the board.

26...♕d6 27 ♕xd6 ♘xd6 28 ♖bc1

Balashov excels in technical situations, and this endgame is a textbook example of how to exploit the potential of the two bishops.

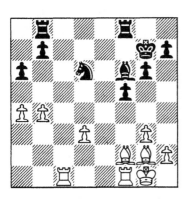

28...♖f7 29 ♖c5 ♗g5 30 h4 ♗d2 31 ♗d4+ ♔h6 32 ♖d5 ♖d7 33 ♗f3 ♖bd8

33...♗xb4 34 g4 fxg4 35 ♗xg4 ♖f7 36 ♖b1 a5 37 ♖xb4 axb4 38 ♖xd6 should be good for White.

34 ♗b6 ♖e8 35 ♗c5 ♖ed8 36 g4 fxg4 37 ♗xg4 ♘f5 38 ♖xd7 1-0

1 e4 c5 2 d3 ♘c6 3 g3 g6 4 ♗g2 ♗g7 5 ♘c3 d6 6 f4 e6 7 ♘f3 ♘ge7 8 0-0 0-0 9 ♗e3 ♘d4 10 e5 ♕b6 11 ♖b1 ♘ef5 12 ♗f2 ♘xf3+ 13 ♕xf3 dxe5 14 fxe5 ♗xe5 15 ♘e4 ♘d4 16 ♕d1 f5 17 ♘d2 ♕c7 18 c3 ♘b5 19 ♕e2

Up to this point we have been following the previous game, Balashov-Pigusov. Black's response here is more pugnacious: instead of grovelling around with his knight on the queenside, he attempts a counterattack on the kingside.

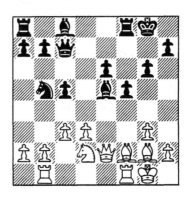

19...♗f6

19...♗g7 is also possible.

20 d4

White can win the pawn back in a couple of different ways, but I think this is the best. For example: 20 ♕e3 ♖d8 21 a4 ♘d6 22 ♕xc5 ♕xc5 23 ♗xc5 ♘f7 24 d4 e5 and Black equalised in Seifried-Bauer, Germany 1994; or 20 ♘b3 c4 21 dxc4 ♘d6 22 c5 ♘f7 and by comparison with the main game, the knight is less well placed on b3.

20...♘d6 21 dxc5 ♘f7 22 ♘c4 e5

It makes sense to go for the kingside counter straightaway. 22...♗d7 didn't work out too badly in Staskin-Horvath, Hungarian Open Championship 1994, but it is less energetic. After 23 ♖fd1 ♘d8 (23...♖ae8 looks stronger) 24 ♘d6 White stood better.

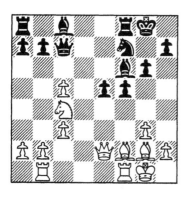

23 ♗d5 ♔g7 24 ♖bd1 ♘g5! 25 ♗e3 f4!

As White has so few pawns around his king, it makes sense to expose it even more.

26 gxf4 exf4 27 ♗d4

White's central control is impressive, but Black will always have counterplay against his king.

27...♗h3 28 ♘d6!?

Bold stuff, but the simple 28 ♖fe1 may have been better. I would still

give White the edge.

28...♗xf1 29 ♖xf1 f3 30 ♕e3 h6 31 h4 ♕d7 32 ♔f2 ♘h7 33 ♔g3 ♗xd4 34 ♕xd4+ ♘f6 35 ♖xf3 h5 36 ♖f4 ♕e7 37 ♖e4 ♕c7 38 ♖e6 ♖ae8 39 ♕e5 ♖xe6 40 ♗xe6 ♔h7 41 b4 b6 42 ♗b3 bxc5 43 bxc5 ♘e8 44 ♗c2 ♘g7 45 ♕g5 ♘f5+ 46 ♔h3 ♕xc5 47 ♘xf5 gxf5 48 ♕xh5+ ♔g7 49 ♕g5+ ♔h7 50 ♕h5+ ♔g7 51 ♕g5+ ½-½

An exciting game. I don't think that Black's play overturns the basic assessment of the 10...♕b6 variation (on balance I feel that White should have the better chances), but at least he was kicking hard.

In the next five games we look at 10...dxe5, a move that Joe Gallagher recommended in his book *Beating the Anti-Sicilians.*

Game 11
Bojkovic-Markovic
Belgrade 1988

1 e4 c5 2 ♘c3 ♘c6 3 g3 g6 4 ♗g2 ♗g7 5 d3 d6 6 f4 e6 7 ♘f3 ♘ge7 8 0-0 0-0 9 ♗e3 ♘d4 10 e5 dxe5

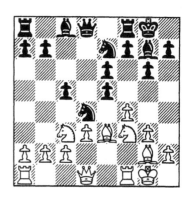

There is no doubt that this is one of

the most reliable methods of meeting
10 e5, but it isn't a reason to give up
the whole variation, and there are a
couple of new ideas for White which
should keep Black players on their
guard.

11 ♘xe5!?

11 fxe5!? is the subject of Game 15.
The position after 11 ♘xe5 reminds
me of a Leningrad Dutch (colours reversed). Considered in those terms,
White isn't doing badly.

11...♖b8!

Clearing the rook from the shadow
of the bishop, and preparing ...b7-b6,
supporting the pawn on c5 which is so
often the source of Black's problems
in this variation.

12 ♘e4 b6 13 c3

The standard move. White's other
possibilities here are dealt with in
Game 14.

13...♘df5

The alternative retreat 13...♘dc6 is
considered in Game 13.

14 ♗f2 ♕c7

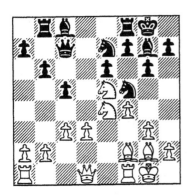

Gallagher's suggested improvement
over 14...♗b7 (see the next game).
White's problem here is that while his
development is good, Black's position

is so solid that it is difficult to build up
an attack. In contrast to other variations of this 'sacrifice' line, the pawn
on c5 is securely protected, and
Black's king position is a rock.

15 ♕a4

A provocative move. White is se-
cretly hoping that Black will play
15...b5, when the queen simply retreats to c2 and the pawn on c5 is
weak again. The knight on e5 is im-
mune: 15...♗xe5 16 fxe5 ♕xe5 17 g4,
followed by ♗g3. If instead of 15 ♕a4
White plays 15 g4, then Gallagher
recommends the highly complicated
piece sacrifice 15...♘d5!? 16 gxf5 exf5
17 ♘g3 ♘xf4.

15...♘d5

15...a5 allows White to break free:
16 g4 ♘d6 17 ♘xd6 ♕xd6 18 d4 cxd4
19 ♗xd4 ♕c7 20 ♕b5 f6 21 ♘c6 ♘xc6
22 ♕xc6 ♕xc6 23 ♗xc6 was a bit better for White in Langner-Potomak,
Czechoslovakian Team Championship 1994.

Although 15...f6 rids Black of the
annoying knight, it doesn't solve all of
his problems: the pawn on e6 is
weaker and the bishop on g7 is now
blocked in. I think White should simply retreat: 16 ♘f3 and then consider
one of the following plans, depending
on how Black plays:

   a) Double rooks on the e-file.

   b) Play for d3-d4.

   c) Play g3-g4 and ♗g3.

16 ♖fe1 ♘fe7

I don't like this retreat. The knight
stands well on f5.

17 ♖ad1

17 d4 is also possible.

17...♖d8 18 d4

This move liberates White's position. Through aimless play, Black has handed over the initiative to his opponent.

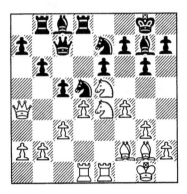

18...cxd4 19 ♗xd4 a6 20 c4 ♘f6

The immediate 20...b5! is stronger, maintaining the knight on d5, though I still prefer White's chances after 21 cxb5 axb5 22 ♕a7 although it's complicated!

21 ♘xf6+ ♗xf6 22 ♗f2 b5 23 ♖xd8+ ♕xd8 24 ♖d1 ♕c7 25 cxb5 ♖xb5 26 ♗f1 ♗xe5 27 fxe5 ♖d5 28 ♖e1 ♔g7 29 ♕f4 ♘g8 30 ♗g2 ♖b5 31 ♖c1 ♕d8 32 b3 ♗b7 33 ♗xb7 ♖xb7 34 ♕c4 ♖b5 35 a4 ♖d5 36 ♕xa6 ♖d1+ 37 ♖xd1 ♕xd1+ 1-0

In the next game we deal with Black's alternatives to 14...♕c7.

Game 12
Kuceva-Gladisheva
Pardubice Open 1992

---

1 e4 c5 2 ♘c3 ♘c6 3 g3 g6 4 ♗g2 ♗g7 5 d3 d6 6 f4 e6 7 ♘f3 ♘ge7 8 0-0 0-0 9 ♗e3 ♘d4 10 e5 dxe5 11 ♘xe5 ♖b8 12 ♘e4 b6 13 c3 ♘df5 14 ♗f2

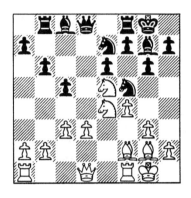

14...♗b7

14...♗a6? is an outright mistake: 15 ♕a4 ♗xd3 16 ♘xd3 ♕xd3 17 ♖ad1 ♕e2 18 ♖d2 ♕h5 19 h3 was winning for White in Kveinys-Bachmeyer, Dresden Open 1994. However, 14...f6!? cuts the Gordian knot. Black rids himself of the knight, but might be storing up trouble for himself as the e6 pawn is weakened. In Papazov-Dao Thien Hai, World U-16 Championship 1993, I think White drifted; he never found a good plan after 15 ♘c4 ♘d5 16 ♖e1 ♕c7 17 a4 ♖d8 18 ♕c2 ♘h6 19 h3 ♘f7 20 ♘ed2 a6 21 a5 b5 22 ♘e3 ♘e7 23 ♘b3 e5 24 ♘g4 h5 25 ♘h2 exf4 26 ♗xc5 ♘f5 with a crushing counterattack. Instead, I would prefer 15 ♘f3 followed by either pressure on the e-file; the d3-d4 break; or g3-g4 – or a combination of all three of these plans.

15 ♕a4

This move is surprisingly difficult to counter. White threatens perhaps ♕xa7; and perhaps ♘d7; and he might flick in g3-g4, depending on Black's response. The alternatives are weaker:

a) 15 ♘c4? (again White plays aimlessly) 15...♘d5 16 ♕e1 ♕c7 17 ♖d1

♖bd8 18 ♔h1 ♖fe8 19 ♗g1 h6 20 ♕f2 b5 with a winning initiative in Langner-Stohl, Czechoslovakia 1992.

b) 15 ♕e2 ♕c7 16 g4? (a nice idea, but simply a mistake in this case) 16...♘d5! (it is well worth remembering this motif: support for the knight on e5 is undermined) 17 gxf5 exf5 18 ♗g3 fxe4 wrecking White's position in Paulic-Renet, Belgrade GMA 1988.

15...a5

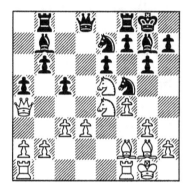

Again there are several alternatives here:

a) 15...♕c7?! 16 g4 ♘d6 17 ♕d7 winning material!

b) 15...f6 16 ♘d7 b5 17 ♕xa7 ♘c6 18 ♘exf6+ ♗xf6 19 ♗xc6 ♗xc6 20 ♘xb8 ♕xb8 21 ♕xb8 ♖xb8 22 ♗xc5 was analysed by Stohl who assesses the ending as slightly better for White. Since then, this position has actually been reached in a game – which ended in a draw, after many adventures. I would broadly concur with Stohl, but the situation is unclear enough that all three results are possible.

c) 15...♔h8 is given by Stohl, with the idea of 16 g4 f6 17 gxf5 exf5 'unclear', but that looks good for Black to me after 18 ♘xf6 ♗xf6 19

♗xb7 ♖xb7. After 15...♔h8, White could just plonk a rook in the middle.

d) 15...♘d5 is also slapped with an unclear symbol by Stohl, which is reasonable. If 16 ♘d7?! (16 ♖fe1!) then Black should play 16...♘fe3! 17 ♘xf8 ♗xf8 18 ♗xe3 ♘xe3 19 ♖f2 ♘xg2 20 ♖xg2 f5! winning back material.

16 ♖ad1

16 ♘d7 doesn't work here due to 16...b5 17 ♕xb5 ♗xe4 18 ♕xb8 ♕xd7.

16...♕c7 17 ♕d7! ♖fc8

Not 17...♗xe5? 18 fxe5 ♕xd7 19 ♘f6+.

18 g4 ♘h6 19 h3

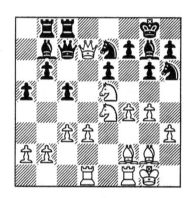

Black is in a tangle. The knight on h6 is out of play, and it is difficult to get rid of the queen on d7 without harming the position in some way.

19...♘d5 20 ♘d6 ♗c6 21 ♕xc7 ♖xc7 22 ♘xc6 ♖xc6 23 ♘b5 ♖cc8 24 ♗xd5 exd5 25 d4 c4 26 f5 ♗f8 27 ♗g3 ♖b7 28 f6 a4 29 ♘d6 ♗xd6 30 ♗xd6 g5 31 ♖de1 ♖d7 32 ♗b4 ♔h8 33 ♖e5 ♖g8 34 ♔g2 ♖g6 35 ♖e8+ ♖g8 36 ♗f8 1-0

Most players have favoured 13...♘df5, as in Games 11 and 12, but 13...♘dc6 is arguably a more reliable move, as we see in the next game.

Game 13
Shchekachev-Galliamova
Kstovo Open 1994

1 e4 c5 2 ②c3 ②c6 3 g3 g6 4 ②g2 ②g7 5 d3 d6 6 f4 e6 7 ②f3 ②ge7 8 0-0 0-0 9 ②e3 ②d4 10 e5 dxe5 11 ②xe5 ③b8 12 ②e4 b6 13 c3 ②dc6

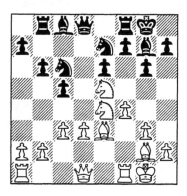

14 ♕a4!?

Tempting Black into taking the knight. The attempt to win a pawn with 14 ②xc6?! ②xc6 15 ②xc5 rebounds on White: 15...bxc5 16 ②xc6 ③xb2 17 ②xc5 ②xc3. White must tread with great care, and it is interesting to see that one of the masters of the variation could make little headway against Black's defence: 14 ②c4 ♕c7 15 ♕e2 ②a6 16 ③ad1 ½-½ Balashov-Cvitan, Warsaw 1990. To be more precise, he didn't even make an attempt.

14...②b7

Sensibly, Black declines the offer. It is more trouble than it is worth to take either of the pawns, e.g. 14...②xe5 15 fxe5 ②xe5 (or 15...♕xd3 16 ②g5 ②d5 17 ②f6+ ②xf6 18 exf6

with good compensation for White) 16 ②h6 ③e8 17 ②f4!

15 ③ae1 ♕c7! 16 d4 b5

The simplest way of coping with White's temporary initiative seems to be 16...cxd4 17 cxd4 f6 (the e6 pawn is easy enough to defend and, having rid himself of the knight on e5, Black has more manoeuvring space).

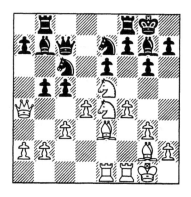

17 ♕c2 cxd4 18 cxd4 ②d5 19 ②f2 ②xe5 20 ♕xc7 ②f3+ 21 ②xf3 ②xc7 22 ③c1 ②e8 23 ♔g2 ③d8 24 ②c5

24 ③fd1 would have given White some advantage: he controls the c-file and has more space.

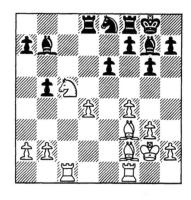

24...②xf3+ 25 ♔xf3 ②d6 26 g4 ②c4 27 ②b3 ③d5 28 ③c2 a5 29 ②d2 ②xd4 30 ②xc4 bxc4 31 ③xc4 ②xb2

32 ♖b1 ♗a3 33 ♖b7 ♗b4 34 ♗d4 ♖dd8 35 f5 exf5 36 gxf5 ♖d5 37 f6 ♖f5+ 38 ♔g2 ♗d6 39 ♖d7 ♗e5 40 ♖c5 ♖g5+ 41 ♔f3 ♗xf6 42 ♖xg5 ♗xg5 43 ♖d5 ♗d8 44 ♖d7 ♗h4 45 ♖a7 ♗e1 46 ♗b6 ♖c8 47 ♗xa5 ♗xa5 48 ♖xa5 ♖c3+ 49 ♔f2 ♔g7 50 a4 ♖a3 51 ♖a6 h5 52 ♔g2 g5 53 ♖a7 h4 54 ♖a6 g4 55 ♖a5 ♔g6 56 ♖a8 ♔g5 0-1

So far we have looked at games where White has played 13 c3 followed by a rapid ♕a4, often leading to obscure tactics. In the next game we look at what happens when White tries a different tack.

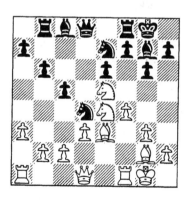

Game 14
Bastian-Pieper Emden
German Bundesliga 1986/87

1 e4 c5 2 ♘c3 ♘c6 3 g3 g6 4 ♗g2 ♗g7 5 d3 e6 6 ♗e3 d6 7 f4 ♘ge7 8 ♘f3 ♘d4 9 0-0 0-0 10 e5 dxe5 11 ♘xe5 ♖b8 12 ♘e4 b6 13 a3!?

Another idea is 13 a4 ♗b7 14 c3 ♘df5 15 ♗f2 ♕c7 16 ♘c4 ♘d5 17 ♕e2 (in view of White's later play, 17 ♖fe1 followed by ♕c2 or ♕b3 and a4-

a5 might have been more to the point) 17...♖bd8 18 ♖fe1 ♖fe8 19 ♕c2 ♗a8 20 ♕b3 ♘f6 21 a5 ♘d5 22 axb6 axb6 23 ♖a6 ♗b7 24 ♖a7 ♖a8 25 ♖xb7 ♕xb7 26 ♘ed6 ♘xd6 27 ♘xd6 ♕d7 28 ♘xe8 ♖xe8 29 ♗xd5 exd5 30 ♖xe8+ ♕xe8 31 ♕xb6 and White should have cleaned up in Olesen-Moskow, New York 1993. White's strategy was straightforward and reliable.

13...♘df5 14 ♗f2 ♘d6 15 b4

15 ♕e2, to support the knight on e5, might have been an improvement, and only then b2-b4.

15...♘xe4 16 ♗xe4

16 dxe4 ♕c7 17 bxc5 bxc5 is more comfortable for Black.

16...♕c7 17 bxc5

17...f6?

After 17...bxc5! White would still have had a few problems to solve on the a1-g8 diagonal, and after the future exchange of light-squared bishops, his king would feel a touch exposed.

18 cxb6 axb6 19 ♘c4 f5 20 ♗g2 ♗xa1

How could Black even consider taking this exchange? His game rapidly goes downhill now.

21 ♕xa1 ♗a6 22 ♘e5 b5 23 ♘f3 ♗b7 24 ♘g5 ♗c8 25 ♖e1 ♕d6 26 ♕a2 ♖f6 27 ♕b2 ♖f8 28 ♕b3 h6 29 ♘xe6 ♖f7 30 ♗c5 ♕d7 31 ♘g5 1-0

Game 15
Bergonzi-Kropff
Asuncion San Cristobal Open 1995

---

1 e4 c5 2 ♘c3 ♘c6 3 g3 g6 4 ♗g2 ♗g7 5 d3 d6 6 f4 e6 7 ♘f3 ♘ge7 8 0-0 0-0 9 ♗e3 ♘d4 10 e5 dxe5 11 fxe5

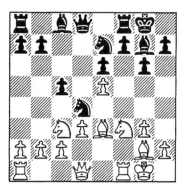

In a sense, 11 fxe5 is more in keeping with the spirit of the whole variation than the more popular 11 ♘xe5 (see Games 11–14): the f-file is opened, as well as the c1–h6 diagonal, making an attack on Black's king more likely. That's White's idea: to get into f6 and deliver checkmate! Alright, so that's the theory, but the reality might not square up to it. Read on ...

11...♘ef5

This move was analysed by Stohl, but there is an important alternative that he failed to consider: 11...♘ec6!? According to my sources, this has only been played once, when after 12 ♘e4 Black had to make an important decision. In the game Lyrberg-Ernst, Gausdal 1993, he chose 12...♘xe5 13 ♘xe5 ♗xe5 14 c3 ♘f5 15 ♗xc5 ♖e8 16 d4 ♗g7 17 g4 (17 ♕f3!?) 17...♘e3 18 ♕f3 ♘xf1 19 ♘d6 ♖e7 20 ♖xf1 f6 21 ♘xc8 ♖xc8 22 ♗xe7 ♕xe7 23 ♖e1 ♖c7 24 ♕e3 e5 25 g5 fxg5 26 ♗d5+ ♔h8 27 dxe5 b6 28 ♔h1 ♖c8 29 e6 ½-½. White could still play for a win, but objectively, Black should hold the position. What is clear in this line is that White has the better chances.

However, it seems to me that 12...♘xf3+! is a stronger move: 13 ♕xf3 (13 ♗xf3 might be a better try, although after 13...♘xe5 14 ♗xc5 ♖e8 15 ♗g2 [15 ♘d6? ♗f8! or 15 d4 ♘xf3+ 16 ♕xf3 ♗xd4+] 15...♘d7 16 ♗a3 ♗xb2! 17 ♗xb2 ♕b6+ it is not clear whether White has enough for the pawn) 13...♘xe5 and now:

a) 14 ♕f4 f5 15 ♗xc5 (15 ♘xc5 ♘g4!) 15...fxe4 16 ♗xf8 ♕xf8 17 ♕xe4 ♕e7 is tricky, but I would assess it in Black's favour.

b) 14 ♕e2 f5! (this is the key move, forcing White to capture on c5 with the knight) 15 ♘xc5 ♘g4! (the essential follow-up, grabbing one of the bishops) 16 c3 ♘xe3 17 ♕xe3 e5 and again, I prefer Black.

12 ♗f2

12 ♗f4!? wasn't mentioned by Stohl in his analysis, but it may be better than the text move. After 12...♘xf3+ 13 ♕xf3 g5 (if Black doesn't eliminate the pawn on e5 then White will have a wonderful attacking position after he plays ♘e4) 14 ♗c1 ♗xe5 15 ♘e4 f6 16 c3 ♕c7 17 ♕f2 ♖d8 (17...b6 is met by ♘xg5, and although Black could attempt to hold on to the pawn by

playing 17...c4 this would be a painful experience: 18 d4 ♗d6 19 ♘xd6 ♛xd6 20 b3 with oodles of compensation. White's bishops sizzle, and Black's king is potentially weak) 18 ♘xc5 ♖b8 19 ♗h3 (19 ♗e4!?) 19...♖d5 20 ♗xf5 exf5 21 d4 ♗d6 22 ♛f3 ♛f7 23 ♗e3 ♗xc5 a draw was agreed in Franke-Kishnev, Germany 1993. The final position is complicated, but after 24 dxc5 ♗e6 25 ♗d4 ♖d7 26 ♖ae1 I would give White the edge, as he has the plan of doubling rooks along the e-file.

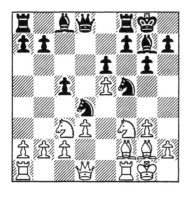

12...♖b8 13 ♘e4 b6 14 ♘xd4 cxd4 15 ♘f6+ ♗xf6 16 exf6 ♛xf6 17 g4 ♘d6 18 ♗g3 ♛e7 19 ♗e5 f6 20 ♗xd4 e5 21 ♗c3 ♘b5!?

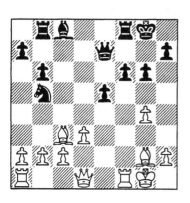

All these moves were mentioned by Stohl. Black has the better chances because of his strong pawn centre and White's weak king position. This is borne out by the game.

22 ♗d5+ ♔g7 23 d4 ♘xc3 24 bxc3 e4 25 ♛e2 f5 26 ♛g2 ♛d6 27 c4 ♔h8 28 c3 ♗d7 29 a4 ♖be8 30 a5 b5 31 ♖ab1 bxc4 32 ♗xc4 f4 33 ♖b7 f3 34 ♛g3 ♛xg3+ 35 hxg3 ♗xg4 36 ♗f7 e3 37 ♗xe8 f2+ 38 ♔h2 e2 39 ♖bb1 exf1♛ 40 ♖xf1 ♗e2 41 ♖xf2 ♖xf2+ 42 ♔g1 ♖f3 43 d5 ♖xc3 44 d6 ♗g4 0-1

In principle 11 fxe5 appeals to me, but 11...♘ec6 may be a problem. My analysis needs checking, however!

Black's chief problem in the positions that arise after 10 e5 is how to develop his queen's bishop. In the following two games Black aims at solving this question with 10...♗d7 straightaway, rather than taking any of the pawns offered in the centre. So long as he sticks to this policy, Black has every chance of equalising. Matthew Sadler's games are model examples of Black's strategy in this line.

Game 16
Lane-Sadler
London Lloyds Bank Masters 1992

1 e4 c5 2 ♘c3 d6 3 g3 g6 4 ♗g2 ♗g7 5 d3 ♘c6 6 f4 e6 7 ♘f3 ♘ge7 8 0-0 0-0 9 ♗e3 ♘d4 10 e5 ♗d7

It looks extraordinary to leave everything hanging in the centre, but, strangely enough, it seems that White is unable to take advantage of the situation.

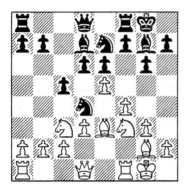

11 ♘e4

11 ♘xd4 isn't bad, but it doesn't promise White a theoretical advantage, e.g. 11...cxd4 12 ♗xd4 dxe5, when 13 ♗xe5? is very unfortunate (instead 13 fxe5 ♗c6 14 ♗c5 ♗xe5 15 ♗xc6 ♗d4+ 16 ♗xd4 ♕xd4+ 17 ♔h1 ♘xc6 18 ♕f3 is balanced) after 13...♕b6+ 0-1 Kristensen-Feher, Aarhus 1992, on account of 14 ♔h1 f6 winning a piece.

If 11 exd6 then Black will win the pawn back, transposing to one of the lines considered later in this chapter after 11...♘ef5 12 ♗f2 ♗c6 13 ♘e4 ♘xf3+ (not 13...b6 14 ♘e5). In general, in this particular variation it is a mistake to release the tension too soon (and this comment applies to both sides).

11...♘ef5 12 ♗f2 ♘xf3+

This is the critical move. Black's alternatives are unappealing:

a) 12...dxe5? (releasing the tension too early!) 13 ♘xe5 (Black didn't understand the idea behind 10...♗d7: now the light-squared bishop won't reach the long diagonal) 13...b6 14 g4 ♘e7 15 ♗h4 f6 16 ♗xf6 ♗xf6 17 ♘xf6+ ♖xf6 18 ♘xd7 ♕xd7 19 ♗xa8

winning in Pavasovic-Applebury, Budapest 1994.

b) 12...♗c6? looks good but White has the cunning 13 ♘fd2!, when the knight on d4 is suddenly in a spot of trouble, e.g. 13...dxe5 14 fxe5 ♗xe5 15 ♘c4 ♗g7 16 c3 ♘b5 17 ♗xc5 ♖e8 18 a4 ♘c7 19 ♘ed6 ♗xg2 20 ♔xg2 ♘xd6 21 ♘xd6 ♖e7 22 ♕f3 ♖d7 23 ♘xf7 with a won position for White in Langner-Obsivac, Czechoslovakian Team Championship 1992.

13 ♕xf3

The alternative recapture, 13 ♗xf3, is considered in the next game.

13...♗c6!

This is the whole point of 10...♗d7: Black brings his bishop to the long diagonal to counter the bishop on g2. Once again, capturing in the centre with 13...dxe5?! is not in the spirit of 10...♗d7: 14 ♗xc5 ♖e8 15 fxe5 ♗xe5 16 g4 ♗c6 17 ♕f2 ♕h4 18 h3 ♕xf2+ 19 ♖xf2 ♘h4 20 ♘f6+ ♗xf6 21 ♗xc6 ♖ac8 22 ♖xf6 ♖xc6 23 ♗e3 ♖xc2 24 ♗g5 winning, Papazov-Apro, European U-14 Championship 1992. It is better to get the bishop to the long diagonal first.

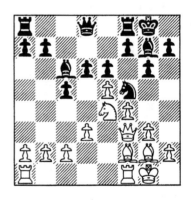

14 c3 ♖c8!

14...dxe5?! 15 ♗xc5 exf4 (or 15...♘d6 16 fxe5 ♗xe4 17 dxe4 ♗xe5 18 ♖ad1 ♕c7 19 ♗d4) 16 ♕xf4 e5 17 ♕f2 ♕xd3 (if 17...♖e8 18 g4) 18 ♖ad1 ♕b5 19 g4 ♘h6 20 ♗xf8 ♖xf8 21 ♘d6 ♘xg4 22 ♘xb5 ♘xf2 23 ♖xf2 ♗xb5 24 ♗xb7 with a winning ending, Pavasovic-Shumiakina, Ljubljana 1992.

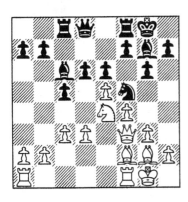

15 exd6

Instead, White played 15 ♖fd1 in Relange-Berestetzky, European Junior Championship 1991, after which Black committed the sin of releasing the tension too early: 15...dxe5? 16 ♗xc5 ♖e8 17 ♗xa7 and White had simply won a pawn. Instead, 15...b6 was correct, when play will follow along similar lines to the main game if he captures on d6, or instead White could play 16 d4!? maintaining the pawn on e5. Chances are balanced.

15...♘xd6 16 ♕e2 b6 17 ♖fd1 ♕d7

Although there appears to be little to choose between the two sides, I would favour Black here. Why? Because he has a clear plan (pressure on the d3 pawn combined with a potential break in the centre after ...♖fe8 and ...e6-e5) while White isn't quite sure what to do. If he attempts an attack on the kingside then it is likely to rebound (Black has four pawns around his king, White only three, plus the f-pawn has already advanced, exposing the white king); while Black is also well placed to meet the break in the centre, as we shall see.

18 h4?!

White has no realistic attacking chances, so this move merely weakens White's king. It would have been better to play 18 d4 immediately.

18...♖fe8 19 d4 ♘xe4 20 ♗xe4 ♗xe4 21 ♕xe4 ♕b5 22 ♖d2 cxd4 23 ♗xd4 ♖ed8 24 ♕b7 ♗xd4+ 25 cxd4 ♕a5 26 ♕g2 ♖c4 27 ♕f2 ♖dc8 28 a3 ♕a4 29 ♔h2 ♖d8 30 ♖ad1 ♖d5 31 ♕e3 a5 32 f5 ♖xf5 33 b3 ♕xa3 34 d5 ♕c5 35 ♕e2 ♖c1 36 d6 ♖f2+ 0-1

A fine positional performance from Sadler.

Game 17
Sale-Sadler
Cannes Open 1995

1 e4 c5 2 ♘c3 d6 3 g3 ♘c6 4 ♗g2 g6 5 d3 ♗g7 6 f4 e6 7 ♘f3 ♘ge7 8 0-0 0-0 9 ♗e3 ♘d4 10 e5 ♗d7 11

♘e4 ♘ef5 12 ♗f2 ♘xf3+! 13 ♗xf3

13 ♕xf3 was seen in the previous game, Lane-Sadler.

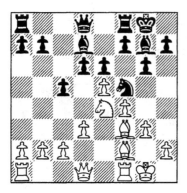

13...♗c6!

At the risk of sounding monotonous: it is simply a mistake to release the tension before the bishop reaches the long diagonal. 13...dxe5?! 14 fxe5 (not 14 ♗xc5? exf4 15 ♗xf8 ♕xf8 with compensation for the exchange in Relange-Chevalier, Paris 1991) 14...♗xe5 15 ♘xc5 ♗c6 16 ♗xc6 bxc6 17 c3 ♖b8 18 ♕e2 ♗g7 19 ♘e4 ♕c7 20 ♗c5 ♖fd8 21 g4 ♘h6 22 ♖f2 ♖d5 23 ♗e3 ♔h8 24 ♗f4 e5 25 ♗xh6 ♗xh6 26 g5 ♗g7 27 ♖af1 with the better chances for White, Geurink-Simons, Groningen Open 1994.

14 c3

Not 14 exd6?! as after the continuation 14...b6 15 c3 ♖c8 16 ♕e2 ♘xd6 17 ♖fd1 ♕e7 18 d4 c4 19 ♘g5 ♕b7 20 ♗xc6 ♕xc6 21 ♕f3 ♕d5 Black had a big positional advantage in the game Turner-Wolff, London Lloyds Bank Masters 1994.

14...h5

As usual, White was hoping for 14...dxe5 15 fxe5 ♗xe5 16 ♗xc5 with a slight pull.

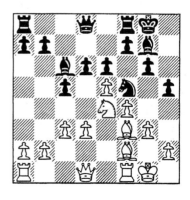

15 exd6?!

I'm still not happy with this move. I would offer two alternatives:

a) 15 ♘xd6!? ♘xd6 16 ♗xc5 ♘f5 17 ♗xf8 ♗xf8 18 ♗xc6 bxc6 19 ♖f2. Two pawns and a rook is usually good value for two minor pieces, but in this case Black's knight is well-anchored, and his king position secure, so anything could happen.

b) 15 d4 is reasonable, holding the pawn on e5.

15...b6 16 ♘f6+ ♗xf6 17 ♗xc6 ♖c8 18 ♗b7 ♖b8 19 ♗e4 ♕xd6

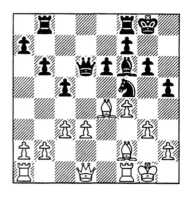

There is little to choose between this and 19...♘xd6, which was played in Kveinys-Dokhoian, Bonn 1994. That game is worth looking at as

White's strategy is far better than in Sale-Sadler: 20 ♕e2! (the queen should be on this side of the board, where it can protect the king if necessary) 20...♕c7 21 ♗f3 ♖fd8 22 ♖ad1 ♘f5 23 ♖fe1 ♖d6 24 ♗e4 ♘e7 25 h3 ♗g7 26 g4 (White can get away with this advance as he has so many pieces around his king) 26...hxg4 27 hxg4 f5, when chances are balanced and the game eventually ended in a draw.

20 ♕a4?!

The queen is on the wrong side of the board!

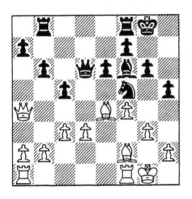

20...♕c7 21 ♕a6 b5 22 ♖ac1 ♖fc8 23 ♖fe1 ♖d8 24 b4 ♗e7 25 a4 ♖d6 26 ♕a5 ♕xa5 27 bxa5 ♖a6 28 axb5 ♖xb5 29 ♖b1 ♖bxa5 30 ♖b8+ ♔g7 31 ♖c8 ♖a1 32 ♖xa1 ♖xa1+ 33 ♔g2 ♘d6 34 ♖c7 ♗d8 35 ♖c6 ♘xe4 36 dxe4 ♖a2 37 ♔f3 ♖c2 38 ♗xc5 ♖xc3+ 39 ♔e2 ♔h7 40 ♔d2 ♗a5 0-1

Whereas Black's kingside was rock solid, White's queenside, and eventually his kingside, were a little shaky. Black exploited the weaknesses skilfully.

Without doubt, 10...♗d7 is a sound

move, but I don't believe that we have seen the best yet from White in this variation. I have pointed out plenty of instances where there is room for improvement.

In the final game of this chapter Black takes a hot pawn and suffers for it in typical fashion.

Game 18
Claesen-Dgebuadze
World Student Ch., Leon 1996

1 e4 c5 2 ♘c3 ♘c6 3 g3 g6 4 ♗g2 ♗g7 5 d3 e6 6 f4 d6 7 ♘f3 ♘ge7 8 ♗e3 ♘d4 9 0-0 0-0 10 e5 ♘ec6?!

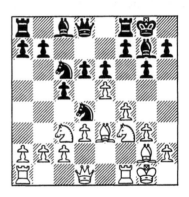

This attempt to steer away from the normal continuations of 10...♘ef5, 10...♕b6, 10....dxe5 and 10...♗d7 cannot be recommended. The d6 and c5 squares aren't given sufficient protection. White immediately looks to exploit this weakening in Black's position.

11 ♘e4 dxe5 12 ♘xe5 ♘xe5 13 fxe5 ♗xe5 14 c3 ♘f5 15 ♗xc5 ♖e8 16 d4 ♗g7

A standard kind of position has arisen in which White's better development provides him with excellent prospects.

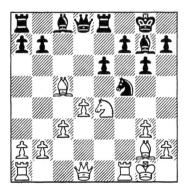

17 ♕f3 h5 18 ♖ad1 ♗d7 19 ♘d6 ♗c6 20 d5 ♗xd5 21 ♖xd5 exd5 22 ♘xf5 gxf5 23 ♕xf5 ♕c7 24 ♗d4

Now White has a blistering attack.

Black's extra exchange is irrelevant.

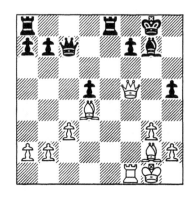

24...♗xd4+ 25 cxd4 ♖ad8 26 ♗xd5 ♖d7 27 ♕g6+ ♔f8 28 ♕xh5 ♖xd5 29 ♕h8+ ♔e7 30 ♖e1+ ♔d6 31 ♕xe8 ♕d7 32 ♕b8+ ♔c6 33 ♕xa7 ♖xd4 34 ♖c1+ ♔d5 35 ♕xd4+ 1-0

Summary

The popularity of 10 e5 has waned over the last few years as Black has found adequate responses. For instance, Hjartarson's play in Game 3 was extremely solid; 10...fxe5 (Games 11–15) is sensible; and the lines with 10...♗d7 (Games 16 and 17) also look sound for Black. However, I hope I have shown that the possibilities in this complex position are far from exhausted. In my opinion it is time for White to try out this line again.

1 e4 c5 2 ♘c3 ♘c6 3 g3 g6 4 ♗g2 ♗g7 5 d3 d6 6 f4 e6 7 ♘f3 ♘ge7 8 0-0 0-0 9 ♗e3 ♘d4 10 e5!? *(D)* **10...♘ef5**

10...♕b6 11 ♖b1 ♘ef5 12 ♗f2 ♘xf3+ 13 ♕xf3 dxe5 14 fxe5 ♗xe5 15 ♘e4 ♘d4 16 ♕d1 f5 17 ♘d2 ♕c7 18 c3 ♘b5 19 ♕e2

19...a6 – *Game 9*; 19...♗f6 – *Game 10*

10...dxe5

11 ♘xe5 ♖b8 12 ♘e4 b6 *(D)*

13 c3

13...♘df5 14 ♗f2

14...♕c7 – *Game 11*; 14...♗b7 – *Game 12*

13...♘dc6 – *Game 13*

13 a3 – *Game 14*

11 fxe5 – *Game 15*

10...♗d7 11 ♘e4 ♘ef5 12 ♗f2 ♘xf3+ *(D)*

13 ♕xf3 – *Game 16*; 13 ♗xf3 – *Game 17*

10...♘ec6 – *Game 18*

11 ♗f2 ♘xf3+ (11...♖b8 – *Game 7*; 11...d5 – *Game 8*)

12 ♕xf3 ♘d4 (12...♗d7 – *Game 6*)

13 ♕d1 dxe5 (13...♖b8 – *Game 1*; 13...d5 – *Game 8* [by transposition])

14 fxe5 ♗xe5 (14...♖b8 – *Game 5*)

15 ♘e4 f5 16 ♘xc5 ♕d6 (16...♕c7 – *Game 4*)

17 b4 (17...♘c6 – *Game 3*; 17...♖b8 – *Game 2*)

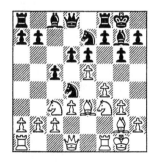

10 e5

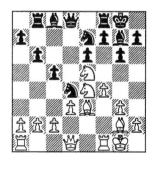

12...b6

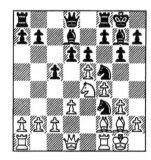

12...♘xf3 +

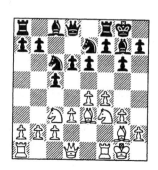

CHAPTER TWO

Main Line:
Alternatives after 9 ♗e3

1 e4 c5 2 ♘c3 ♘c6 3 g3 g6 4 ♗g2 ♗g7 5 d3 d6 6 f4 e6 7 ♘f3 ♘ge7 8 0-0 0-0 9 ♗e3

In this chapter we shall be looking at games where White plays 9 ♗e3 but after 9...♘d4 declines to play the pawn sacrifice with e4-e5 (Games 19-24); or else Black refuses to play 9...♘d4, thus avoiding the possibility of the pawn sacrifice altogether (Games 25-27).

The emphasis in this chapter is on new ideas. After 9...♘d4, for example, I haven't included any games with the older 10 ♖b1 and 10 ♕d2, as very little has changed theoretically and Black has had few problems (see the introductory section on pushing the b-pawn for a discussion of Black's typical strategy). Instead I have placed the emphasis on fresh ideas or areas where there is room for innovation.

1 e4 c5 2 ♘c3 ♘c6 3 g3 g6 4 ♗g2 ♗g7 5 d3 d6 6 f4 e6 7 ♘f3 ♘ge7 8 0-0 0-0 9 ♗e3 ♘d4 10 ♗f2

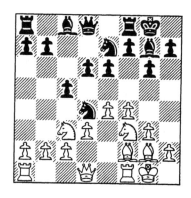

White retreats the bishop so that it is now possible to exchange off the knight on d4. This move has a solid, if somewhat uninspired, reputation and there is nothing in recent games to alter this assessment. As we saw in the first chapter, Spassky has employed this idea, sometimes using it to enter the e4-e5 pawn sacrifice line (Spassky-Hjartarson, Game 3, for instance).

10...b6!? 11 ♘xd4 cxd4 12 ♘e2 e5 13 c3 dxc3 14 ♘xc3 ♗e6 15 d4

15 ♕d2!? – compare with the next

game.

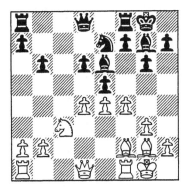

15...exf4 16 gxf4 d5

16...♕d7 17 ♗h4 (17 f5 ♗c4!) 17...f6 18 d5 ♗h3 is unclear according to Stohl.

17 ♗h4 f6 18 ♕b3 ♕d7 19 ♘xd5 ♘xd5 20 exd5 ♗f7 21 ♖ae1 ♖fe8 22 f5 ♖xe1 ½-½

The position is roughly level after 23 ♗xe1 ♖d8.

Game 20
Abramovic-Koch
Paris Championship 1989

1 e4 c5 2 ♘c3 ♘c6 3 g3 g6 4 ♗g2 ♗g7 5 d3 d6 6 f4 e6 7 ♘f3 ♘ge7 8 0-0 0-0 9 ♗e3 ♘d4 10 ♗f2 e5!?

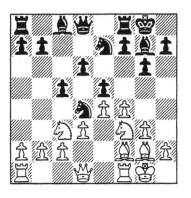

Now that White has retreated the bishop to f2, this move looks logical to me as the f4 pawn lacks support.

11 ♘xd4 cxd4 12 ♘e2 ♗e6 13 c3 dxc3 14 ♘xc3

14 bxc3 doesn't seem much better: 14...♕d7 15 d4 ♗g4 16 dxe5 dxe5 17 ♕xd7 ♗xd7 18 ♗c5 ♖fe8 19 f5 ♗b5 20 f6 ♗xe2 21 ♖f2 ♗xf6 22 ♖xf6 ♖ac8 23 ♗xa7 ♖xc3 and Black was a pawn up in Lenart-Wells, Hungarian Team Championship 1994.

14...♕d7

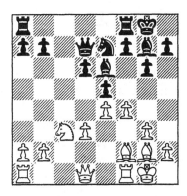

Compare this position with the previous game (Abramovic-Stohl); Black is virtually a whole tempo up. 14...d5!? was another possibility.

15 ♕d2 exf4 16 ♕xf4 ♘c6 17 ♕d2 ♘d4 18 ♗e3 f5 19 ♗h6 ♔h8 20 ♖ad1 ♖ac8 21 ♖f2 b5 22 exf5 ♖xf5 23 ♖xf5 ♗xf5 24 ♗xg7+ ♕xg7 25 ♖e1 ♗h3 26 ♗h1 ♖f8 27 ♘d5 ♗e6 28 a3 ♖c8 29 ♕f2 ♖c2 30 ♕e3 ♖xb2 ½-½

Game 21
Todorcevic-Portisch
Szirak Interzonal 1987

1 e4 c5 2 ♘c3 d6 3 f4 g6 4 ♘f3

♗g7 5 d3 ♘c6 6 g3 e6 7 ♗g2 ♘ge7 8 0-0 0-0 9 ♗e3 ♘d4 10 ♗f2 ♘ec6

Probably the most common response to 10 ♗f2.

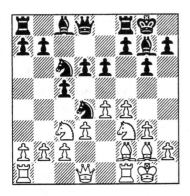

11 ♘d2!?

An interesting idea. White ducks the challenge and hopes to drive the knight back from d4. It is more common to play 11 ♘xd4 ♘xd4, when in this position Spassky played 12 e5 against Hjartarson (Game 3). White tried another strategy in Davies-Fossan, Gausdal 1992: 12 ♖b1!? ♖b8 13 a3 b6 14 ♕d2 ♗b7 15 ♘d1 d5 16 e5 ♘c6 17 b4 ♕e7 18 ♘e3 ♕c7 19 ♘g4 d4 20 ♘f6+ ♔h8 21 bxc5 bxc5 22 ♘e4 when with his space advantage, and beautifully placed knight on e4, White had a clear advantage.

11...♖b8 12 ♘cb1 ♘e7

Although White has lost time retreating the knights, Black must also regroup.

13 c3 ♘dc6 14 a4 b6 15 ♘f3

The interesting 15 ♘a3!? was also possible.

15...e5 16 ♘bd2 ♗a6 17 ♕e2?

An ugly move. White's queen is caught in a crossfire of pins. 17 ♕c2 looks more sensible.

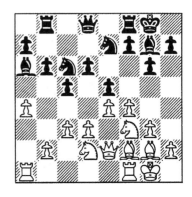

17...exf4 18 gxf4 ♖e8 19 ♖fe1 ♘d5 20 ♗g3 ♗h6 21 f5 ♘f4 22 ♗xf4 ♗xf4 23 ♘f1 d5 24 ♕f2 dxe4 25 dxe4 ♘e5 26 ♘xe5 ♗xe5 27 ♘e3 ♕g5 28 a5 ♗d3 29 axb6 axb6 30 ♖a7 ♗xe4 31 ♘g4 ♕xg4 32 ♖xe4 ♗xh2+ 33 ♔xh2 ♖xe4 34 ♗xe4 ♕xe4 35 fxg6 ♕xg6 36 ♖xf7 ♕h5+ 0-1

An impressive game from Portisch.

Game 22
Hort-Afifi
Tunis Interzonal 1985

1 e4 c5 2 ♘c3 ♘c6 3 f4 g6 4 ♘f3 ♗g7 5 g3 e6 6 ♗g2 ♘ge7 7 d3 0-0 8 ♗e3 ♘d4 9 ♗f2 d6 10 0-0 ♖b8

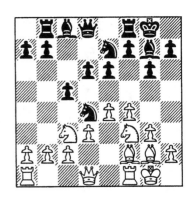

The fact that Black has such a choice of reasonable moves in this position is a fair indication that this is not the most critical variation in the Closed Sicilian.

11 a4 ♘ec6 12 ♘e1

The same idea from Game 21 of ducking the knight on d4 with the intention of driving it out later with c2-c3. Except that White never quite gets around to it here.

12...a6 13 g4!? b5 14 h4

Brutal! Hort's strategy is noteworthy: instead of opening the a-file, he prefers to let Black pass with the b-pawn, thus ensuring that the queenside remains closed.

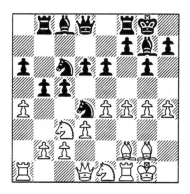

14...b4 15 ♘b1 ♕b6 16 ♘d2 ♘a5 17 ♖b1 ♗d7 18 b3 f5 19 ♗e3 fxg4 20 ♕xg4 ♕d8 21 ♖f2 ♕e7 22 ♘df3 ♘ac6 23 ♗h3 ♖bd8 24 ♕g5 ♗f6 25 ♕g3 ♕g7 26 ♔h1 e5 27 ♘g2 ♘xf3 28 ♖xf3 exf4 29 ♘xf4 ♘d4 30 ♖f2 ♗e5 31 ♖bf1 ♗xf4 32 ♗xf4 ♖xf4 33 ♖xf4 ♘e2 34 ♕g5 ♖e8 35 ♖f7 ♕xf7 36 ♖xf7 ♗xh3 37 ♖f2 1-0

Before we leave our discussion of 9...♘d4, here are a couple of games that deal with offbeat alternatives for

White in the main line.

Game 23
Fries Nielsen-Jansa
Esbjerg 1981

1 e4 c5 2 g3 ♘c6 3 ♗g2 g6 4 d3 ♗g7 5 f4 e6 6 ♘f3 ♘ge7 7 ♘c3 d6 8 0-0 0-0 9 ♗e3 ♘d4 10 ♘g5

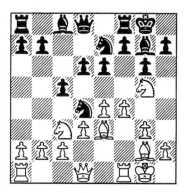

I had to include this game. White's idea is inspired: although he loses time by moving the knight, he hopes to prove that by playing ...h7-h6, Black weakens his kingside; which he does!

10...h6 11 ♘h3 ♔h7 12 ♕d2 e5 13 ♘d1 ♗g4 14 ♘df2 ♗f3

14...♘f3+ would have been a mistake due to 15 ♗xf3 ♗xf3 16 fxe5 dxe5 17 ♗xc5.

15 c3 ♗xg2 16 ♔xg2 ♘e6 17 g4 exf4 18 ♘xf4 ♘xf4+ 19 ♗xf4 d5 20 ♕e2 ♕d7 21 ♖ae1 b6 22 ♕f3 ♖ad8 23 ♕h3 ♘c6 24 ♕h4

see following diagram

Threatening 25 ♗xh6 and g4-g5.

24...f6 25 ♕g3 f5 26 exf5 gxf5 27 g5 hxg5 28 ♕xg5 ♖de8 29 ♘h3 ♕f7 30 ♔h1 ♘e5 31 ♕g3 ♕f6 32 ♘g5+ ♔g8 33 ♕h4 ♕g6 34 ♖g1 ♘xd3 35

♖xe8 ♖xe8 36 ♘h3 ♕h7 37 ♗h6 ♖e1 38 ♕d8+ ♔f7 39 ♘g5+ ♔g6 40 ♘xh7+ 1-0

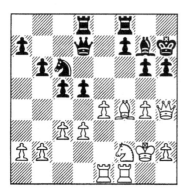

Game 24
Piceu-Vaklinov
European U-18 Championship 1996

1 ♘f3 c5 2 g3 ♘c6 3 ♗g2 g6 4 0-0 ♗g7 5 d3 e6 6 e4 ♘ge7 7 ♘c3 0-0 8 ♗e3 ♘d4 9 ♘h4 d6 10 f4

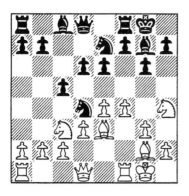

Instead of to g5, as in the previous game, the knight has gone to h4, and this strategy works here as well.

10...f5 11 ♕d2 ♗d7 12 ♘d1 ♖b8 13 c3 ♘dc6

Black's knight retreats, so White's knight can return to a better square.

14 ♘f3 b6 15 exf5 ♘xf5
Or 15...exf5 16 d4!

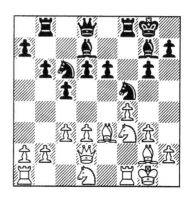

16 d4 cxd4 17 cxd4 ♕f6 18 ♘c3 ♘xe3 19 ♘e4 ♕e7 20 ♕xe3 ♖bc8 21 ♖ad1 ♖fe8 22 ♕a3 d5 23 ♘d6 ♘a5 24 ♘xe8 ♕xa3 25 bxa3 ♖xe8 26 ♖c1 ♗b5 27 ♖fe1 ♘c6 28 ♖ed1 ♗c4 29 ♔f2 ♘e7 30 ♗f1 ♗xa2 31 ♖c7 ♘f5 32 ♗b5 ♖f8 33 ♗d7 ♗b3 34 ♗xe6+ ♔h8 35 ♖d3 ♗c4 36 ♗xf5 gxf5 37 ♖e3 1-0

In order to avoid the complicated 9...♘d4 10 e5 variation, many Black players have switched to 9...b6 in recent years.

Game 25
Bastian-Loew
German Championship, Binz 1995

1 e4 c5 2 ♘c3 ♘c6 3 g3 g6 4 ♗g2 ♗g7 5 d3 d6 6 f4 e6 7 ♘f3 ♘ge7 8 0-0 0-0 9 ♗e3 b6

With this move Black supports the c-pawn and declares his intention to complete his development with ...♗b7. The drawback is that this allows White to carry out an advance in the centre with ...

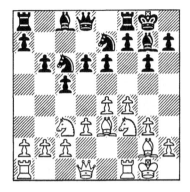

10 d4

... although I have my doubts as to whether this is really a move White wants to play.

10...d5!?

This was recommended by Joe Gallagher in *Beating the Anti-Sicilians*, but I'm not convinced of its effectiveness. White cannot play 11 dxc5 as 11...d4 wins a piece, while 11 e5 is unattractive due to the forced variation 11...&f5 12 &f2 &a6 13 &e1 cxd4 14 &xd4 &xd4 15 &xd4 &xd4 16 &xd4 &c7 (Gallagher), when Black has a pleasant positional advantage: pressure down the c-file and ...f7-f6 is in the air, opening up the position for the dark-squared bishop. For 10...&a6 see the next game.

11 exd5 &f5!

If 11...exd5 then White can capture on c5: 12 dxc5 d4 13 &xd4 and Black has problems on the long diagonal.

12 &f2 &cxd4 13 &e5

It is important to stay active. Other moves give Black an easy time: 13 dxe6 (13 &xd4 &xd4 14 dxe6 &xe6 is similar) 13...&xe6 (13...&xe6 is recommended by Gallagher, but I see nothing wrong with this natural

recapture) when Black was more active than his opponent in the game Ma.Zelic-Belamaric, Croatian Team Championship 1995.

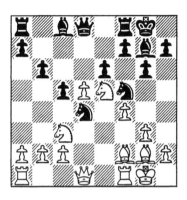

13...&a6 14 &e1 &c8

Instead, if 14...exd5?! 15 &xd5 &c8 16 c3 &e6 17 &a4 (Laurent-Nelson, Cappelle la Grande 1995), then White is a tempo up on Abramovic-Razuvaev, Paris 1989 (see the next note).

15 dxe6 &xe6 16 &d5 &b7

17 c4!?

It seems strange to give Black the d4 square for his knights, but if the knight on d5 is to be maintained, then this move is necessary. The stem game which Gallagher quotes is Abramovic-

Razuvaev, Paris 1989, which continued 17 c3 ♗a8! 18 ♘d7 ♖e8! 19 ♕a4 ♔h8! 20 ♘e5 ♗xe5 21 ♖xe5 f6 22 ♖ee1 ♗xd5 ... and by super-precise play Black had emerged with an extra piece.

17...♘fd4 18 ♕a4!

This is the crucial difference between the two sides: White has an active square for his queen and can connect his rooks; Black's queen is stuck in the middle.

18...a5

18...♖a8!? is a possible improvement.

19 ♕d7!

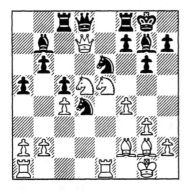

Surprising and strong.

19...♗xe5 20 ♖xe5 ♗xd5 21 ♕xd5 ♕c7 22 ♖ae1 ♖cd8 23 ♕e4 ♖fe8 24 h4

White has a fantastic attack.

24...♘f5 25 h5 ♘d6 26 ♕e2 ♘d4 27 ♕d3 ♖xe5 28 ♖xe5 ♘6f5 29 hxg6 hxg6 30 ♗d5 ♘c6 31 ♖xf5!? gxf5 32 ♕xf5 ♖d6 33 g4 ♘d4 34 ♕e4 ♕d7 35 f5 ♖h6

The preliminary to an attempt to invade the white kingside. Bastian now misses the best way to cope with Black's threats.

36 ♗g3

36 g5! was the move.

36...♕d8 37 ♔g2 ♕f6 38 g5 ♕xg5 39 ♕e8+ ♔h7 40 ♕xf7+ ♕g7 41 ♕xg7+ ♔xg7 42 ♗e5+ ♔f8 43 f6 ♔e8 44 ♔g3 ♔d7 45 f7 ♔e7 46 ♗c7 ♖g6+ 47 ♔h4 ♖f6 48 ♔h5 ♘e6 49 ♗g3 ♘f4+ 0-1

The wrong result! White should have won this game.

Game 26
Abramovic-Damljanovic
Yugoslav Championship 1989

1 e4 c5 2 ♘c3 ♘c6 3 g3 g6 4 ♗g2 ♗g7 5 d3 e6 6 f4 ♘ge7 7 ♘f3 d6 8 0-0 0-0 9 ♗e3 b6 10 d4 ♗a6

I think that this is stronger than 10...d5. Alternatively, 10...cxd4?! 11 ♘xd4 ♗a6 12 ♖f2 ♘a5 13 f5 ♘c4 14 ♗c1 ♗xd4 15 ♕xd4 e5 16 ♕d3 ♕c8 17 f6 should have given White a winning attack in Hartvig-Gabrielsen, Copenhagen 1996.

11 ♖f2

Of course 11 ♖e1 is also perfectly playable.

11...♕c7!

This is stronger than capturing on d4.

12 a4 ♖ad8 13 ♘b5 ♗xb5 14 axb5 ♘xd4 15 ♘xd4 cxd4 16 ♗xd4 e5 17 ♗c3 d5!?

The position is messy, but it seems to me that the odds are in Black's favour. Alternatively, 17...exf4 18 gxf4 (18 ♗xg7 fxg3) 18...♗xc3 19 bxc3 d5 wasn't bad for Black in Kovacevic-Paunovic, Yugoslavia 1989. White's position looks rather ragged.

18 exd5 exf4 19 ♗xg7 fxg3 20 hxg3 ♔xg7 21 ♕d4+ ♔g8 22 g4 ♘c8 23 c4 ♘d6 24 b3 ♕e7 25 b4 ♖c8 26 ♖c2?

White should have tried 26 ♗f1, when the position is complex and too close to call.

26...♘xb5 27 ♕d2 ♕f6! 28 ♖ac1 ♘d4 29 ♕c3 ♖ce8 30 c5 ♕f4 31 ♖d2 ♘e2+ 32 ♖xe2 ♖xe2 33 ♖f1 ♕xg4 34 ♖f2 ♖xf2 35 ♔xf2 ♖e8 0-1

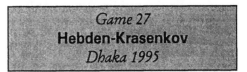

Game 27
Hebden-Krasenkov
Dhaka 1995

1 e4 c5 2 ♘c3 ♘c6 3 g3 g6 4 ♗g2 ♗g7 5 d3 d6 6 f4 e6 7 ♘f3 ♘ge7 8 0-0 0-0 9 ♗e3 b6 10 ♗f2

It isn't necessary to play 10 d4, though the bishop move hardly tests Black's strategy.

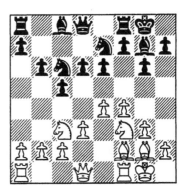

10...♗b7 11 ♕d2 e5

It is logical to play this move when the bishop has retreated to f2: the pawn on f4 lacks support. Alternatively, 11...♕d7 12 ♖ae1 ♘d4 13 ♘h4 f5 14 ♔h1 e5?! (misjudged; Black's position is fine after 14...♖ae8) 15 ♘d5 ♘xd5 16 exd5 ♖ae8 17 c3 ♘b5 18 ♗e3 ♖f7 19 a4 ♘c7 20 c4 and Black's minor pieces on the queenside were misplaced in Spassky-Krasenkov, Oviedo Rapidplay 1991.

12 ♖ae1 ♕d7 13 ♗e3 ♘d4 14 ♘h4 f6 15 f5!? g5 16 ♘f3 d5 17 ♘xd5 ♘xd5 18 exd5 ♘xf5 19 ♗h3 ♗xd5 20 ♘h4 gxh4 21 ♗xf5 ♕c6 22 ♕e2 ♗e6 23 ♕g4 ♗xf5 24 ♖xf5 hxg3 25 hxg3

With his unskaeable grip on the kingside light squares, White has reasonable compensation for the pawn.

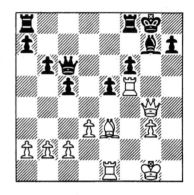

25...♖f7 26 ♖e2 ♔h8 27 ♖h2 ♗f8 28 ♖fh5 ♖c8 29 ♕g6 ♕d7 30 ♖f5 ♖g7 31 ♕xf6 ♗e7 32 ♕xe5 ♗d6 33 ♕d5 ♖xg3+ 34 ♔f2 ♖xe3 35 ♖f7 ♗g3+ 36 ♔xe3 ♖e8+ 37 ♔d2 ♗f4+ 38 ♔c3 ♕xd5 ½-½

Summary

After 9...♘d4 10 ♗f2 (Games 19-22) is a sound alternative to 10 e5, and White's results with it are by no means bad. I think Black's most interesting response to 10...e5, attempting to exploit the slight weakening of the f4 square (Game 20). Instead of 9...♘d4, 9...b6!? (Games 25-27) has been scoring very well for Black. The only way for White to exploit the omission of ...♘d4 is to play 10 d4 himself, and then my bet is that we will be seeing more of 10...♗a6 (Game 26) in the future, rather than 10...d5 (Game 25).

1 e4 c5 2 ♘c3 ♘c6 3 g3 g6 4 ♗g2 ♗g7 5 d3 d6 6 f4 e6 7 ♘f3 ♘ge7 8 0-0 0-0 9 ♗e3

9...♘d4
       9...b6 *(D)*
           10 d4
                10...d5 – *Game 25*; 10...♗a6 – *Game 26*
           10 ♗f2 – *Game 27*

10 ♗f2 *(D)*
       10 ♘g5 – *Game 23*; 10 ♘h4 – *Game 24*

10...b6
       10...♘xf3+ 11 ♗xf3 ♘c6 12 ♗g2 ♘d4 13 e5 transposes to
       10 e5 ♘ef5 11 ♗f2 ♘xf3+ 12 ♕xf3 ♘d4 13 ♕d1 in Chapter 1
       10...e5 – *Game 20*
       10...♘ec6 *(D)*
            11 ♘xd4 ♘xd4 12 e5 transposes to 10 e5 ♘ef5 11 ♗f2 ♘xf3+
            12 ♕xf3 ♘d4 13 ♕d1 in Chapter 1
            11 ♘d2 – *Game 21*
       10...♖b8 – *Game 22*
11 ♘xd4 – *Game 19*

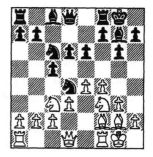

    9...b6   *10 ♗f2*   *10...♘ec6*

CHAPTER THREE

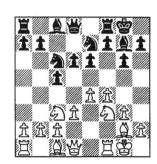

Main Line: White does not play 9 ♗e3

1 e4 c5 2 ♘c3 ♘c6 3 g3 g6 4 ♗g2 ♗g7 5 d3 d6 6 f4 e6 7 ♘f3 ♘ge7 8 0-0 0-0

This chapter contains games where White plays 6 f4, but does not follow up with 9 ♗e3, the standard move which we saw in the first two chapters. Although 9 ♗e3 is by far the most popular move, there are alternative strategies which deserve more than a second glance. If you are looking to catch your opponent out with something that is a little offbeat, then you might find what you are looking for here.

There are certain advantages to delaying, or completely omitting, ♗e3, the main one being that if Black plays his knight into d4, it can be exchanged off straightaway by the knight on f3 as there is no pawn fork to worry about. We shall start off with games in which White plays a controlled strategy (Games 28-33), then move on to the crude (Games 34-36) and, finally, the bizarre (Game 37 and 38), which often involves something down the h-file.

Game 28
Spassky-Geller
Sukhumi Candidates 1968

1 e4 c5 2 ♘c3 d6 3 g3 ♘c6 4 ♗g2 g6 5 d3 ♗g7 6 f4 e6 7 ♘f3 ♘ge7 8 0-0 0-0 9 a3

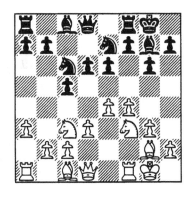

White secures his queenside position before committing himself in the centre or kingside. The point is to forestall Black's plan of ...b5-b4, but also, under the right circumstances (protecting the knight on c3 for a start) to play b2-b4, putting pressure on Black's queenside and centre. Surprisingly few players have tried this idea in exactly this position, but it looks sensible to me. At this point a reasonable idea for Black is to attempt to transpose into the next game with 9...♖b8.

9...♗d7 10 ♖b1 ♖c8 11 ♗d2

Now White is ready to play b2-b4, but Black jumps in to stop it.

11...♘d4 12 ♘e2

Another plus of playing ♖b1: the pawn on b2 is covered.

12...♗a4 13 b3 ♗c6 14 c4!

Increasing his control over the centre.

14...♘xf3+ 15 ♗xf3 d5 16 ♗e3 d4 17 ♗d2 ♕d7 18 g4 f5 19 ♘g3

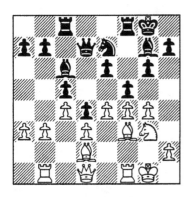

Since White has the potential to play on both sides of the board, I prefer his position, although the situation is just messy. Geller counterattacks well and by the end it is Spassky who is fighting for the draw.

19...♔h8 20 ♕e2 ♖ce8 21 ♗g2 e5 22 b4 exf4 23 ♗xf4 cxb4 24 axb4 b5 25 cxb5 ♗xb5 26 gxf5 ♘d5 27 ♗h3 gxf5 28 ♕h5 ♘xf4 29 ♖xf4 ♗xd3 30 ♖xf5 ♕c6 31 ♖c5 ♕h6 32 ♕xh6 ♗xh6 33 ♖d1 ♗xe4 34 ♘xe4

♖xe4 35 ♖c8 ♗e3+ 36 ♔g2 ♖xc8 37 ♗xc8 ♖e7 38 ♔f3 ♔g7 39 ♗a6 ♖f7+ 40 ♔e4 ♖f4+ 41 ♔d3 ♖f2 42 ♖a1 ♔f6 43 ♔e4 ♖f4+ 44 ♔d3 ♖f2 45 ♔e4 ♔g5 46 ♗c4 ♖c2 47 ♖a5+ ♔h4 48 ♗f7 h6 49 ♖xa7 ♖b2 50 ♖a4 ♔g5 51 ♗c4 ½-½

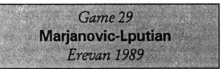

Game 29
Marjanovic-Lputian
Erevan 1989

1 e4 c5 2 ♘c3 ♘c6 3 g3 e6 4 ♗g2 g6 5 d3 ♗g7 6 f4 ♘ge7 7 ♘f3 0-0 8 0-0 d6 9 ♗d2

This idea is closely connected to that in the previous game – indeed, it could potentially transpose. 9 ♗d2 was also a favourite of Spassky's, but this game has put a dampener on the whole variation for White.

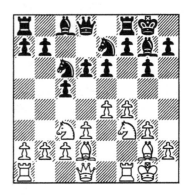

9...b5!

If Black can get away with playing this immediately, then why not go for it?

10 a3 ♖b8 11 ♖b1 c4!

An important novelty at the time this game was played. Black's most natural move here, 11...a5?!, is actually a mistake due to 12 a4! b4 (or

12...bxa4 13 ♘xa4 and Black's pawn advance has been halted and the a-pawn isolated) 13 ♘b5 ♗a6 14 c4! and the knight on b5 has been secured. This is the positional trick that I mentioned in the introduction.

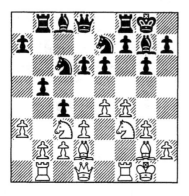

12 h3?!

A waste of time. 12 ♗e3 d5 13 dxc4 bxc4 14 ♘d4 ♘xd4 15 ♗xd4 dxe4 16 ♗xg7 ♕xd1 17 ♖fxd1 ♔xg7 18 ♘xe4 ♗b7 is given as unclear by Lputian. I can't imagine that either side should lose if they play sensibly.

12...b4!

Black has a powerful initiative.

13 axb4 cxd3 14 cxd3 ♕b6+ 15 ♔h2 ♘xb4 16 ♗e1 ♗a6 17 ♗f2 ♕c7 18 ♘e1 ♖fc8

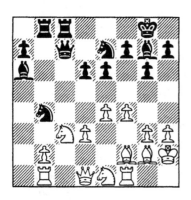

Lputian reckons that 18...e5! is even stronger: 19 ♗e3 d5 20 exd5 ♘f5 with a vicious attack in the making.

19 ♖c1 ♕d7 20 ♕d2 ♘ec6 21 ♖a1 ♘d4 22 ♖a3 ♖c7 23 ♗e3 ♘b5 24 ♖b3 ♘c6 25 ♘xb5 ♗xb5 26 ♘f3 ♖cb7 27 ♖a1 a5 28 ♖a2 ♕c7 29 e5 dxe5 30 ♘xe5 ♘xe5! 31 fxe5 ♗xe5 32 ♗xb7 ♗xg3+ 33 ♔g1 ♕xb7 34 ♖xa5 ♕d5 35 ♖c3 ♕d8 36 ♗a7 ♖b7 37 ♕g2 ♕xa5 38 ♕xb7 ♕a1+ 39 ♔g2 ♕xb2+ 40 ♔xg3 ♕xc3 41 ♕b8+ ♔g7 42 ♗e3 ♗xd3 43 ♕d6 e5 44 ♗c5 ♗c4+ 45 ♔f2 ♕c2+ 46 ♔g1 ♕c1+ 47 ♔h2 ♕f4+ 48 ♔g2 h5 0-1

A complicated game, but the odds were heavily in Black's favour.

Game 30
Gabriel-Miladinovic
World Junior Ch., Singapore 1990

1 e4 c5 2 ♘c3 ♘c6 3 g3 g6 4 ♗g2 ♗g7 5 d3 e6 6 f4 d6 7 ♘f3 ♘ge7 8 0-0 0-0 9 ♘e2

Christian Gabriel from Germany regularly practised this well-motivated move a few years ago. White swings the knight round to the kingside and intends to cover the d4 square by playing c2-c3. The drawback is that it is time consuming and gives Black an easy plan: the advance of the b-pawn.

9...♖b8

The most critical response. Games 31, 32 and 33 consider 9...b6, 9...♗d7 and 9...d5 respectively.

10 c3

White did without c2-c3 in Kostrov-Al.Sokolov, Kstovo Open 1994: 10 ♔h1 b5 11 g4 f5 12 gxf5 exf5 13 ♘g3 ♔h8 14 ♕e1 ♕c7 15 ♕f2 (if White is going to play this crudely, then how about 15 h4 here?) 15...♘d4 16 c3 ♘xf3 17 ♕xf3 c4 18 ♖e1 ♗b7 when White's centre is under enormous pressure.

10...b5! 11 ♕c2 b4! 12 ♗e3 bxc3!

In a previous round in the same tournament, Black had played less accurately: 12...♕a5 13 ♘d2 ♖d8 14 g4 bxc3 15 bxc3 ♕c7 16 f5 f6 17 ♘f4 e5 18 ♘h3 ♗d7 19 a3!? ♖f8 20 ♖f2 ♘a5 21 ♕a2+ ♔h8 22 ♖af1 ♗c6 23 g5 with a strong attack, Gabriel-Markowski, World Junior Championship, Singapore 1990.

13 bxc3 ♗a6

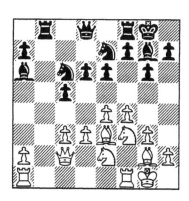

Although White's position is alright, it is difficult to build up an

attack on the kingside when his centre and queenside are so sensitive. The game is finely balanced.

14 ♖fd1 ♕a5 15 g4 ♖fc8 16 ♗f2 ♕a3 17 ♖ab1 ♗b5 18 ♕b2 ♕xb2 19 ♖xb2 ♗a4 20 ♖dd2

Not 20 ♖db1 ♗c2!

20...♘a5 21 e5 dxe5 22 ♘xe5 ♖xb2 23 ♖xb2 g5 24 ♗g3 gxf4 25 ♗xf4 ♘d5 26 ♗xd5 exd5 27 ♘g3 ♖e8 28 ♘h5 ♗h8 29 g5 ♖xe5 30 ♗xe5 ♗xe5 31 ♘f6+ ♔g7 32 ♘xd5 ♗c6 33 ♖e2 ♗d6 34 ♘f6

34 c4!? might have been a better try.

34...♔g6 35 h4 h6 36 ♘e4 ♗xe4 37 ♖xe4 hxg5 38 hxg5 ♔xg5 39 ♖a4 ♗c7 40 ♔g2 f5 41 d4 cxd4 42 ♖xd4 ♗b6 43 ♖a4 ♘c6 44 ♔f3 ♘e5+ 45 ♔g3 ♘d3 46 ♔f3 f4 0-1

Game 31
Gabriel-Stangl
Altensteig 1992

1 e4 c5 2 ♘c3 ♘c6 3 g3 g6 4 ♗g2 ♗g7 5 d3 d6 6 f4 e6 7 ♘f3 ♘ge7 8 0-0 0-0 9 ♘e2 b6

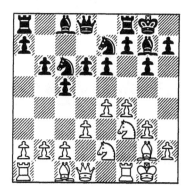

Simple development, but as we have seen, 9...♖b8 is more to the point.

10 c3 ♗a6 11 g4 f5 12 gxf5 gxf5

This justifies White's strategy: the knight will find a good square on h5. I don't see what is wrong with 12...exf5. This position is worth investigating. I suppose that Black must have been worried about 13 ♘g5 ♕d7 14 ♕b3+, although after 14...♔h8 I don't see how White should continue.

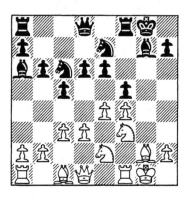

13 ♘g3 ♕d7 14 ♖e1 ♖ae8 15 ♘h5 ♘g6 16 ♗e3 ♘d8 17 ♕d2 ♗b7 18 ♖ad1 fxe4 19 dxe4 ♗xe4 20 ♕xd6 ♕b7 21 ♕d7 ♖e7 22 ♕xb7 ♘xb7 23 ♘g5 ♗xg2 24 ♔xg2 h6 25 ♘e4 ♖f5 26 ♘eg3 ♖ff7 27 ♗c1 ♘h4+ 28 ♔h3 ♘f5 29 ♘xf5 ♖xf5 30 ♔g4 ♗f8 31 ♖xe6 ♖ff7 32 f5 c4 33 ♗e3 ♖c7 34 ♖g6+ ♔h7 35 ♘f6+ 1-0

Game 32
Prasad-Kuzmin
New Delhi 1984

1 e4 c5 2 ♘c3 ♘c6 3 g3 g6 4 ♗g2 ♗g7 5 d3 d6 6 f4 e6 7 ♘f3 ♘ge7 8 0-0 0-0 9 ♘e2 ♗d7

see following diagram

10 c3 ♕b6 11 ♔h1 f5 12 ♖b1 ♕a6

Black attacks on the light squares in an original manner, and perhaps he

should have got more from the position.

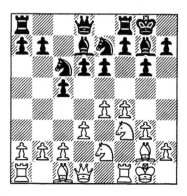

13 ♗e3 ♖ac8 14 a3 ♘d8 15 e5 ♘f7

15...dxe5!? 16 ♘xe5 ♗xe5 17 fxe5 ♗c6 is slightly risky as it weakens the kingside, but is consistent with the light-square strategy he has decided to adopt.

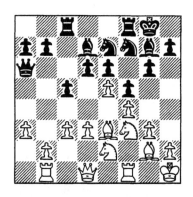

16 exd6 ♕xd6 17 c4 ♗c6 18 b4 cxb4 19 axb4 a6 20 ♕b3 ♖fd8 21 ♖bd1 ♕d7 22 ♘c3 h6 23 ♗b6 ♖e8 24 d4 ♘d6 25 d5 exd5 26 cxd5 ♗b5 27 ♘e5 ♖xc3 28 ♕xc3 ♗xf1 29 ♖xf1 ♘e4 30 ♘xd7 ♗xc3 31 ♖d1 ♘c8 32 ♗c5 ♖d8 33 ♗xe4 ♖xd7 34 ♗f3 ♘d6 35 ♖c1 ♗f6 36 ♗xd6 ♖xd6 37 ♖c8+ ♗d8 38 ♖b8 ♖d7 39 ♗d1 ♔f8 40 ♗a4 ♖xd5 ½-½

Game 33
Stanec-Lendwai
Austrian Championship 1995

1 e4 c5 2 ♘c3 ♘c6 3 g3 g6 4 ♗g2 ♗g7 5 d3 d6 6 f4 e6 7 ♘f3 ♘ge7 8 0-0 0-0 9 ♘e2 d5

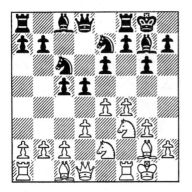

10 e5 d4?!

I don't like this move very much at all. If Black is going to play 9...d5, then he should at least be consistent and play 10...f6. Leaving the pawn on e5 gives White the chance to build up a strong attack (compare with Davies-Fossan which I mentioned in the notes to Game 21; White also establishes a knight on e4 in that game).

11 ♘g5! b6 12 ♘e4 ♗a6 13 b3 ♘d5 14 g4 h6 15 ♖f3 ♖c8 16 ♖h3 ♖c7 17 g5

see following diagram

White's strategy is blunt but effective. If 17...h5, then 18 ♘g3 and ♘xh5.

17...hxg5 18 ♘xg5 ♗b7 19 ♘g3 ♘e3 20 ♗xe3 dxe3 21 ♘3e4 e2 22 ♕e1 ♘d4 23 ♖c1 ♗xe4 24 ♘xe4 ♖d7 25 c3 ♘f5 26 ♕xe2 ♕e7 27 ♘g3

27 ♘g5! was the move.

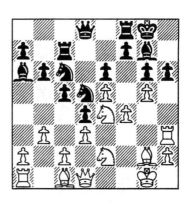

27...♖fd8 28 ♗e4 a6 29 ♘h1 ♗xe5 30 ♗xf5 ♗xf4 31 ♖f1 ♕g5+ 32 ♗g4 f5 33 ♖xf4 ♕xf4 34 ♕xe6+ ♔g7 35 ♗e2 ♕c1+ 36 ♗f1 ♕xc3 37 ♕xb6 ♖d6 38 ♕b7+ ♖8d7 39 ♕f3 ♖e6 40 ♘f2 ♕d4 41 ♕a8 ♖d8 42 ♕a7+ ♖d7 43 ♕b8 ♖d8 44 ♕c7+ ♕d7 45 ♕xc5 ♖c8 46 ♕b4 ♖c1 47 ♕d2 ♕c6 48 ♘d1 f4 49 ♕b2+ ♖f6 50 ♘f2 ♕c5 51 ♖h7+ ♔xh7 52 ♕xf6 ♕e3 53 ♕f7+ ♔h6 54 ♕f8+ ♔h7 55 ♕f7+ ♔h6 56 ♕f8+ ♔h7 ½-½

Black should have been put away out of the opening.

Game 34
Hennigan-Kuznecov
Oakham Young Masters 1986

1 e4 c5 2 ♘c3 ♘c6 3 g3 g6 4 ♗g2 ♗g7 5 d3 d6 6 f4 e6 7 ♘f3 ♘ge7 8 0-0 0-0 9 g4

With this move we are edging from the aggressive into the crude. If White were given one more move, then he could play f4-f5!?, sacrificing a pawn to get a good shot at his opponent's king. This is all very well, but 9 g4 allows

Black to reveal one of the main points of his piece formation:

9...f5!

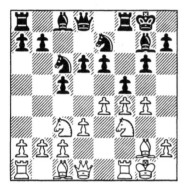

This is a crucial move in Black's counterattack. It isn't just that White is prevented from playing f4-f5; it means that the pawn is fixed on f4, restricting the scope of the bishop on c1. Playing a move like 9 g4 is risky. Although it looks like jolly good fun to launch an attack from the beginning of the game, the whole exercise can easily rebound: White's king might find itself exposed in a few more moves.

10 gxf5 exf5

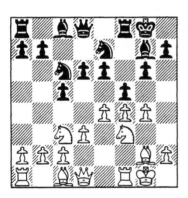

For 10...gxf5 see the next game. In principle I prefer the recapture with

the e-pawn: Black's king keeps its pawn cover. The only drawback can be if the a2-g8 diagonal becomes a little sensitive, or White can put the d5 square to good use.

11 ♗e3 ♔h8 12 ♕d2 ♗e6 13 ♖ae1 ♕d7 14 ♘g5

14 d4 runs into 14...fxe4 15 ♘xe4 ♗d5 and White should lose a pawn.

14...♗g8 15 ♘d5

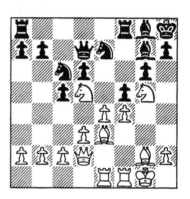

White's strategy is a bit obvious, but Black falls for it nevertheless. There is really no need to capture the knight on d5. 15...h6 is the move, when White will either have to exchange on e7, or make a miserable retreat to h3. After 16 ♘h3 ♖ae8, the position is still complicated, but Black has enough pieces protecting his king, and he can decide exactly when, and if, he wishes to exchange the knight on d5.

15...♘xd5 16 exd5 ♘d4 17 c3 ♘b5 18 ♗f2 ♘c7

18...♖ae8 doesn't solve Black's problems: 19 d4! b6 20 ♘e6 ♗xe6 21 dxe6 ♖xe6 22 dxc5, when White's bishops are impressive.

19 c4 ♖ae8 20 d4 b6 21 b3 ♗f6 22 ♖xe8 ♖xe8 23 ♖e1

White has a pleasant space advantage, but in the remainder of the game Black is a little too cooperative in helping him to exploit it.

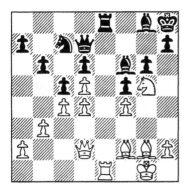

23...♗xd4 24 ♗xd4+ cxd4 25 ♕xd4+ ♕g7 26 ♕xg7+ ♔xg7 27 ♖xe8 ♘xe8 28 ♘f3 ♔f6 29 ♔f2 ♘c7 30 ♘d4 ♗f7

30...a6, preventing White's coming knight manoeuvre, was a better defensive try.

31 ♘c6 a5 32 ♘a7 ♘a6 33 ♘c8 ♘b4 34 a4 ♘d3+ 35 ♔e3 ♘c5 36 ♘xd6 ♘xb3 37 ♘c8 ♗e8 38 ♘xb6 ♘c5 39 ♔d4 ♘b3+ 40 ♔c3 ♘c5 41 ♗f3 ♘xa4+ 42 ♘xa4 ♗xa4 43 c5 g5 44 fxg5+ ♔xg5 45 c6 ♔f6 46 ♔c4 ♔e7 47 ♔c5 ♗b3 48 d6+ ♔e8 49 c7 ♗e6 50 ♗c6+ ♔f8 51 d7 1-0

> *Game 35*
> ## Hennigan-Muir
> *British Championship 1987*

1 e4 c5 2 ♘c3 ♘c6 3 g3 g6 4 ♗g2 ♗g7 5 d3 d6 6 f4 e6 7 ♘f3 ♘ge7 8 0-0 0-0 9 g4 f5 10 gxf5 gxf5

For 10...exf5 see the previous game. By capturing with the g-pawn, Black keeps as many pawns in the centre as possible (that's the good news), but leaves his kingside position slightly weaker (bad news). If I were playing 9 g4, I think I would be very glad to see Black recapture like this: it justifies White's blunt strategy.

11 ♘e2!

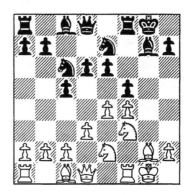

With this move Hennigan pinpoints the shortcomings of 10...gxf5: the knight is heading for h5.

11...♖b8 12 ♘g3

As well as looking at h5, the knight keeps up the pressure on the f5 pawn.

12...b6 13 ♔h1 ♗b7 14 c3!

Covering the d4 square.

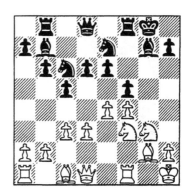

14...♕d7 15 ♕c2 ♘g6 16 exf5 exf5 17 ♗d2 ♖be8 18 ♖ae1 ♖e7 19 ♘h5 ♖fe8 20 ♖xe7 ♖xe7 21 ♖e1 ♖xe1+

22 ♗xe1

White has the better chances as his pieces are slightly more active. However, the game should still be a draw.

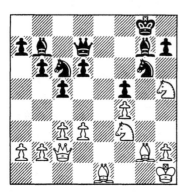

22...♕e6 23 ♕b3 ♕xb3 24 axb3 ♗h6 25 ♘h4 ♘xf4 26 ♘xf5 ♗g5 27 ♘xf4 ♗xf4 28 ♗g3 ♗xg3 29 hxg3

Suddenly Black is unable to protect his d-pawn.

29...♘a5 30 ♘xd6 ♗xg2+ 31 ♔xg2 ♘xb3 32 ♔f3 h5 33 ♘c8 ♘c1 34 ♔e3 ♔f7 35 ♘xa7 ♔e6 36 ♘c8 ♔f5 37 ♘xb6 ♔g4 38 ♘d7 ♔xg3 39 ♘xc5 h4 40 ♘e4+ ♔g2 41 ♘g5 ♘b3 42 d4 h3

43 ♘xh3 ♔xh3 44 ♔f4 ♔h4 45 d5 ♔h5 46 ♔f5 ♔h6 47 d6 ♘c5 48 b4 ♘d7 49 ♔e6 1-0

Game 36
Kurcubic-Garcia del Blanco
World Student Ch., Leon 1996

1 e4 c5 2 ♘c3 ♘c6 3 f4 g6 4 ♘f3 ♗g7 5 g3 d6 6 ♗g2 e6 7 0-0 ♘ge7 8 d3 0-0 9 ♕e1

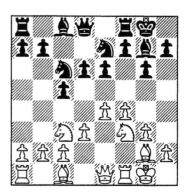

White nudges the queen one square across the board; all very subtle.

9...♖b8

In view of what follows, I would suggest 9...f5, frustrating White's plan.

10 a4 a6 11 g4 f5 12 ♕h4

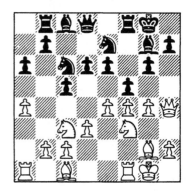

Perhaps not so subtle. In fact, extremely crude, but the kingside is definitely where the queen belongs, and there is no obvious way for Black to exploit this early demonstration.

12...&d4 13 &f2 &ec6 14 &g3 b5 15 axb5 axb5 16 &g5

We have encountered this idea before. White plays the knight to g5, with no particular idea in mind; in fact Black can chase away immediately.

16...h6 17 &f3

A waste of time? No. The g6 square has been weakened. In the game Black fails to contain White's attack.

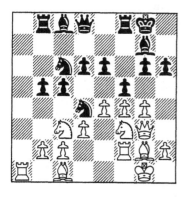

17...b4 18 &d1 &xf3+ 19 &xf3 &d4 20 &g2 &h7 21 &e3 fxg4 22 &xg4 h5 23 &e3 &f6 24 f5 exf5 25 exf5 &xf5 26 &xf5 &xf5 27 &a7+ &g7 28 &e3 g5 29 &xf5 &xf5 30 &e4 &f6 31 &xg5 &xg5+ 32 &xg5 &bf8

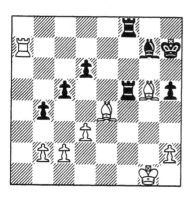

33 &xf5+ &xf5 34 &h4 &g6 35 b3

&d4+ 36 &g2 &f4 37 &g3 &f6 38 &d7 &e5 39 &xe5 dxe5 40 &d5 &f5 41 &xc5 &f4 42 &c4+ &e3 43 &g3 &f4 44 &c8 &d2 45 &c5 &g4+ 46 &h3 &d4 47 &g3 &g4+ 48 &f2 &f4+ 49 &g2 &g4+ 50 &h1 h4 51 h3 &f4 52 &g2 e4 53 &c4 exd3 54 cxd3 &f8 55 &xb4 &g8+ 56 &g4 &h8 57 b4 &xd3 58 &f3 &h5 59 &f4 &h6 60 &g4 &e3 61 &g5 &b6 62 &xh4 &b5+ 63 &f6 &f3 64 &c4 &g3 65 h4 &b8 66 &e7 &b6 67 &d7 &h6 68 b5 1-0

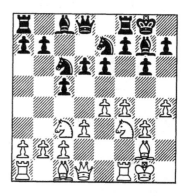

Game 37
Van der Weide-Langeweg
Dutch Ch. Semi-Final 1992

1 e4 c5 2 &c3 &c6 3 g3 g6 4 &g2 &g7 5 d3 d6 6 f4 e6 7 &f3 &ge7 8 0-0 0-0 9 h4

Now we come on to the bizarre. Somehow this move is very appealing. Van der Weide has made it his speciality, with mixed results.

9...e5

Quite logical; meeting a wing attack with an advance in the centre. This seems more effective than 9...h5 10 &g5 &d4 11 &e2 and after expelling

the knight, White's attack continues.
10 ♘g5!?

Preventing ...♗g4, but also opening up the possibility of playing f4-f5. Nevertheless, 10 h5 ♗g4 11 hxg6 hxg6 12 ♕e1 is worth considering.

10...exf4 11 gxf4 h6 12 ♘h3 f5

Black thought he was being crafty in Van der Weide-Los, Leeuwarden Open 1993, but he soon came unstuck: 12...d5 13 f5! dxe4 (13...gxf5 14 exd5 ♘d4 15 ♕h5!) 14 f6 ♗xf6 15 ♖xf6 ♕d4+ 16 ♖f2 and White managed to consolidate his extra piece.

13 h5 gxh5 14 ♕xh5 ♕e8 15 ♕xe8 ♖xe8

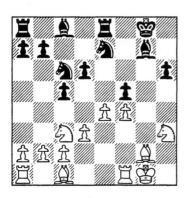

White's strategy has been successful: he has the better pawn structure and goes into the ending with a slight advantage.

16 ♘b5 ♖d8 17 c3 ♖b8 18 ♗e3 a6 19 ♘c7 b6 20 ♘d5 ♘xd5 21 exd5 ♘e7 22 ♗f2 ♗f6 23 ♖fe1 ♘g6 24 ♗f3 ♖b7 25 ♗h5 ♖g7 26 ♔h2 ♔h7 27 ♖e3 ♘e7 28 ♗f3 ♗d7 29 ♖g1 b5 30 ♖xg7+ ♔xg7 31 c4 ♔f8 32 b3 ♖b8 33 ♘g1 a5 34 ♘e2 a4 35 ♔g2 axb3 36 axb3 ♖a8 37 ♘g3 ♖a3 38 ♗d1 ♖a1 39 ♖e1 ♗c3 40 ♖h1 ♗g7 41 ♗h5 ♖a2 42 ♖b1 b4 43 ♔f3 ♗e8

44 ♗xe8 ♔xe8 45 ♖e1 ♔d7 46 ♖xe7+ ♔xe7 47 ♘xf5+ ♔d7 48 ♘xg7 ♖b2 49 ♗h4 ♖xb3 50 ♔e2 ♖b1 51 ♔d2 ♖g1 52 ♗f6 ♖g4 53 f5 ♖g2+ 54 ♔c1 ♖g1+ 55 ♔c2 ♖g2+ ½-½

Game 38
Haik-Mednis
Cannes Open 1994

1 e4 c5 2 ♘c3 ♘c6 3 f4 g6 4 g3 ♗g7 5 ♗g2 d6 6 d3 e6 7 ♘h3

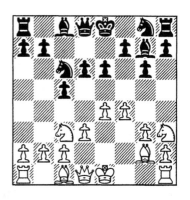

It is not uncommon for the knight to develop to h3 in the Closed Sicilian, but it is usually combined with ♗e3 and ♕d2 with the idea of exchanging the dark-squared bishops. In this case, White has an aggressive plan in mind.

7...♘ge7 8 ♘f2 ♖b8

Black has an inkling that White is planning something blunt on the kingside and hangs back with castling for a moment. He clearly had no desire to get embroiled in the manic complications that might follow after 8...0-0 9 h4!? (with the rook still on h1, this is too tempting to resist) 9...h5 10 g4 hxg4 11 ♕xg4 (11 ♘xg4!? f5 12 ♘f2) 11...♘d4 12 ♔d1. In these variations, White's king is in just as much danger as Black's. Anything could happen.

9 g4 h5 10 g5

Black was probably relieved to see the kingside close, but the space which White has gained on the kingside is pleasant.

10...♘d4 11 0-0 b5

The advance of the b-pawn only helps White to gain play on the queenside. Perhaps it would have been wiser to play the more modest 11...b6 followed by ...♗b7. The pawn on c5 would have had sufficient support – see the rest of the game, but also think back to Chapter 1 where the c5 pawn is often a problem for Black.

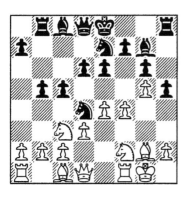

12 ♘e2 b4 13 a3 a5 14 axb4 axb4 15 ♘xd4 ♗xd4 16 ♕e1 0-0 17 c3 ♗g7 18 ♗e3 ♕b6 19 e5 bxc3 20 bxc3 d5 21 ♖b1 ♕xb1 22 ♕xb1 ♖xb1 23 ♖xb1 d4 24 cxd4 ♘f5 25 ♗d2 ♘xd4 26 ♘e4 ♗d7 27 ♘xc5 ♗c6 28 ♘e4 ♖d8 29 ♖b6 ♗xe4 30 ♗xe4 ♗f8 31 ♔f1 ♖c8 32 ♗e3 ♘c2 33 ♗f2 ♘b4 34 d4 ♖d8 35 ♔e2 ♘d5 36 ♗xd5 ♖xd5 37 ♔d3 ♖a5 38 ♗e1 ♖d5 39 ♖b8 ♔g7 40 ♔c4 ♗e7 41 ♖b7 ♗f8 42 ♖a7 ♖d8 43 ♗a5 ♖b8 44 ♗c7 ♖b4+ 45 ♔c3 ♖b5 46 ♗d8 ♖b8 47 ♗a5 ♔g8 48 ♗c7 ♖b5 49 ♖a8 ♔g7 50 ♗d8 ♖b7 51 ♗f6+ ♔g8

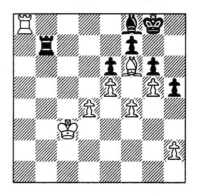

52 d5 exd5 53 ♔d4 h4 54 ♔xd5 h3 55 ♔c6 ♖b2 56 ♗e7 ♖xh2 57 ♖xf8+ ♔g7 58 ♖a8 ♖c2+ 59 ♔d5 1-0

Summary

Lputian's novelty in Game 29 has removed any danger which might have existed in the system with 9 ♗d2, and this probably also applies to Game 28, which is likely to transpose. 9 ♘e2 (Games 30–33) is sensible but, if handled correctly, a bit tame. 9 g4 (Games 34 and 35) just looks too crude to me, so long as Black plays 9...f5, and recaptures on f5 with the e-pawn. I can't believe that 9 h4 (Game 37) is terribly good, but it's fun, and I'll be giving it a punt in the next blitz game I play.

1 e4 c5 2 ♘c3 ♘c6 3 g3 g6 4 ♗g2 ♗g7 5 d3 d6 6 f4 e6

7 ♘f3
> 7 ♘h3 – *Game 38*

7...♘ge7 8 0-0 0-0 *(D)* **9 a3**
> 9 ♗d2 – *Game 29*
> 9 ♘e2 *(D)*
>> 9...♖b8 – *Game 30*
>> 9...b6 – *Game 31*
>> 9...♗d7 – *Game 32*
>> 9...d5 – *Game 33*
> 9 g4 f5 10 gxf5
>> 10...exf5 – *Game 34*
>> 10...gxf5 – *Game 35*
> 9 ♕e1 – *Game 36*
> 9 h4 – *Game 37*

9...♗d7 *(D)*
> 9...♖b8 10 a3 – *Game 29* (by transposition)

10 ♖b1- *Game 28*

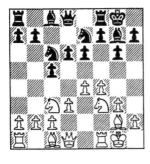
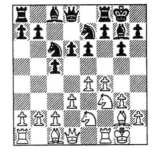
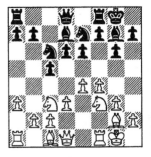

8...0-0	9 ♘e2	9...♗d7

CHAPTER FOUR

6 f4 e5

1 e4 c5 2 ♘c3 ♘c6 3 g3 g6 4 ♗g2 ♗g7 5 d3 d6 6 f4 e5

If Black wants to engage in a more open position than those that occur after 6 f4 e6, then he might choose to reply to 6 f4 with 6...e5. When the centre is so fluid, it is difficult for White to embark on some of the attacking ideas contained in the first three chapters (though it isn't clear one would wish to prevent these anyway). By meeting 6 f4 with 6...e5, one could argue that Black is doing half White's job for him, as he voluntarily opens the f-file. On the other hand, Black often gains the e5 square for his minor pieces, so it's a trade off. In Games 39-41 White meets 6...e5 with the straightforward 7 ♘f3; and in Games 42-48 he plays 7 ♘h3, which, according to existing theory, is meant to be the better move. We shall see.

If, having reached the end of the chapters on 6 f4, you are still waiting for a discussion of 6...♘f6, then I would refer you to Game 60: I have included this system in the chapter on

6 ♗e3 as it often transposes.

The poor reputation of 7 ♘f3 can be traced back to the following game. Larsen plays the opening a little carelessly, and Portisch emerges with a slight, but permanent, advantage in the form of the two bishops and pressure on White's centre.

> *Game 39*
> **Larsen-Portisch**
> *Rotterdam Candidates 1977*

1 e4 c5 2 ♘c3 ♘c6 3 g3 g6 4 ♗g2 ♗g7 5 d3 d6 6 f4 e5 7 ♘f3

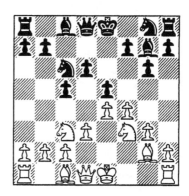

7...♘ge7 8 0-0 0-0 9 ♗e3

The speculative 9 f5 is considered in Game 41.

9...♘d4 10 ♕d2 exf4

10...♗g4 is the subject of the next game.

11 ♗xf4

11 gxf4 is similar to Games 34 and 35 if Black chooses to block with 11...f5. In fact, this may be a slightly improved version from White's viewpoint as Black has already committed himself to ...♘d4.

11...♘xf3+

Here 11...♗g4 isn't terribly good: 12 ♘xd4 cxd4? (12...♗xd4+ 13 ♗e3 and White stands comfortably: after the exchange of bishops White doubles rooks on the f-file) 13 ♘b5 a6 14 ♘xd6 g5 15 ♘xb7 ♕b6 16 ♗d6 ♕xb7 17 ♕xg5 ♗e2 18 e5 was winning for White in Fahnenschmidt-Gauglitz, German Bundesliga 1994.

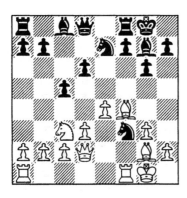

12 ♖xf3

This recapture is never commented on in theory books, but 12 ♗xf3 is no better and no worse. For instance, 12...♗h3 13 ♗g2 ♗xg2 14 ♕xg2 ♕d7 15 g4! (Spassky likes to play in this way on the kingside as well) 15...b5 16 ♖ae1 b4 17 ♘d1 ♘c6 18 ♔h1 ♖ad8 19 ♘e3!? ♘e7, as in Benschop-Cameron, Dutch Women's Championship 1989. White has the slightly freer position, although Black flunked the challenge: what would have happened if Black had taken the pawn? 19...♗xb2!? 20 ♘c4 ♗e5 21 ♗g5 ♖c8 22 ♘xe5 ♘xe5 23 ♖f4 ♕e6 24 ♖ef1 is one plausible line, when White has attacking chances in return for the pawn.

12...♕b6!

A well-timed move. White would like to get on with his kingside attack by doubling rooks on the f-file, exchanging bishops with ♗h6, for example, but he must first deal with the threat to b2. If he tries 13 b3, then the knight's support is undermined and Black can exploit this with 13...♕b4. If 13 ♘d1, then 13...♗g4. So White is reduced to playing ...

13 ♖b1

... but assigning a whole rook to the defence of a lousy pawn is hardly desirable. White must also take care that Black doesn't throw in a discovered check with ...c5-c4 at some awkward moment.

13...♗e6

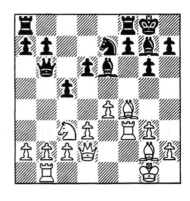

14 ♗g5?!

That one is a waste of time: the knight was going on a trip anyway. Portisch's second at the event, Forintos, recommends 14 ♖ff1 instead, and that does remove the rook from its vulnerable square. 14 ♔h1 is also reasonable (it might be useful to keep the rook on f3 for a moment, in case it becomes possible to double on the f-file).

14...♘c6 15 ♗e3?

14 ♗g5 wasn't great, but it seems to me that this is the real blunder. Instead, 15 ♖ff1 should be alright for White.

15...♘e5 16 ♖ff1 ♘g4 17 ♗f4 c4+ 18 ♔h1 cxd3 19 cxd3 ♗d4!

This forces the win of the two bishops, and from here on, White's king is insecure.

20 h3 ♘e3 21 ♖fe1 ♘xg2 22 ♔xg2 ♕c6! 23 ♗e3 ♗h8 24 ♖bc1 ♕d7! 25 ♔h2! a6

25...♗xh3 26 ♘d5 confuses the issue enough to make Black think twice about capturing.

26 ♕g2

Both 26 g4 and 26 h4 create too many holes in White's kingside.

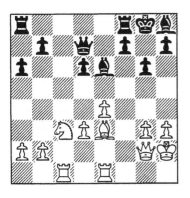

26...♖ac8 27 d4 ♕d8 28 d5 ♗d7 29 ♗f4 ♕e7 30 ♕d2 ♗e5 31 ♖f1 ♖ce8 32 ♖ce1 f6 33 a3 h5 34 ♘e2 g5 35 ♗xe5 ♕xe5 36 ♘d4 h4 37 ♖g1 ♔f7 38 ♘f3 hxg3+ 39 ♖xg3 ♕f4 40 ♖f1 ♕xd2+ 41 ♘xd2 ♖c8 42 ♖xg5 ♖h8 43 e5 dxe5 44 ♘e4 ♖c2+ 45 ♔g1 ♖h6 46 ♖g3 f5 47 b4 b6 48 ♘g5+ ♔e7 49 ♘f3 ♔f6 50 ♖g8 ♖xh3 51 ♖b8 f4 52 ♖xb6+ ♔f5 53 ♖f2 ♖g3+ 54 ♔f1 ♗b5+ 55 ♔e1 ♖xf2 56 ♔xf2 ♔e4 57 ♘d2+ ♔xd5 58 a4 ♗d3 59 ♖f6 ♖e3 60 ♘b3 ♖e2+ 61 ♔g1 ♖b2 62 ♘c5 ♗e2 63 ♖b6 ♔d4 64 ♘d7 ♗f3 65 ♖e6 ♔e3 66 ♖xe5+ ♗e4 0-1

A positional masterpiece from Portisch.

Game 40
Romanishin-J.Horvath
Euro Club Cup, Balatonbereny 1993

1 e4 c5 2 ♘c3 ♘c6 3 g3 g6 4 ♗g2 ♗g7 5 d3 d6 6 ♗e3 e5 7 ♕d2 ♘ge7 8 f4 ♘d4 9 ♘f3 0-0 10 0-0 ♗g4

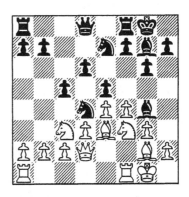

11 ♘h4 exf4 12 ♗xf4

Another idea is 12 ♖xf4!? ♗e6 13 ♖f2 d5 14 ♗h6 ♖c8 15 ♗xg7 ♔xg7 16 ♖af1 f6 17 exd5 ♘xd5 18 ♘e4 and White had the better chances in

Lijedahl-Spassky, Gothenburg 1973. As is so often the case, if White can exchange the dark-squared bishops, then he has the better chances due to the weak squares around Black's king.

12...♕d7 13 ♖f2 b5 14 ♗h6 ♖ae8 15 ♖af1 b4 16 ♗xg7 ♔xg7 17 ♘d1

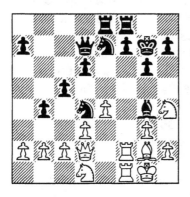

17...♗xd1!

Black appreciates that the knight will contribute greatly to White's attack if it arrives at e3, so he hacks it off.

18 ♕xd1 d5!

Another good move. Black is fighting for the initiative. If he doesn't, then White will build up unopposed on the kingside. Nevertheless, I still prefer White.

19 c3 bxc3 20 bxc3 ♘dc6 21 ♕f3 d4 22 ♕f6+ ♔g8 23 c4

see following diagram

23 ♘f3!? is worth a thought.

23...♕e6 24 ♕g5 ♕e5 25 ♕d2 f6 26 ♗h3 ♔g7 27 ♘g2 g5! 28 ♕d1 ♕d6 29 ♘e1 ♘e5 30 ♗f5 ♖b8 31 h4 ♖b6 32 ♗xh7 ♘f7 33 ♗f5 ♕xg3+ 34 ♘g2 ♘e5 35 ♖f3 ♘xf3+ 36 ♖xf3 ♕b8 37 ♖f1 ♘xf5 38 exf5 ♖h8 39 ♖e1 gxh4 40 ♕g4+ ♔f7 41 ♕g6+

♔f8 42 ♖e6 ♖b1+ 43 ♔f2 ♕g3+ 44 ♕xg3 hxg3+ 45 ♔e2 ♔f7 46 ♖c6 ♖e8+ 47 ♔f3 ♖f1+ 48 ♔xg3 ♖g8+ 49 ♔h2 ♖xf5 0-1

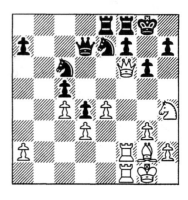

1 g3 c5 2 ♗g2 ♘c6 3 e4 d6 4 d3 g6 5 f4 ♗g7 6 ♘f3 e5 7 0-0 ♘ge7 8 ♘c3 0-0 9 f5!?

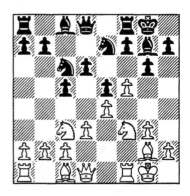

I'm surprised that this hasn't been seen more often. I haven't a clue what's going on, but it seems to create enough panic in Black's camp judging by the two games which I've unearthed.

9...gxf5 10 ♘h4

This must be stronger than 10 ♘g5, though Black failed to find the right answer in Pikryl-Kupcik, Moravian Championship 1994: 10...h6 (I suspect that 10...f6 is the right move, when I can't see anything better for White than retreating the knight to f3. Nevertheless, it is worth looking at the rest of the game, as White plays a sensational attack) 11 exf5 ♗xf5 12 ♖xf5 ♘xf5 13 ♗e4 ♘cd4 14 ♕h5 hxg5 15 g4 ♕f6 16 gxf5 ♕h6 17 ♕xh6 ♗xh6 18 f6 ♘xc2 19 ♖b1 ♘d4 20 h4 ♔h8 21 ♔f2 ♘e6 22 ♘d5 ♖fe8 23 hxg5 ♗g7 24 ♗d2 ♖ac8 25 ♖h1+ ♔g8 26 fxg7 ♔xg7 27 ♖h7+ ♔f8 28 g6 1-0.

10...fxe4 11 dxe4 ♘d4?!

Risky. The knight could find itself offside in a couple of moves if Black isn't careful. 11...f5 is critical, but White has a wide choice of responses. I like 12 ♗g5.

12 ♘d5! ♘xd5 13 exd5

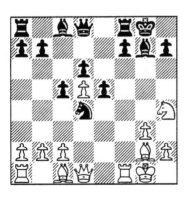

13...♗f6

Also risky, but the more orthodox 13...f5 (13...♗d7 14 c3 ♘b5 15 ♗e4 is also promising for White) wasn't very good: 14 c3 ♘b5 15 ♕h5 ♕e8 (or 15...♕d7 16 ♗h3) 16 ♕xe8 ♖xe8 17

♘xf5 and White has a large positional advantage thanks to the bishop pair and kingside pawn majority.

14 ♗h6

Or perhaps even 14 c3!? ♗xh4 15 cxd4 (15 gxh4 ♘f5!) 15...♗g5 16 dxe5 dxe5 17 d6 and White has compensation for the pawn.

14...♗xh4 15 gxh4 ♕xh4 16 ♗xf8 ♗g4?

Black would have still been very much in the game after 16...♔xf8.

17 ♗e7 1-0

Game 42
Baum-Howell
German Bundesliga 1992

1 e4 c5 2 ♘c3 ♘c6 3 g3 g6 4 ♗g2 ♗g7 5 d3 d6 6 ♘h3 e5 7 f4

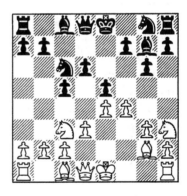

7 ♘h3 has proved to be a more popular move than 7 ♘f3 in recent years, thanks to its adoption by the likes of Spassky, but also because there are a couple of tricky lines which the unwary can easily stumble into. The unwary here is James Howell who, in spite of being a good deal stronger than his opponent, is unable to recover from his difficult start.

7...♘ge7 8 0-0

Black's best move here is 8...exf4 – see Games 44-46; but there are quite a few players who have played the seemingly natural ...

8...0-0?

... only to be shocked by ...

9 f5! f6

If the pawn is accepted then Black falls prey to a vicious attack. Here are just a couple of examples to give a flavour of the carnage, although I could have provided many more: 9...gxf5 10 exf5 ♗xf5 (10...♘xf5 11 ♕h5 also gives White a strong attack) 11 ♖xf5 ♘xf5 and now:

a) 12 ♗e4 ♕d7? (12...♘cd4 13 ♕h5 transposes to the next variation) 13 ♕g4 ♘ce7 14 ♘d5 ♕e6? 15 ♘xe7+ ♘xe7 16 ♗xh7+ 1-0 Seret-Juglard, Belfort Open 1989.

b) 12 ♕h5 ♘cd4 13 ♗e4 ♕f6 14 ♘d5 ♕g6 15 ♘e7+ (15 ♕d1!, e.g. 15...♕e6 16 ♘g5! ♕d7 17 c3 f6 18 ♘xh7!) 15...♘xe7 16 ♗xg6 fxg6 17 ♕d1 h6 18 c3 ♘f3+ 19 ♔g2 ♖f7 20 ♗e3 b6 21 a4 ♖af8 and Black had compensation for the queen in Kroeze-Kharlov, Leeuwarden 1994. This is the best that I have seen Black do with this variation but I think 15 ♕d1 would have been a killer.

10 g4

By declining the pawn sacrifice Black has staved off immediate disaster, but his long-term prospects are poor: White's kingside pawn wedge is formidable and he has a clamp on the centre, making it impossible for Black to organise counterplay. The win takes time, but there is a feeling of inevitability about it.

10...♘d4 11 ♗e3 g5?

This allows White complete freedom to build on the kingside.

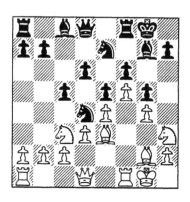

12 ♘d5 h6 13 ♔h1 ♖f7 14 ♘g1 ♗f8 15 c3 ♘xd5 16 exd5 ♘b5 17 ♘e2 ♘c7 18 ♘g3 ♗d7 19 ♗e4 ♗e8 20 ♔g2 ♖h7 21 ♖h1 h5 22 gxh5 ♗h6 23 ♕d2 ♗f7 24 c4 ♕f8 25 ♗f3 g4 26 ♗xg4 ♗xe3 27 ♕xe3 b5 28 ♔f2 ♖b8 29 b3 ♗e8 30 ♖ag1 ♔h8 31 ♖g2 a5 32 ♖hg1 a4 33 ♗d1 ♗d7 34 ♘e4 axb3 35 axb3 ♘e8 36 h6 bxc4 37 dxc4 ♗xf5 38 ♕g3 ♖xh6 39 ♕g8+ ♕xg8 40 ♖xg8+ ♔h7 41 ♘xd6 ♖xh2+ 42 ♔e1 ♘xd6 43 ♖xb8 ♖b2 44 ♖f8 ♘e4 45 d6 ♖d2 46 ♖f7+ ♔h6 47 ♖xf6+ ♘xf6 48 ♔xd2 ♘e4+ 49 ♔c1 ♘xd6 50 ♗c2 ♗xc2 51 ♔xc2 e4 52 ♖g8 e3 53 ♔d3 ♘f5 54 ♖c8 ♘d4 55 ♔xe3 ♘xb3 56 ♖g8 1-0

Game 43
Sale-Psakhis
Portoroz Open 1995

1 e4 c5 2 ♘c3 d6 3 g3 ♘c6 4 ♗g2 g6 5 d3 ♗g7 6 f4 e5 7 ♘h3 ♘ge7 8 0-0 ♘d4

Spassky won a famous game (playing White) with this line against

Hort in 1978, and it is surprising that Psakhis chose to repeat it. His opponent even manages to improve on Spassky's play. 8...h6 9 ♗d2 (9 f5!? looks inviting: 9...gxf5 10 ♕h5 with similar play to the main game) 9...♗e6 10 g4 exf4 11 ♘xf4 ♕d7 12 h3 ♗d4+ 13 ♔h1 h5 14 g5 ♗e5 15 ♘xe6 fxe6 16 h4 0-0-0 17 ♗h3 gave White a slight advantage in Spassky-Tan Lian Ann, Manila Interzonal 1976.

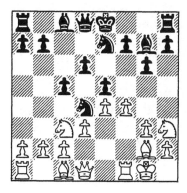

9 f5!

This sacrifice again.

9...gxf5 10 ♕h5!

This move is never commented on in theoretical works, but if I were playing White I would want to make sure that I had something worked out against 10...♘xc2 before playing my queen out. In fact, after a little examination, I think Black would have to be suicidal to take the pawn: 10...♘xc2? 11 ♘g5! ♘g6 (11...♘xa1 12 ♘xf7!) 12 exf5 ♘xa1 13 ♘xf7 ♔xf7 14 fxg6+ is the end for Black.

10...h6 11 ♖f2 ♗e6 12 ♗e3 ♕d7

After 12...fxe4 White could simply recapture on e4 with the pawn which would guarantee good compensation, but it is tempting to pile on the

pressure straightaway with 13 ♖af1.

13 ♖af1 0-0-0 14 ♗xd4!

This appears to be even stronger than the move played by Spassky: 14 ♘d5 fxe4 15 ♘xe7+ ♕xe7 16 ♗xd4 cxd4 17 ♖xf7 ♕e8 18 ♗xe4 ♖f8 19 ♗f5 ♕xf7 20 ♕xf7 ♖xf7 21 ♗xe6+ ♖fd7 22 ♖f7 ♔c7 23 ♗xd7 ♖xd7 24 ♖xd7+ ♔xd7 25 ♔g2 with a clear advantage to White in the endgame in Spassky-Hort, Bugojno 1978.

14...cxd4

14...exd4 15 exf5 ♘xf5 16 ♘d5 is very similar to the game.

15 exf5 ♘xf5

15...dxc3 (or 15...♗xf5 16 ♖xf5! ♘xf5 17 ♘d5) 16 fxe6 fxe6 17 ♖f7 leaves White with a clear advantage.

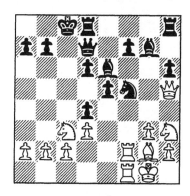

16 ♘d5 ♘e3 17 ♖xf7! ♘xd5 18 ♖xd7 ♖xd7 19 ♕g6 ♘c7 20 ♘f2 ♖e7 21 ♗h3 d5 22 ♗xe6+ ♘xe6 23 ♘g4 ♘d8 24 b4 ♖he8 25 b5 e4 26 ♕f5+ ♔b8 27 ♕xd5 e3 28 ♘xh6 ♗xh6 29 ♕d6+ ♔a8 30 ♕xh6 ♘f7 31 ♕h5 e2 32 ♖e1 ♘d6 33 ♕d5 ♘f7 34 ♔g2 ♖e6 35 a4 ♘h6 36 h3 ♖e5 37 ♕xd4 ♘f5 38 ♕c3 ♘e3+ 39 ♔g1 ♘f5 40 ♔h2 ♖5e6 41 a5 ♘e3 42 g4 ♔b8 43 ♔g1 ♘f1 44 ♕d4 ♖f8 45 ♖xe2 1-0

A convincing victory by White. It is worth bearing in mind that Black is a much stronger player than his opponent, but even he could find no answer to the attack.

1 e4 c5 2 ♘c3 ♘c6 3 g3 g6 4 ♗g2 ♗g7 5 d3 d6 6 f4 e5 7 ♘h3 exf4

This is by far the best way for Black to play. By capturing on f4 here (or after 7...♘ge7 8 0-0) Black rules out any nonsense with f4-f5.

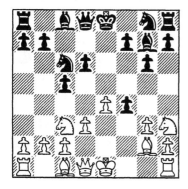

8 ♘xf4

Theory has tended to favour 8 ♗xf4 (see Games 45-46), but it is not entirely clear which is better. It is interesting to see that Spassky, the great expert, isn't sure himself: he has used both recaptures. On the surface, it would seem that Black has left himself with a poor pawn structure compared to White. Not so fast! Although White has d5 under control, Black will be able to use the e5 square for his minor pieces, and the bishop on g7 is a tremendous piece, searing right across the board.

8...♘ge7

8...♘f6 is similar. The game Bolehradski-Knezevic, Yugoslav Team Championship 1992, provided an excellent example of how not to play for White: 9 h3 0-0 10 ♗e3 ♖b8 11 0-0 b5 12 ♖b1 (this leaves the a-pawn vulnerable; it is better to play 12 a3) 12...b4 13 ♘cd5 ♘xd5 14 ♘xd5 ♗e6 (this is the point: White cannot avoid the exchange of the knight, and in this particular position, that's bad and now he gets done on the dark squares) 15 ♕d2 ♗xd5 16 exd5 ♘d4 17 c3? (17 g4) 17...bxc3 18 bxc3 ♘b5 19 ♖b3 ♕a5 20 ♖c1 ♗e5 21 ♔h2 ♖b6 22 c4 ♕xd2 23 ♗xd2 ♘d4 and White's position was ugly in Bolehradski-Knezevic, Yugoslav Team Championship 1992.

9 0-0 0-0 10 ♗e3 ♖b8

10...♘e5 was played in Spassky-Franke, German Bundesliga 1981, when the game continued 11 h3 ♗e6 12 ♕d2 ♕d7 13 a3 ♖ae8 14 ♔h2 b6 15 g4! ♕d8 16 ♔h1 ♗c8 17 ♕e1 ♗b7 18 ♕g3 and White had the better chances. Spassky likes playing g3-g4 and supporting the pawn front with ♕g3; compare with this game and Spassky-Portisch (Game 45) for instance.

11 a3

Also possible is 11 ♕d2 b5 12 a3 a5 13 ♖ab1 b4 14 ♘cd5 ♘xd5 15 ♘xd5 ♗e6 16 ♘f4 ♗d7 17 c3 ♘e5 18 ♔h1 and now, instead of closing the queenside with 18...b3 (Spassky-Franco, Buenos Aires 1979), Black should have just covered the d5 square with 18...♗c6, when chances would have been about equal.

11...♘e5 12 ♔h1 b6 13 ♕e2 ♗b7
14 g4 ♘7c6 15 h3 ♕d7 16 ♕f2 ♘e7
17 ♕g3

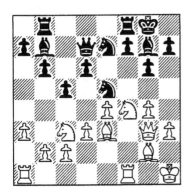

There we go again. Spassky achieves his favourite formation, although it isn't clear what he should do now.

17...♔h8 18 ♖f2 b5 19 ♖af1 a5 20 ♗c1 b4 21 axb4 axb4 22 ♘cd5

22 ♘d1 looks better.

22...♘xd5 23 exd5

White's knight on f4 just gets in the way of the rooks and bishops, although 23 ♘xd5 is also pleasant for Black: 23...♗xd5 24 exd5 ♖a8. It is difficult for White to generate play on the kingside, while Black is able to probe on the other flank. However, it might make a difference if Black has a pawn on h6. Confused? See the next few games where White plays the recapture ♗xf4!

23...♖fe8 24 ♗e4 b3 25 c3 c4 26 dxc4 ♘xc4 27 ♗g2 ♗a6 28 ♖d1 ♖e7 ½-½

I imagine that Spassky was relieved to hear Black offer a draw here: he has a rotten position. Black will double rooks on the e-file; he can use e5 for his minor pieces; and White's king is a little exposed.

1 e4 c5 2 ♘c3 ♘c6 3 g3 g6 4 ♗g2
♗g7 5 d3 d6 6 f4 e5 7 ♘h3 exf4 8
♗xf4

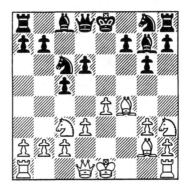

It looks more logical to recapture with the knight on f4, securing control over the d5 square, but as we saw in the previous game, Black can cover with the knight on e7 and bishop on e6. By keeping the bishop's diagonal open, White hopes to exchange off the dark-squared bishops, and thereby weaken Black's king position.

8...♘ge7 9 0-0 h6

Portisch is alert to Spassky's idea and instead of castling, first plugs a few holes. Don't think that White's strategy has all been in vain though: the pawn on h6 gives White a tiny weakness to latch on to, and it can make all the difference to an attack. For 9...0-0 10 ♕d2 see the next game.

10 ♖b1

10 ♕d2 is worth considering. In order to castle Black must play 10...g5, and while his king is secure in the short-term; in the long-term there is a tendency for the kingside to unravel, e.g. 11 ♗e3 0-0 12 ♘f2 with a tense scrap in prospect.

10...0-0 11 a3

Spassky is fond of these prophylactic measures on the queenside. I'm fairly certain it was never his intention to play for b2-b4, but he is ready to meet Black's plan of ...b5-b4.

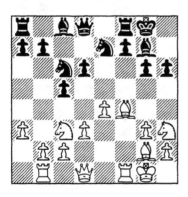

11...♗e6 12 ♗e3

Its job completed, the bishop drops back to allow the knight into play.

12...♘e5 13 ♘f4 ♗d7 14 ♔h1 ♖c8 15 ♕d2 ♔h7 16 h3 ♗c6 17 g4 ♕d7 18 ♖f2 b6

As Forintos points out, 18...b5 can be met by 19 b4!

19 ♖bf1 ♗b7 20 ♕e2 ♖ce8 21 ♗c1 ♔g8 22 ♕e3 b5 23 ♕g3

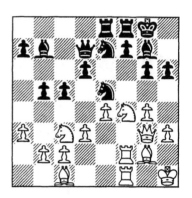

Spassky has achieved his desired attacking formation, just as in the previous game. Is there any difference at all? What happens if Black continues as Sax did by playing 23...a5 24 ♘cd5 ♘xd5 25 ♘xd5 ♗xd5 26 exd5 here? This position is very similar to one which I considered in the previous game. Black is a little less advanced with his play on the queenside, although that is hardly significant. But look at the kingside. Black's pawn stands on h6 rather than h7, and that gives White something to bite on. The plan is ♗e4 followed by ♕h4. Such plans reveal the strength of Spassky's attacking formation of g3-g4 and ♕g3.

23...b4

Premature. This spoils Black's pawn structure.

24 axb4 cxb4 25 ♘d1 d5 26 d4 ♘5c6 27 exd5 ♘xd4 28 c4 bxc3 29 bxc3 ♘b3 30 ♗a3 ♖c8 31 c4 ♘a5 32 ♖e2 ♖fe8 33 ♖fe1 ♗f8 34 ♘h5 ♘xd5 35 cxd5 gxh5 36 gxh5+ ♗g7 37 ♗b2 f6 38 ♗xf6 ♖xe2 39 ♖xe2 ♕f7 40 ♖e6 1-0

Boris at his best.

1 e4 c5 2 ♘c3 ♘c6 3 g3 g6 4 ♗g2 ♗g7 5 d3 e5 6 f4 d6 7 ♘h3 ♘ge7 8 0-0 exf4 9 ♗xf4 0-0

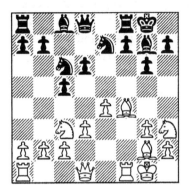

Black decides not to mess around and castles straightaway, but the exchange of bishops proves to be awkward for him.

10 ♕d2 b6 11 ♗h6! ♘d4 12 ♖f2 ♗b7 13 ♗xg7 ♔xg7 14 ♘f4 ♘e6 15 ♖af1 ♘xf4 16 ♖xf4

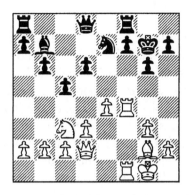

Black's king is less secure, and he has less control over the centre. For instance, White has the option to break with d3-d4, although in the game he gets side-tracked into a hunt for bigger game..

16...♕d7 17 ♗h3!

This unusual tactic gains an immediate reward. Of course if 17...♕xh3 18 ♖h4 and ♕h6+.

17...♕e8? 18 ♗e6! fxe6 19 ♖xf8 ♕xf8 20 ♖xf8 ♖xf8 21 ♘b5 d5 22 ♕g5 ♘c6 23 exd5 exd5 24 ♕xd5 ♖f5 25 ♕g2 ♖f6 26 ♘c7 ♖f7 27 ♘e8+ 1-0

Summary

It is difficult for White to find a significant improvement in Game 39, so it must be concluded that 7 ♘f3 is solid, but uninspired – unless you wish to play like the gentleman in Game 41, although I suspect this pawn sacrifice should carry a health warning. Good for a giggle, though. 7 ♘h3 is more dangerous, particularly if Black allows one of the f4-f5 pawn sacrifices (Games 42 and 43). If Black captures on f4, then on due reflection my preference would be for ♗xf4 (Games 45 and 46), rather than ♘xf4 (Game 44), although I'm prepared to be convinced otherwise. There's not much in it. In these kind of positions where manoeuvring dominates, an understanding of the different plans and set-ups plays a much greater role than following a prescribed variation in routine fashion.

1 e4 c5 2 ♘c3 ♘c6 3 g3 g6 4 ♗g2 ♗g7 5 d3 d6 6 f4 e5

7 ♘f3
>   7 ♘h3
>>   7...♘ge7 8 0-0 *(D)*
>>>   8...0-0 – *Game 42*
>>>   8...♘d4 – *Game 43*
>>>   8...exf4 9 ♗xf4 – see 7...exf4 8 ♗xf4 ♘ge7 9 0-0 below
>>   7...exf4 *(D)*
>>>   8 ♘xf4 – *Game 44*
>>>   8 ♗xf4 ♘ge7 9 0-0
>>>>   9...h6 – *Game 45*; 9...0-0 – *Game 46*

7...♘ge7 8 0-0 0-0 *(D)* 9 ♗e3
>   9 f5 – *Game 41*

9...♘d4 10 ♕d2 exf4
>   10...♗g4 – *Game 40*

11 ♗xf4 – *Game 39*

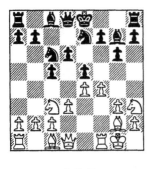

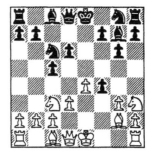

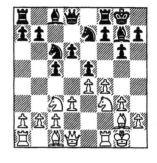

8 0-0	*7...exf4*	*8...0-0*

CHAPTER FIVE

6 ♗e3

1 e4 c5 2 ♘c3 ♘c6 3 g3 g6 4 ♗g2 ♗g7 5 d3 d6 6 ♗e3

To Closed Sicilian sophisticates, 6 f4 is just too brutal: how can such a direct attack possibly succeed? Black can see that White is intent on an assault, and prepare himself accordingly. In recent years, the more subtle practitioners of the opening have tended to opt for ♗e3 and ♕d2 before playing f2-f4, so that they can exchange bishops, and only then hit their opponents over the head on the kingside. If White can exchange off the dark-squared bishops, then he not only improves his attacking chances, but he also loosens Black's hold over the centre. By refraining from f2-f4, White also retains more flexibility. He might attack with h2-h4 instead, or break in the centre, or play f2-f4 eventually anyway, depending on how Black develops. Sounds good in theory, and it's not bad in practice either. In Games 47-51 Black plays the most logical move: 6...e5. Games 52-55 feature 6...e6; then we move on to 6...♖b8

(Games 56-58); 6...♘f6 (Games 59 and 60) and 6...b5 (Game 61).

Game 47
Fritsche-Kengis
German Bundesliga 1994/95

1 e4 c5 2 ♘c3 ♘c6 3 g3 g6 4 d3 ♗g7 5 ♗e3 d6 6 ♕d2 e5

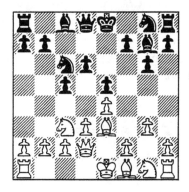

If White is going to exchange dark-squared bishops, then it makes sense for Black to erect a pawn front on the black squares. That way he maintains a hold over the centre if the bishops are exchanged.

7 ♗g2 ♘ge7 8 ♗h6

Having got this far White invariably goes for the exchange, but 8 h4!? is worth checking out (Game 51). Note that 8 f4 ♘d4 transposes to a position that commonly arises from 4 ♗g2 ♗g7 5 d3 d6 6 f4 e5 7 ♘f3 ♘ge7 8 0-0 0-0 9 ♘f3 ♘d4 10 ♕d2 ♗g4 after 9 ♘f3 0-0 10 0-0 ♗g4 (see Game 40), although Romanishin has also experimented with 10 0-0-0!?

8...♗xh6

8...0-0 is more commonly played (see Games 48-50) but it isn't clear that it is a better move.

9 ♕xh6 ♘d4

Black gives up the idea of castling kingside for the moment, but counterattacks in the centre and queenside.

10 0-0-0

I prefer castling queenside to other moves, although 10 ♖c1 was successful in Rohde-Dlugy, USA Championship 1986: 10 ♖c1 ♗e6 11 ♘f3 ♕b6 12 ♘d1 ♕a5+ 13 c3 ♘xf3+ 14 ♗xf3 ♕xa2 15 0-0 ♘c6 16 ♘e3 0-0-0 when White was allowed to build up a strong attack on the queenside. But why not 16...♕xb2 instead? White has compensation, but I don't believe it's enough.

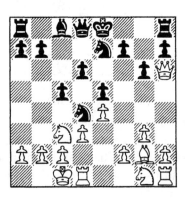

10...♗e6

10...b5!? raises the stakes.

11 ♘d5

11 ♕g7?! ♔d7! 12 ♗h3 ♕f8 13 ♕xf8 ♖hxf8 gave Black the better ending in Bakhrakh-Yurenko, St Petersburg Open 1994.

11...♗xd5 12 exd5 ♕a5 13 ♔b1 ♘ef5 14 ♕c1 ♕b6 15 c3 ♘b5

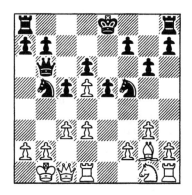

Black's early initiative has faded leaving his queen and knight misplaced on the queenside. I would prefer to play White, but Kengis eventually manages to subdue his weaker opponent.

16 ♘f3 h6 17 ♖he1

17 g4!? ♘e7 18 ♘d2 was also possible.

17...♔f8 18 ♘d2 ♔g7 19 ♘c4 ♕d8 20 f4 f6 21 g4 ♘h4 22 ♗e4 ♕d7 23 f5 g5 24 ♕e3 ♖ad8 25 ♘d2 a5 26 ♕e2 a4 27 a3 ♘c7 28 d4 cxd4 29 cxd4 ♘b5 30 dxe5 dxe5 31 ♖c1 h5 32 h3 ♔h6 33 ♕c4 ♖h7 34 ♕b4 ♘d4 35 ♖e3 b5 36 ♔a2 ♕a7 37 ♖cc3 ♖hd7 38 ♖c5 ♔g7 39 ♖ec3 ♘e2 40 ♖d3 ♘f4 41 ♖dc3 ♘e2 42 ♖e3 ♘d4 43 ♘f1 ♖f7 44 ♘g3 hxg4 45 hxg4 ♘b3 46 ♖cc3 ♕d4 47 ♖e1 ♘d2 48 ♘h5+ ♔h6 49 ♖c6 ♘xf5 50

♘xf6 ♕xb4 51 axb4 ♘d4 52 ♖h1+
♔g7 53 ♖h7+ ♔f8 54 ♖h8+ ♔e7 55
♖c7+ ♔xf6 56 ♖xf7+ ♔xf7 57 ♖xd8
♘xe4 58 ♖d7+ ♔f6 59 ♖d8 ♔e7 60
♖g8 ♘c2 61 ♖g6 ♘xb4+ 62 ♔a3
♘xd5 63 b3 axb3 64 ♔xb3 ♘df6 65
♔b4 ♘xg4 66 ♔xb5 ♘e3 67 ♖a6 g4
68 ♖a3 ♘c2 69 ♖a8 g3 70 ♔c4 ♔f7
71 ♖a7+ ♔f6 0-1

Game 48
Becke-Steiger
RLN 1983

**1 e4 c5 2 ♘c3 ♘c6 3 g3 g6 4 ♗g2
♗g7 5 d3 d6 6 ♗e3 e5 7 ♕d2 ♘ge7
8 ♗h6 0-0**

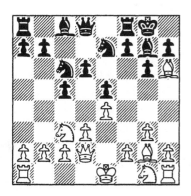

9 h4

Going for mate on the h-file. Black
is not going to fall for that, is he?
Probably not, but he has to be careful.
For 9 ♗xg7 see Games 49 and 50.

9...♗xh6

It looks odd to invite White's queen
into the heart of the kingside, but this
is actually the best move. Instead,
9...f6?! is less good: 10 ♗xg7 ♔xg7 11
h5 g5 12 h6+! ♔h8 13 f4! (Black's
kingside is a bit shaky: the pawn on
h6 is a long-term problem for the

black king) 13...♘g6 14 ♘d5 (14 f5!?
♘ge7 15 ♘h3) 14...gxf4 15 gxf4 f5 16
exf5 ♗xf5 17 fxe5 ♘gxe5 18 0-0-0 was
fun for White in Franke-Gupta, German Bundesliga 1988/89.

10 ♕xh6 f6!

This is the trick: if White plays 11
h5, then Black closes the kingside with
11...g5 and traps the queen on h6.

11 ♕d2

This retreat is the most sensible
move. C.Morrison-Howell, London
Lloyds Bank Masters 1988, shows
what might happen if White ploughs
on blindly with his attack: 11 ♘d5?!
♘xd5 12 exd5 ♘e7 13 ♗e4 ♖f7 14 h5
g5 15 f4 exf4 16 gxf4 g4 17 0-0-0 ♗f5
18 ♘f3 (or 18 ♘e2 ♔h8 and ...♘g8)
18...gxf3 19 ♖dg1+ ♔h8 20 ♗xf5 ♘xf5
21 ♕g6 ♕d7 0-1.

11...♘d4 12 ♘ge2 ♗d7

12...♗g4! is stronger. In that case I
don't see that White has any advantage at all.

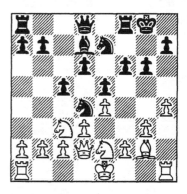

**13 ♘d1 ♗g4 14 ♘xd4 cxd4 15 c4
♘c6 16 f3 ♗e6 17 ♘f2 ♔g7 18 ♗h3
♗xh3 19 ♘xh3 h6 20 0-0 a5 21
♔g2 ♕e7 22 ♖ae1 g5 23 ♘f2 ♘d8
24 ♖h1 ♘e6 25 hxg5 hxg5 26 ♘g4
♖h8 27 ♖xh8 ♖xh8 28 ♕xa5 ♔g6 29**

♖h1 ♖xh1 30 ♔xh1 ♘c5 31 ♕d2
♕h7+ 32 ♔g2 ♕d7 33 b3 ♕c8 34
♘f2 ♘e6 35 ♕b4 ♘c5 36 ♕b6 ♕d7
37 ♕a7 ♔g7 38 ♕a8 f5 39 b4 ♘a4
40 exf5 ♘c3 41 f6+ ♔xf6 42 ♕f8+
♔g6 43 ♘e4 ♘xe4 44 fxe4 ♕g4 45
♕xd6+ ♔h5 46 ♕f6 ♕e2+ 47 ♕f2
♕xd3 48 ♕f3+ ♕xf3+ 49 ♔xf3 g4+
50 ♔e2 ♔g5 51 a4 ♔f6 52 c5 ♔e6
53 b5 ♔d7 54 a5 ♔c7 55 ♔d3 ♔d7
56 ♔c4 ♔c7 57 ♔b4 ♔d7 58 ♔b3
♔c7 59 ♔c4 ♔d7 60 c6+ ♔c7 61
cxb7 ♔xb7 62 ♔b3 ♔a7 63 ♔b4
♔b7 64 ♔c4 ♔c7 65 a6 ♔b6 66
♔b4 ♔a7 67 ♔c5 d3 68 ♔c6 d2 69
b6+ ♔xa6 70 b7 d1♕ 71 b8♕ ½-½

White had nothing from the opening.

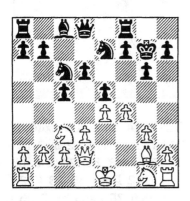

Game 49
Spassky-De Firmian
London Lloyds Bank Masters 1984

---

1 e4 c5 2 ♘c3 d6 3 g3 ♘c6 4 ♗g2
g6 5 d3 ♗g7 6 ♗e3 e5 7 ♕d2 ♘ge7
8 ♗h6 0-0 9 ♗xg7 ♔xg7 10 f4

9 h4 is fun if Black doesn't know
what he is doing, but this is more reliable. Boris knows best.

10...♗e6

Solid, but I think 10...♘d4 is more
to the point – see the next game.
11 ♘f3 f6 12 0-0 ♘d4 13 ♘h4

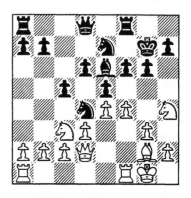

Without the dark-squared bishop,
Black's pawn structure is strong but
inflexible. If he advances one of his
centre pawns, then the rest of the
structure creaks, and this gives White
time to develop an attack. Spassky is
preparing ♘d1, followed by c2-c3, and
then ♘e3. De Firmian is aware of
that, and tries too cut across his plan.
13...♕b6 14 ♖f2!

14 ♘d1 c4! 15 ♔h1 cxd3 16 ♕xd3
♖ac8 is getting a bit too busy for
White.

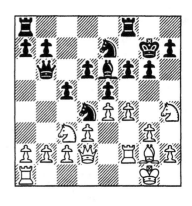

14...c4
Not 14...♕xb2 15 ♖b1 ♕a3 16

♖xb7 with the initiative, but 14...♖ac8 looks quite solid.

15 dxc4 ♗xc4 16 b3 ♗g8 17 ♘a4 ♕c7 18 c3 ♘dc6 19 c4!? ♘d4 20 ♖c1 ♖ad8 21 ♗h3 h6 22 ♘g2 b5 23 cxb5 ♕b7 24 ♘e3 ♘xb5 25 ♘c3 ♘xc3

If 25...♘d4 26 ♖cf1 and White is on the attack.

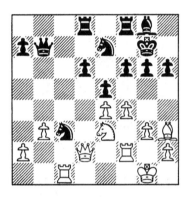

26 ♕xc3 ♕xe4 27 ♗g2 ♕d4 28 ♕xd4 exd4 29 ♘c2 ♘f5 30 ♖d1 ♖fe8 31 ♘xd4 ♘xd4 32 ♖xd4 ♖e1+ 33 ♗f1 ♖d7 34 ♖fd2 d5 35 ♔f2 ♖a1 36 ♗g2 ♔f8 37 ♖a4 ♗e6 38 ♔e3 g5 39 ♔d4 gxf4 40 gxf4 ♖e1 41 ♖a5 ♔f7 42 ♗xd5 ♖f1 43 ♔e4 f5+ 44 ♔e3 ♖e7 45 ♗xe6+ ♖xe6+ 46 ♔d3 ♖xf4 47 ♖xa7+ ♔f6 48 ♔c2 ♖f1 49 b4 f4 50 b5 f3 51 ♖a6 ♔e7 52 ♖xe6+ ♔xe6 53 b6 f2 54 ♔d3 ♖b1 55 ♖xf2 ♖xb6 56 ♔c4 ♖a6 57 ♔b5 ♖a3 58 ♖d2 ♔f5 59 ♔b4 ♖a8 60 a4 ♖b8+ 61 ♔c5 ♖c8+ 62 ♔b5 ♖b8+ 63 ♔a6 ♖c8 64 ♖a2 ♔e6 65 a5 1-0

Game 50
Narayana-King
Calcutta Open 1993

---

1 e4 c5 2 ♘c3 d6 3 g3 ♘c6 4 ♗g2 g6 5 d3 ♗g7 6 ♗e3 e5 7 ♕d2 ♘ge7 8 ♗h6 0-0 9 ♗xg7 ♔xg7 10 f4 ♘d4

We saw 10...♗e6 in the previous game.

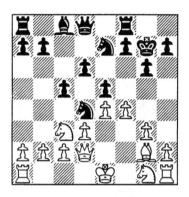

11 ♘f3 ♗g4 12 0-0 ♗xf3!

A few years before this game I had reached the same position and played 12...f6?! 13 ♖f2 ♕b6 (the right idea but a couple of moves too late) 14 ♘e1! ♗e6 15 ♘d1 ♖ac8 16 c3 ♘dc6 17 ♘e3 (now Black is stuck for a plan) 17...exf4 18 gxf4 f5 19 ♘d5! ♗xd5? (19...♕d8 is better, but 20 ♘c2 is good for White since Black's kingside is draughty) 20 exd5 ♘b8 21 c4 ♘d7 22 ♘f3 h6 23 ♖e1 ♘g8 24 ♕c3+ ½-½ Seppeur-King, German Bundesliga 1985/86, but White stands well, e.g. 24...♖f6 25 ♘g5 ♕b4!? 26 ♘e6+ ♔h7 27 ♕xb4!? cxb4 28 ♖fe2.

12...♕d7? should have lost a pawn in Ljubojevic-Van der Wiel, Tilburg 1983, to 13 fxe5! ♘xf3+ 14 ♗xf3 dxe5 15 ♗xg4 ♕xg4 16 ♕f2 (Van der Wiel)
13 ♗xf3 ♕b6!

I prepared this after my game with Seppeur, but it took me seven years before I had a chance to play it!
14 ♘d1

I think it would have been better to

play 14 ♖ab1 or 14 ♖f2.

14...c4 15 ♔h1 cxd3 16 ♕xd3

16 cxd3 keeps a stronger centre. In view of what now happens, White should certainly have played this. Now he is quickly overrun.

16...♖ac8 17 c3 ♘xf3 18 ♖xf3 f5

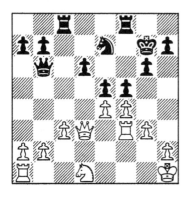

White's position is a wreck and he simply doesn't have time to coordinate his position.

19 b3 d5! 20 ♖f1 dxe4 21 ♕d7 ♖fe8 22 ♘b2 ♖cd8 23 ♕a4 exf4 24 gxf4 ♘c6 25 ♘c4 ♕c5 26 ♕a3 ♕xa3 27 ♘xa3 ♖d3 28 ♖ac1 ♖ed8 29 ♘b5 a6 30 ♘c7 ♔f6 31 c4 ♘e7 0-1

Game 51
Hort-Portisch
Wijk aan Zee 1968

1 e4 c5 2 ♘c3 ♘c6 3 g3 g6 4 ♗g2 ♗g7 5 d3 d6 6 ♗e3 e5 7 ♕d2

White can try 7 ♘h3, hoping to transpose to positions from Chapter 4 (Game 44). However, if Black is alert, he will play 7...h5!? 8 0-0 ♘ge7 9 f4 ♗g4 10 ♕d2 h4 with a pleasant initiative, as in Uritzky-Soffer, Israeli Championship 1996.

7...♘ge7

7...♘f6 is probably best met by 8 h3, preserving White's options and preventing ...♘g4.

8 h4!?

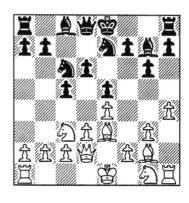

8 ♗h6 is invariably played here, but Hort is a 'natural' player and likes to go his own way.

8...h5 9 ♘h3 ♘d4 10 f4 ♗g4 11 0-0 exf4 12 ♘xf4 0-0 13 ♖f2 ♔h7 14 ♖af1

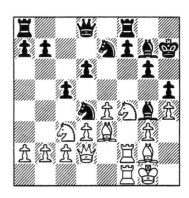

White's attack has developed with great speed. I like the doubled rooks.

14...♕d7 15 ♘cd5 ♘g8

Otherwise a knight would land on f6.

16 ♔h2 ♘c6 17 ♘h3 f6

Proof that Black is already in some trouble.

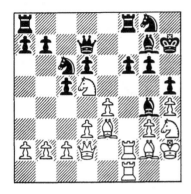

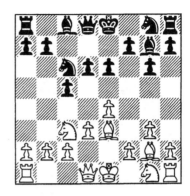

18 c3 ♘e5 19 d4 ♘c4 20 ♕d3 ♘xe3
21 ♘xe3 ♘h6 22 ♘f4 cxd4 23 cxd4
♕e8 24 ♗h3 ♗xh3 25 ♔xh3 ♕d7+
26 ♔g2 ♖ae8 27 d5 ♖e7 28 e5 f5
29 e6 ♕e8 30 ♘c4 ♕b8 31 ♘e3
♕e8 32 ♖c2 a6 33 ♘c4 ♕b8 34
♘b6 ♖c7 35 ♖e2 ♖e8 36 ♘d7 ♕d8
37 ♘h3 ♗f6 38 ♘f2 ♕e7 39 ♖c2
♖ec8 40 ♖fc1 ♖xc2 41 ♖xc2 ♖xc2
42 ♕xc2 ♗d4 43 ♕c7 ♘g8 44 ♘h3
♗xb2 45 ♕xb7 ♗c1 46 ♕xa6 ♕g7
47 ♘g5+ ♗xg5 48 hxg5 ♕b2+ 49
♔h3 ♕a1 50 ♘f8+ ♔h8 51 ♕e2 ♔g7
52 e7 ♕h1+ 53 ♕h2 ♕e4 54 e8♕
♕xe8 55 ♘e6+ ♔h7 56 ♕b2 ♕f7 57
♕b4 ♘e7 58 a4 ♔g8 1-0

A heavyweight struggle.

1 ♘c3 c5 2 e4 ♘c6 3 g3 g6 4 ♗g2
♗g7 5 d3 d6 6 ♗e3 e6 7 ♕d2 ♘ge7

This is rarely played, and with some
justification: it does nothing to cross
White's plan. Note also that 7...♘d4 is
well countered by 8 ♘d1 followed by
c2-c3, when the knight is forced into
an embarrassing retreat.

8 ♗h6 ♗xh6

8...0-0? wouldn't be very bright due
to 9 h4! Compare with Games 48-50:
this really is powerful now. Black will
simply be a move down on Game 48
if he tries 9...♗xh6 10 ♕xh6 f6 11
♕d2 e5.

9 ♕xh6 ♘d4 10 0-0-0 ♘ec6

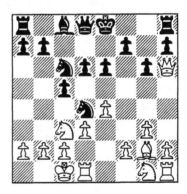

At the moment Black has reasonable control in the centre, but so long
as White plays steadily and doesn't
rush his attack, then he stands well.
Black's basic problem is simple: he
cannot castle.

11 ♘ge2 ♗d7 12 ♘xd4 cxd4 13
♘e2 ♕a5 14 ♔b1 ♕a4 15 c3 dxc3
16 ♘xc3 ♕b4 17 d4 ♖c8 18 ♕g7
♖f8 19 ♖he1 ♘a5 20 ♘d5 ♕a4 21

♛f6 ♘c6

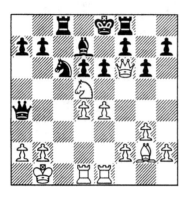

22 ♖c1

Apparently, 22 ♛h4 wins: 22...h6 (22...exd5 23 exd5+ ♘e5 24 ♛f6!) 23 ♘f6+ ♚e7 24 e5 dxe5 25 ♗xc6 and a double check to follow.

22...♛a5 23 ♛h4 h6 24 ♘f6+ ♚e7 25 ♘d5+ ♚e8 26 b4 g5 27 bxa5 gxh4 28 ♘f6+ ♚e7 29 ♘xd7 ♚xd7 30 a6 ♘xd4 31 ♖ed1 ♖xc1+ 32 ♚xc1 ♖c8+ 33 ♚b2 ♘c6 34 axb7 ♖b8 35 ♚c3 ♖xb7 36 f4 ♖b5 37 ♖d2 ♖c5+ 38 ♚b2 ♘a5 39 ♖d4 ♖c4 40 ♖d3 h3 41 ♗f3 ♖b4+ 42 ♚c2 ♘c6 43 a3 ♘d4+ 44 ♚c3 ♖a4 45 ♗h5 ♘b5+ 46 ♚d2 ♚e7 47 ♖b3 a6 48 ♗e2 ♖xe4 49 ♗xb5 axb5 50 ♖xb5 d5 51 ♖b7+ ♚f6 52 ♖a7 h5 53 ♖a8 ♚g7 54 f5 ♖g4 55 fxe6 fxe6 56 ♖e8 ♖e4 57 ♚d3 ♚f7 58 ♖a8 ♖e1 59 ♖h8 ♖h1 60 ♖xh5 ♖xh2 61 ♚c3 ♖h1 62 a4 h2 63 ♚b2 d4 0-1

Well saved, but the theoretical assessment of 7...♘ge7 is doubtful.

Game 53
Smyslov-Kottnauer
Moscow-Prague 1946

---

1 e4 c5 2 ♘c3 ♘c6 3 g3 g6 4 ♗g2

♗g7 5 d3 e6 6 ♗e3 d6 7 ♛d2 ♛a5

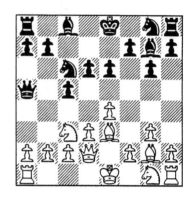

If Black is going to play with ...e7-e6, then delaying the development of the king's knight is his best policy. 7...♛a5 is another Gallagher recommendation from *Beating the Anti-Sicilians*. By pinning the knight on c3, and then establishing the knight on d4, Black hopes to tie White up for long enough to divert him from the kingside. This is a sound strategy. White must attempt to prove that the queen is misplaced on the queenside.

8 ♘ge2

The most straightforward, and I think the best, way to develop.

8...♘d4 9 0-0 ♘e7 10 ♚h1

How about 10 a3 followed by ♖ab1 and, with a bit of luck, b2-b4? It is tempting to gain a tempo on the queen. 10 ♘c1 is also playable, with the idea of ♘b3.

10...♗d7

ECO gives as its main line: 10...♘ec6 11 a3 ♘xe2 12 ♛xe2 ♘d4 13 ♛d2 0-0 14 ♖ab1 (14 ♖ac1 would best be met by 14...♖e8! 15 ♗h6 ♗h8) 14...♖b8 15 f4 f5 'unclear', Panbuk-chan-Popov, Sofia 1978, which doesn't really help us much.

11 f4 Ïb8 12 g4

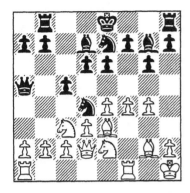

A well-motivated move. Smyslov sees that Black's queen is far from the kingside, so he seizes the chance to begin an attack.

12...h5

Or 12...0-0 13 f5!

13 f5! &e5 14 fxg6 Øxg6 15 g5 Øxe2 16 Ýxe2 &xc3 17 bxc3 Ýxc3 18 Ýf2 Ýg7 19 d4

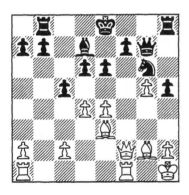

White has tremendous compensation for the pawn: two bishops and Black's weakened kingside. The situation is still unclear, but Smyslov gets there in the end after a fluctuating struggle.

19...b6 20 Ïad1 &b5 21 Ïfe1 0-0 22 Ýg3 Ïbc8 23 d5 exd5 24 Ïxd5

Ïcd8 25 &d2 h4 26 Ýb3 &c6 27 Ïf5 Ýd4 28 Ïf6 c4 29 Ýc3 Ýxc3 30 &xc3 Ïfe8 31 Êg1 Ïd7 32 &h3 Ïde7 33 Ïxd6 &xe4 34 &f6 &xc2 35 &xe7 &a4 36 Ïd8 Ïxd8 37 &xd8 1-0

1 e4 c5 2 Øc3 e6 3 g3 Øc6 4 &g2 g6 5 d3 &g7 6 &e3 d6 7 Ýd2 Ïb8

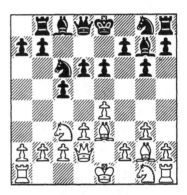

A common move, but there remain many unanswered questions surrounding it.

8 Øge2

A few years previously, Romanishin had preferred 8 Øh3 Ød4 9 0-0 b5 10 Êh1 b4 11 Ød1 h6 12 f4 (perhaps 12 c3!? – isn't it better to keep the bishop's diagonal open?) 12...Øe7 13 &g1 0-0 14 Øe3 f5 15 exf5 exf5, although he didn't get very far; Romanishin-Geller, Sochi 1983.

I'm not sure why 8 Øf3 (threatening d3-d4) isn't seen more often, e.g. 8...Ød4 (8...e5!?) 9 &xd4 cxd4 10 Øb5 Ýb6 (10...e5 is also met by 11 Ýb4) 11 Ýb4 Êd7 12 e5 (12

♘d2!? is worth a shot, when 12...a6 13 ♘c4 ♕c5 14 ♕xc5 dxc5 15 ♘b6+ ♔e7 16 ♘a3 is slightly better for White) 12...dxe5 13 ♘d2 a5 14 ♕a4 ♔d8 15 ♘c4, as in Zakharov-Karpesov, USSR 1981. This position is assessed as slightly better for White by *ECO*.

8...♘d4 9 0-0

Here 9 ♗xd4?! cxd4 10 ♘b5 ♕b6 11 ♕b4 ♔e7 12 ♕b3 a6 13 ♘a3 ♕xb3 14 axb3 b5 is a little better for Black.

9...♘e7

For the more popular 9...b5 see the next game.

10 ♗h6! ♘xe2+

Or 10...♗xh6 11 ♕xh6 ♘xc2 12 ♖ac1 ♘b4 13 d4 with a strong attack.

11 ♘xe2 ♗xb2

If 11...0-0 12 ♗xg7 ♔xg7 13 d4!

12 ♖ab1 ♗f6

Black's king is caught in the middle, so White blows open the centre.

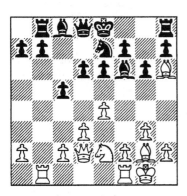

13 d4! cxd4 14 ♘xd4 a6 15 ♖fd1 ♗d7 16 ♘f3 ♘c8 17 e5 dxe5

Not 17...♗xe5? 18 ♘xe5 dxe5 19 ♗g7 ♖g8 20 ♗xe5 ♖a8 21 ♖xb7.

18 ♘g5 ♗e7 19 ♘e4 ♖g8

Black is also in trouble after 19...f6 20 ♗g7 ♖g8 21 ♗xf6! ♗xf6 22 ♘xf6+ ♕xf6 23 ♕xd7+ ♔f8 24 ♕c7.

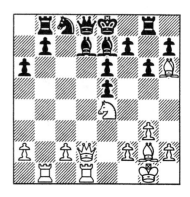

20 ♗g5 ♗xg5 21 ♘xg5 b5 22 ♘e4 ♘b6 23 ♕d6 ♖c8 24 ♕xe5 f5 25 ♘d6+ ♔e7 26 ♘xc8+ ♘xc8 27 ♕c5+ ♔f6 28 ♗c6+- ♖g7 29 ♕d4+ e5 30 ♕h4+ 1-0

A crisp attack from Romanishin.

> *Game 55*
> **Spassky-Portisch**
> *Mexico 1980*

1 e4 c5 2 ♘c3 ♘c6 3 g3 g6 4 ♗g2 ♗g7 5 d3 d6 6 ♗e3 ♖b8 7 ♘ge2 ♘d4 8 0-0 e6 9 ♕d2 b5

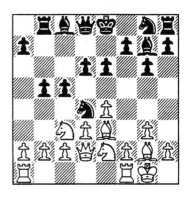

The move order was a little different to the last game, but don't let that put you off. It's the same variation. In the last game Black played 9...♘e7

instead of 9...b5.

10 ♘d1 ♘e7

Or 10...b4 11 f4?! (11 ♘c1 should transpose to the main game with 11...♘e7) 11...♘e7 12 c3 ♘xe2+ 13 ♕xe2 bxc3 14 bxc3 0-0 15 g4?! f5 16 gxf5 exf5 17 e5 ♗a6 with a tremendous position for Black, Waitzkin-Quinn, World U–16 Championship 1992.

11 ♘c1

White's maneuverings with his knights look tortuous, but he is keeping his original aim in mind: to exchange off the dark-squared bishops with ♗h6. 11 ♘xd4 is less effective as is clear from the following: 11...cxd4 12 ♗h6 0-0 13 ♗xg7 ♔xg7 14 f4 f6 15 ♗h3 e5 16 ♘f2 ♗xh3 17 ♘xh3 ½-½ Spassky-Portisch, Mexico Candidates 1980.

11...b4 12 a3

For 12 c3 see the next game.

12...a5 13 axb4 axb4 14 c3 bxc3 15 bxc3 ♘dc6 16 ♗h6

Goal achieved.

16...0-0 17 ♗xg7 ♔xg7 18 ♘e3

White has a slight initiative which he almost manages to convert into a win.

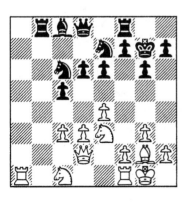

18...d5 19 ♕c2 d4 20 ♘c4 e5 21 ♘b3 dxc3 22 ♕xc3 ♘d4 23 ♘xd4 cxd4 24 ♕a3 f6 25 ♕c5 ♖b7 26 f4 exf4 27 ♖xf4 ♖c7 28 ♕b6 g5 29 ♖ff1 ♘g6 30 ♖a5 ♖cf7 31 ♕c5 ♗e6 32 ♘d6 ♖d7 33 ♖a6 ♕e7

Better is 33...♘e5 34 ♕a3 ♘xd3 35 ♕xd3 ♖xd6 with an equal position. White now gets the better of the forthcoming long endgame but Portisch is a fine defensive player and he holds on for a draw.

34 ♖b1 ♘e5 35 ♕a3 ♖fd8 36 ♖bb6 ♔g6 37 h3 ♔g7 38 ♗f1 ♖f8 39 ♕a1 h6 40 ♔g2 ♖fd8 41 ♘b5 ♗f7 42 ♖xf6 ♕b4 43 ♖ab6 ♘xd3 44 ♘d6 ♕d2+ 45 ♔h1 ♖xd6 46 ♖bxd6 ♖xd6 47 ♖xd6 ♘f2+ 48 ♔g1 ♘xe4 49 ♕xd4+ ♕xd4+ 50 ♖xd4 ♘xg3 51 ♗d3 ♘h5 52 ♖d6 ♘f4 53 ♗f5 ♗g6 54 ♗c8 ♘d3 55 ♔g2 ♘e5 56 ♔f2 h5 57 ♖a6 ♘d3+ 58 ♔e3 ♘f4 59 ♔d4 ♔f7 60 ♖b6 ♔g7 61 ♖b5 ♔f6 62 ♖a5 ♘e2+ 63 ♔e3 ♘f4 64 ♖a6+ ♔g7 65 ♖a2 ♘d5+ 66 ♔d4 ♘f4 67 ♖a5 ♔f6 68 ♔e3 ♘g2+ 69 ♔f3 ♘h4+ 70 ♔f2 ♘f5 71 ♖a6+ ♔g7 72 ♗d7 ♘d4 73 h4 gxh4 74 ♔e3 ♘f5+ 75 ♔f4 ♘h6 76 ♔g5 ♘f7+ 77 ♔xh4 ♘e5 ½-½

1 e4 c5 2 ⚘c3 ⚘c6 3 g3 g6 4 ⚗g2 ⚗g7 5 d3 d6 6 ⚗e3 ⚖b8

A different move order, but this game soon transposes to the previous one. White's other possibilities, 7 f4 and 7 ⚘ge2, are considered in Games 57-58.

7 ⚕d2 b5 8 ⚘ge2 b4 9 ⚘d1 ⚘d4 10 0-0

Not 10 ⚘c1? ⚗g4!

10...e6

10...⚘xe2+!? 11 ⚕xe2 e6 12 ⚕d2 ⚕b6 was suggested by Tringov.

11 ⚘c1 ⚘e7 12 c3

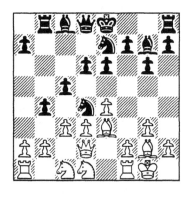

12...bxc3 13 bxc3 ⚘dc6

The position is exactly the same as the previous game except that the a-pawns are still on the board. That keeps a bit more tension on the board.

14 ⚗h6 0-0 15 ⚗xg7 ⚔xg7 16 ⚘e3 ⚗b7

If Black attempts to play in the same way as Portisch then he will come under pressure: 16...d5 17 exd5 exd5 18 ⚘b3! ⚕d6 19 d4 cxd4 20 cxd4.

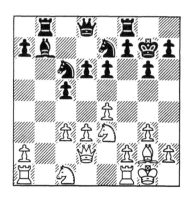

17 ⚘b3 a5 18 a4 ⚗a6 19 ⚖fb1 ⚕b6 20 h4 ⚘e5

20...h5 would have been more sensible.

21 d4 ⚘c4 22 ⚕e1 cxd4 23 cxd4 ⚘xe3 24 ⚕xe3 ⚖fc8 25 ⚔h2 ⚘c6 26 ⚘c5 ⚕a7 27 ⚖xb8 ⚘xb8 28 ⚘xa6 ⚘xa6 29 h5 ⚕e7 30 h6+ ⚔g8 31 ⚖c1 ⚖xc1 32 ⚕xc1 ⚕d8 33 ⚗f1 ⚘b4 34 ⚔g1 f6 35 d5 e5 36 ⚕c4 ⚔f7 37 ⚗h3 ⚕b8 38 ⚗e6+ ⚔e7 39 ⚗g8 f5 40 ⚗xh7 ⚔f6 41 exf5 ⚕h8 42 fxg6 1-0

1 e4 c5 2 ⚘c3 ⚘c6 3 g3 g6 4 ⚗g2 ⚗g7 5 d3 d6 6 ⚗e3 ⚖b8 7 f4

This is hardly ever played here, which surprises me. If Black attempts 7...b5, then it will be met by a counterblast in the centre: 8 e5!

7...⚘d4 8 ⚕d2

The game Romanishin-Stefansson, World Team Championship, Lucerne 1993, continued instead 8 ⚘f3!? ⚗g4 9 0-0 e6 10 ⚕d2 ⚗xf3 11 ⚗xf3 ⚘e7 (11...⚘xf3+!? 12 ⚖xf3 ⚘e7 13 d4 b6 14

♖d1) 12 ♗g2 0-0 13 ♘d1 and White had a pleasant advantage.

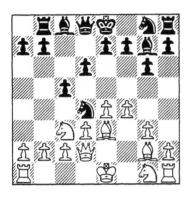

8...b5 9 ♘d1 f5

9...b4 10 c3 bxc3 11 bxc3 ♘c6 12 e5 hands the initiative to White.

10 c3 ♘e6 11 ♘f3 ♘h6 12 ♘f2 ♗b7 13 ♕e2 ♕d7 14 0-0 0-0 15 ♖ae1 ♘d8 16 h3

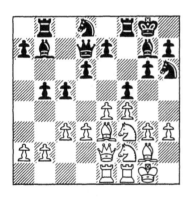

White has the makings of a strong attack, but it takes someone of Hort's calibre to play it so well.

16...♘hf7 17 g4 ♖c8 18 ♔h1 e5 19 exf5 gxf5 20 ♖g1 ♔h8 21 gxf5 exf4 22 f6 ♗xf6 23 ♗xf4 ♕f5 24 ♗h2 ♖c7 25 ♘e4 ♖e7 26 ♘fd2 ♗g7 27 ♖ef1 ♕g6 28 ♕f2 ♖ee8 29 ♕h4 ♘e5 30 ♖xf8+ ♖xf8 31 ♘xc5 ♘xd3 32 ♘xd3 ♕xd3 33 ♕g4 ♗f6 34 ♘e4

♗e7 35 ♘xd6 ♗xg2+ 36 ♕xg2 ♗f6 37 ♘e4 ♕d5 38 ♘xf6 1-0

Game 58
Ljubojevic-J.Polgar
Monaco Rapidplay 1995

1 e4 c5 2 ♘c3 ♘c6 3 g3 g6 4 ♗g2 ♗g7 5 d3 ♖b8 6 ♗e3 d6 7 ♘ge2

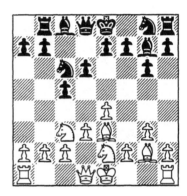

This is also sensible. If Black is going to prepare a wing attack with ...♖b8 then it seems logical to me to continue developing (here) or go for a quick central break (the previous game). I think these moves are more fitting than 7 ♕d2, which is actually more commonly played.

7...b5

7...♘d4 led to some amusing complications in Van der Wiel-Sosonko, Wijk aan Zee 1984: 8 0-0 b5 9 b4!? e6 (after 9...♘xe2+ 10 ♘xe2 ♗xa1 11 ♕xa1 ♘f6 12 bxc5 White would have had excellent compensation for the exchange) 10 a4! a6 11 axb5 axb5 12 ♖b1 ♗d7 13 ♘a2 ♘e7 14 bxc5 dxc5 15 c3 ♘xe2+ 16 ♕xe2 ♖c8 17 f4 0-0 18 ♕f2 and here a draw was agreed, although White has the better position.

8 a3 ♘f6 9 h3 0-0 10 b4

If 10 0-0 then Black continues on the queenside: 10...a5 and White doesn't have the standard positional trick available: 11 a4 b4 12 ♘b5 ♗a6, as White's rook needs to be on b1 for c2-c4 to work. However 11 ♕d2!? is possible: 11...b4 12 axb4 axb4 13 ♘d1 followed by ♗h6 with a tense game ahead.

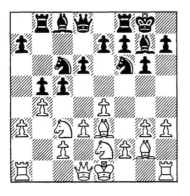

10...♘d7 11 ♖b1 cxb4 12 axb4 a5 13 bxa5 ♕xa5 14 ♗d2

14 ♕d2 b4 15 ♘d1 ♕a2 is irritating.

14...b4 15 ♘d5 e6 16 ♘e3

That was the idea of ♗d2 – to give the knight a square on e3.

16...♗a6 17 0-0 ♘c5

Black's play on the queenside is extremely well developed. Although

Polgar loses her way in the middle (before pulling off the win!) she has certainly won the opening battle.

18 f4 ♕b6 19 f5 b3 20 ♔h2 ♕d8 21 c4 b2 22 ♘g4 h5 23 ♘h6+ ♔h7 24 ♘xf7 ♖xf7 25 fxg6+ ♔xg6 26 ♘f4+ ♖xf4 27 gxf4 ♕e8 28 f5+ ♔f6 29 ♗c3+ e5 30 ♖xb2 ♖xb2 31 ♗xb2 ♗h6 32 ♗c1 ♕h8 33 h4 ♘d4 34 ♗h1 ♗f4+ 35 ♖xf4 exf4 36 ♗xf4 ♔e7 37 ♕g1 ♘e2 38 ♗g5+ ♔d7 39 ♕e3 ♕b2 40 ♗g2 ♗b7 41 ♔h3 ♘c3 42 ♗f6 ♕e2 43 ♕f3 ♕d2 44 ♕xh5 ♕xd3+ 45 ♔h2 ♘3xe4 46 ♕f7+ ♔c6 47 ♗d8 ♘d7 48 ♕e6 ♘e5 49 ♕e8+ ♔c5 50 ♕b5+ ♔d4 51 ♗b6+ ♔c3 52 ♗a5+ ♔c2 53 ♕a4+ ♔b2 54 ♕b4+ ♔c1 55 ♕e1+ ♔c2 56 ♕f1 ♘g4+ 57 ♔g1 ♕e3+ 0-1

Game 59
Uritzky-Rechlis
Israeli Championship 1996

1 e4 c5 2 ♘c3 ♘c6 3 g3 g6 4 ♗g2 ♗g7 5 d3 d6 6 ♗e3 ♘f6

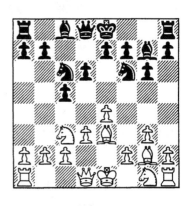

White's best move here is ...

7 h3

... to take away the g4 square from the black knight. Black hopes to prove that he has gained a tempo for his development, but White can take heart that if he throws his f-pawn up the board, it will reach f5 without being blocked by Black's pawn.

7...0-0 8 ♘ge2

8 f4 will probably transpose into Game 60. Another possibility is 8 ♕d2!? ♘d4 9 ♘ce2 e5 10 c3 ♘c6 11 f4 b6 12 ♘f3 exf4 13 ♗xf4 ♗a6 14 0-0 ♖e8 15 c4 b5 16 cxb5 ♗xb5 17 ♖f2 with an attack down the f-file, Ljubojevic-Sunye, Brasilia 1981.

8...♘d7

Or 8...♖b8 9 f4 ♘e8 10 0-0 ♗d7 11 f5 b5 12 ♕d2 b4 13 ♘d1 ♘d4 14 ♘f4 ♘c7 15 h4 with a strong attack, Hamdouchi-Pineda, Erevan Olympiad 1996.

9 g4 ♖b8 10 ♘g3 b5 11 ♕d2 ♘d4 12 f4 b4 13 ♘d1 a5 14 c3 bxc3 15 bxc3 ♘c6 16 0-0 a4 17 e5!?

An enterprising sacrifice. It was possible to continue the attack in standard fashion with 17 f5 and ♗h6, but this is more dynamic, denying Black the use of e5, and opening more lines.

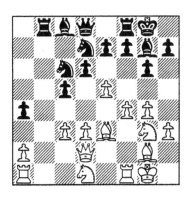

17...♕c7 18 ♘e4 dxe5 19 f5 c4 20 ♗h6 a3 21 ♗xg7 ♔xg7 22 fxg6 fxg6 23 dxc4 ♘a5 24 ♘e3 ♖b2 25 ♕d3

♘f6 26 g5 ♘xe4 27 ♕xe4 ♕c5 28 ♖xf8 ♔xf8 29 ♖f1+ ♔g7 30 ♕f3 ♗f5 31 ♔h1 e6 32 ♖d1 ♕c7 33 c5 e4 34 ♕f1 ♘c6 35 ♕c4 ♗xh3 36 ♕xe4 ♗xg2+ 37 ♘xg2 ♘d8 38 ♕d4+ e5 39 ♕xd8 ♕xd8 40 ♖xd8 ♖xa2 41 ♖a8 ♖a1+ 42 ♔h2 a2 43 c6 ♖c1 44 ♖xa2 ♖xc3 45 ♖a7+ ♔f8 46 c7 ♔e8 47 ♖a8+ ♔d7 48 c8♕+ ♖xc8 49 ♖xc8 ♔xc8 50 ♔g3 ♔d7 51 ♔f3 ♔e6 52 ♔e4 ♔f7 53 ♘e3 ♔e6 54 ♘g4 ♔d6 55 ♘f6 1-0

Game 60
Berg-Dinstuhl
Richmond 1994

1 e4 c5 2 d3 d6 3 g3 g6 4 ♗g2 ♗g7 5 f4 ♘c6 6 ♘f3 ♘f6 7 ♘c3 0-0 8 0-0

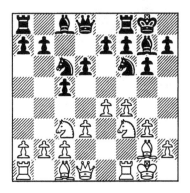

You might be thinking that this game looks a little out of place in this chapter, but it is possible to arrive in this variation via 6 ♗e3 ♘f6 7 h3, as will soon become clear. Black's set-up here has never quite recovered from the mauling it got in the Spassky-Geller Candidates match in 1968 – I won't quote those games again. Instead, I'm giving this more recent effort in which White plays the attack in a slightly different way.

8...♖b8 9 h3 b5

Spassky played 10 a3 and opened the a-file, after which he won brilliantly, but hey, you want to see something new!

10 ♗e3 b4 11 ♘e2 a5 12 g4 ♘e8 13 ♖b1 ♘c7 14 f5 ♘b5 15 h4 a4 16 h5 a3 17 b3 ♘bd4

17...♘c3! 18 ♘xc3 bxc3 and ...♘b4 strikes me as stronger.

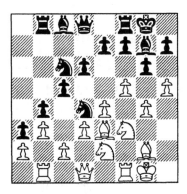

18 ♕d2 ♘xf3+ 19 ♖xf3 ♘e5 20 ♖g3 ♗b7 21 ♖f1 ♖c8 22 hxg6 hxg6 23 ♗h6 ♔h7 24 ♖h3 ♖h8 25 g5 ♗xh6 26 ♖xh6+ ♔g8 27 ♖xh8+ ♔xh8 28 f6 ♔g8 29 ♕f4 ♖c6 30 ♕h4 ♖b6 31 ♘f4 exf6 32 gxf6 d5 33 ♘h3 dxe4 34 ♘g5 ♘f3+ 35 ♖xf3 ♕d4+ 36 ♖f2 1-0

> ### Game 61
> ### Romanishin-Torre
> *Indonesia 1983*

1 e4 c5 2 ♘c3 ♘c6 3 g3 g6 4 ♗g2 ♗g7 5 d3 d6 6 ♗e3 b5

This move enjoyed a period of popularity in the early 1980s, but since then has been seldom encountered.

Hardly surprising. To my eyes it is asking for trouble.

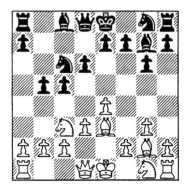

7 e5

A good start: open the centre while Black fiddles around at the side.

7...♕d7

7...♗b7?! 8 exd6 exd6 9 ♘xb5 ♘ge7 was played in Ljubojevic-Miles, London 1982, and now Miles recommends 10 ♘e2 which he assesses as 'slightly better for White'. No one has repeated this with Black, not least Miles himself who varied when he faced Ljubojevic a year later (see the next note).

8 exd6

8 ♘f3 is also fine for White, although Miles managed to work some magic on the position: 8...♘h6 9 exd6 exd6 10 ♘e4 ♘f5 11 ♗g5 (11 ♗f4!? is more dangerous: 11...0-0 12 0-0 ♗b7 13 ♗h3!) 11...0-0 12 0-0 f6 13 ♗c1 (13 ♗d2!? was suggested by Miles) 13...♗b7, when Black was fine in Ljubojevic-Miles, Plovdiv 1983.

8...exd6 9 ♘ge2 ♘ge7

Or 9...b4 10 ♘d5 ♗xb2 11 ♖b1 ♗g7 12 0-0 ♗b7 13 c3 with a slight advantage (Romanishin).

10 d4 b4 11 ♘e4 0-0 12 ♗h6

12 0-0!? was also worth a second

glance here.

12...c4

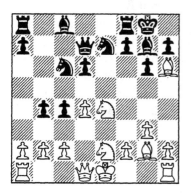

12...&a6 13 &xg7 &xg7 14 d5 ᐃe5

15 0-0 &c4! was Black's best according to Romanishin.

13 &xg7 &xg7 14 d5 ᐃe5 15 f4 ᐃg4 16 h3 ᐃh6 17 g4 f5 18 ₩d4+ &g8 19 ᐃf6+ ᖴxf6 20 ₩xf6 fxg4 21 ₩e6+ ₩xe6 22 dxe6 d5 23 ᐃd4 ᖴb8 24 0-0-0 ᖴb6 25 ᖴhe1 &g7 26 ᖴe5 &b7 27 ᖴde1 ᖴd6 28 ᖴg5 gxh3 29 &xh3 ᖴd8 30 ᖴg3 &f6 31 &d2 ᖴd6 32 a3 c3+ 33 bxc3 bxa3 34 ᖴa1 ᖴa6 35 &f1 ᖴa4 36 &b5 ᖴa5 37 &d3 a2 38 ᖴh3 &g7 39 ᐃb3 ᖴa3 40 ᖴah1 ᐃeg8 41 ᖴa1 ᐃg4 42 f5 g5 43 ᐃd4 ᐃ4f6 44 e7 &f7 45 ᐃb5 1-0

Summary

6...e5 continues to be a sound reply to 6 ♗e3, even if Black has to play with care on some occasions. Black's play in Games 47 and 50 is particularly worth looking at. 6...e6 7 ♕d2 ♕a5 (Game 53) is solid enough, but 7...♖b8 gives White chances for an advantage (Games 54-56) as he is able to exchange bishops on the kingside. 6...♖b8 (Games 57 and 58) is double-edged, but White should be able to build up an attack if he plays correctly – and that is all we can ask for!

1 e4 c5 2 ♘c3 ♘c6 3 g3 g6 4 ♗g2 ♗g7 5 d3 d6 6 ♗e3 *(D)* **6...e5**

    6...e6 7 ♕d2

        7...♘ge7 – *Game 52*; 7...♕a5 – *Game 53*

        7...♖b8 8 ♘ge2 ♘d4 9 0-0

            9...♘e7 – *Game 54*

            9...b5 10 ♘d1 b4 11 ♘c1 ♘e7

                12 a3 – *Game 55*; 12 c3 – *Game 56*

    6...♖b8

        7 ♕d2 b5 8 ♘ge2 b4 9 ♘d1 ♘d4 10 0-0 e6 – Games 55 and 56
        (by transposition)

        7 f4 – *Game 57*; 7 ♘ge2 – *Game 58*

    6...♘f6 7 h3 0-0

        8 ♘ge2 – *Game 59*; 8 f4 ♖b8 9 ♘f3 b5 10 0-0 – *Game 60*

    6...b5 – *Game 61*

7 ♕d2 ♘ge7 *(D)* **8 ♗h6**

    8 f4 ♘d4 9 ♘f3 0-0 10 0-0 ♗g4 – *Game 40* (by transposition)

    8 h4 – *Game 51*

8...♗xh6

    8...0-0 *(D)*

        9 h4 – *Game 48*

        9 ♗xg7 ♔xg7 10 f4

            10...♗e6 – *Game 49*; 10...♘d4 – *Game 50*

9 ♕xh6 – *Game 47*

      6 ♗e3

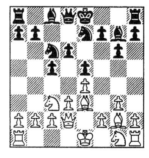

    7...♘ge7

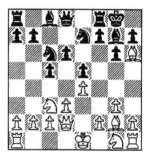

    8...0-0

CHAPTER SIX

6 ♘ge2

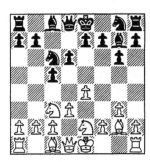

1 e4 c5 2 ♘c3 ♘c6 3 g3 g6 4 ♗g2 ♗g7 5 d3 d6 6 ♘ge2

The advantage of ♘ge2 is its flexibility. White can wait and see how Black develops and then, depending on what is presented, play ♗e3 and ♕d2; play ♗g5; advance the h-pawn; advance the f-pawn, break in the centre or play on the queenside ... Unfortunately, the non-committal nature of the move also applies to Black too: he has a wide choice of options, most of which are reasonable. I think one should pick one's opponent carefully for 6 ♘ge2. If you have the feeling that you are facing a theoretical monster, then this could well be suitable: there isn't a system which is clearly best for Black, so it comes down to an understanding of strategy. This is a subtle way to play: there are many transpositional tricks and a good knowledge of different kinds of positions is helpful.

This chapter is structured as follows: Games 62-64 deal with systems where Black plays an early ...♘f6,

6...e5 is dealt with in Games 65-67 and 6...e6 in Games 69 and 70. Finally, 6...♘d4 is discussed in Game 71.

1 e4 c5 2 g3 ♘c6 3 ♗g2 g6 4 ♘e2 ♗g7 5 0-0 ♘f6 6 ♘bc3 0-0 7 h3 d6 8 d3 ♖b8

8...♘d4 is considered in Game 64.

9 f4

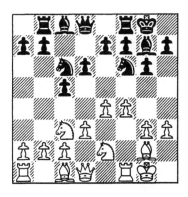

Turner isn't backward about coming forward, and his strategy pays off

here. There is also a more subtle approach: 9 ♗e3 b5 10 ♕d2 b4 11 ♘d1 followed by ♗h6, exchange on g7, and ♘e3. According to how Black plays White can attack on the kingside, or break in the centre.

9...♗d7 10 ♗e3

The even more brutal 10 g4 is discussed in the next game.

10...b5 11 ♕d2

11 a3 is calmer: 11...♘e8 12 d4 cxd4 13 ♘xd4 b4 14 ♘xc6 ♗xc6 15 axb4 ♖xb4 16 ♖xa7 ♖xb2 17 e5 and a draw was soon agreed in Spassky-Fischer, Belgrade 1992.

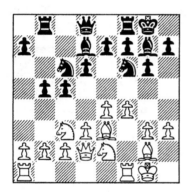

11...b4 12 ♘d1 ♘e8 13 f5 ♘d4 14 g4 a5

After 14...♘xe2+ 15 ♕xe2 a5 16 ♕d2 a4 17 ♗h6 White's attack hasn't been slowed down.

15 ♘xd4 cxd4 16 ♗h6 ♕c7 17 ♗xg7 ♔xg7 18 a3!

The counterplay on the a-file is useful.

18...♕c5 19 axb4 axb4 20 ♕f2 ♗b5

In view of the game continuation it looks advisable to block the kingside completely with 20...g5, though even here White has chances: Black's queen is tied to defending the d-pawn and

that creates problems, e.g. 21 b3 ♘f6 22 ♘b2 and ♘c4.

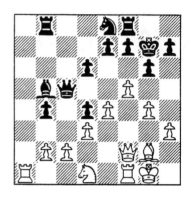

21 b3 ♘f6 22 g5 ♘d7

Or 22...♘h5!? 23 ♖a2!? ♕e5 24 ♖a7 with an attack.

23 ♕h4

Perhaps 23 f6+!? instead.

23...♘e5

Could Black have captured on c2? 23...♕xc2!? 24 f6+ exf6 25 gxf6+ ♔h8 26 ♖f4 (26 ♕h6 ♖g8 27 ♖f4 g5 28 ♖f5 ♖g6 29 ♕h5 ♗xd3) 26...g5 wins for Black.

24 ♘f2

Suddenly White has an attack out of nowhere.

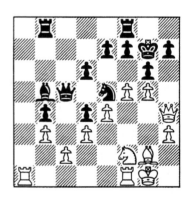

24...♔h8 25 ♘g4 ♗c6 26 f6 ♘xg4 27 hxg4 exf6 28 gxf6 ♖b5 29 ♖a6

♗b7 30 ♕h6 ♖g8 31 ♖f3 ♕g5 32 ♕xg5 ♖xg5 33 ♖xd6 ♗c8 34 ♖xd4 ♗xg4 35 ♖g3 h5 36 ♗f3 ♖c8 37 ♖c4 ♖xc4 38 bxc4 ♔g8 39 ♗xg4 hxg4 40 ♔f1 ♖a5 41 ♖xg4 ♖a2 42 ♖g2 ♔f8 43 ♖e2 ♔e8 44 ♔f2 g5 45 c5 g4 46 c6 ♖a6 47 ♔g3 ♖xc6 48 e5 ♖c3 49 ♖d2 ♖a3 50 ♔xg4 ♖a2 51 ♖h2 ♔d7 52 ♔g3 ♔e6 53 d4 ♖a8 54 ♔f4 ♔d5 55 ♖h7 ♖a7 56 ♔f5 ♔xd4 57 ♖xf7 ♖xf7 58 e6 ♖c7 59 f7 ♖xc2 60 e7 b3 61 f8♕ b2 62 ♕f6+ ♔d3 63 e8♕ b1♕ 64 ♕e4+ ♔d2 65 ♕fd4+ 1-0

One needs strong nerves to play such positions. The game can turn on one move.

Here is another example of a king-side hack. For a while it looked promising, but then ...

Game 63
Maus-Boensch
German Bundesliga 1993

1 e4 c5 2 ♘c3 ♘c6 3 g3 g6 4 ♗g2 ♗g7 5 d3 d6 6 ♘ge2 ♖b8 7 0-0 ♘f6

I feel that if Black is going to play ...♖b8 then he may as well be consistent and follow up with 7...b5 8 f4 b4 9 ♘d5 f5. In Brunthaler-Mainka, Germany 1995, White messed around now with 10 h3, but I think he should have played 10 exf5 gxf5 11 a3 with a double-edged position.

8 f4 0-0 9 h3 ♗d7 10 g4

This is more direct that 10 ♗e3, which we saw in the last game.

10...b5 11 ♘g3 b4 12 ♘ce2 a5 13 f5 a4

In Maus-Moiseev, Germany 1995,

Black varied with 13...♘e8, but White still achieved a powerful attack with 14 ♖b1 a4 15 ♗g5 a3 16 b3 ♘d4 17 ♕d2 ♗c6 18 ♗h6 ♕b6 19 ♔h1 ♘xe2 20 ♘xe2 ♘f6 21 ♕g5 ♔h8 22 ♘f4 ♗xh6 23 ♕xh6.

14 ♗f4 ♘e8

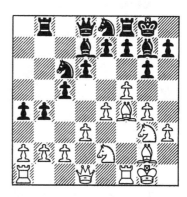

15 ♖b1

15 ♕c1!? is a thought, attempting to gain a tempo on the game. The only way for Black to exploit it is 15...a3 16 b3 ♗b2 17 ♕d2 ♗xa1 18 ♖xa1 ♘g7 19 ♗h6, when White has some attack for the exchange.

15...a3 16 b3 ♘c7 17 ♕d2 ♘b5 18 ♗h6 ♘c3 19 ♗xg7 ♘xe2+ 20 ♘xe2 ♔xg7 21 ♖f2 f6 22 g5 fxg5

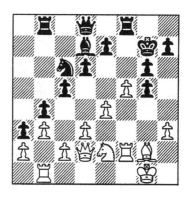

23 ♖bf1

23 ♕xg5! was the way to continue.
23...h6 24 h4

White gets over-excited.

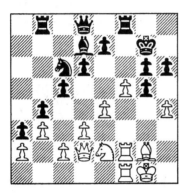

24...gxh4 25 ♘f4 g5 26 f6+ exf6 27 ♘h5+ ♔h7 28 ♘xf6+ ♔h8 29 ♕e2 ♘e5 30 ♕d1 ♗e6 31 ♕h5 ♔g7 32 ♕d1 ♕e7 33 d4 cxd4 34 ♕xd4 ♔h8 35 ♔h2 ♖bd8 36 ♗h3 ♗xh3 37 ♔xh3 ♕g7 38 ♖f5 g4+ 39 ♔g2 ♘f3 40 ♕b6 0-1

Game 64
Spassky-Gipslis
USSR Championship, Baku 1961

---

1 e4 c5 2 ♘c3 ♘c6 3 g3 g6 4 ♗g2 ♗g7 5 d3 d6 6 ♘ge2 ♘f6 7 h3 0-0 8 0-0 ♘d4

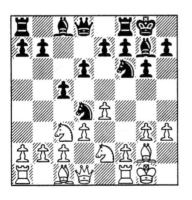

I was surprised to see that *ECO* gives this as its main line.
9 ♘xd4

Not mentioned in *ECO*, but I think we should trust Boris.
9...cxd4 10 ♘e2 ♘d7 11 f4 f5

Black has no desire to allow f4-f5 and be subjected to an attack.
12 ♔h2 ♔h8 13 exf5 gxf5 14 c3 dxc3 15 bxc3 ♕a5 16 ♗e3 ♘c5

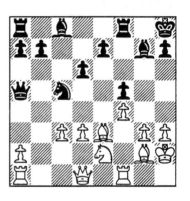

17 ♗d4!

A splendid move, either forcing the exchange of bishops and thus weakening Black's king, or tempting ...
17...e5

Black's pawn front is not particularly stable after this.
18 ♗e3 ♗e6 19 ♖b1 ♖ad8 20 d4 ♘e4 21 ♖xb7

Now that Black has played ..e7-e5, his second rank is also weaker.
21...♕xa2 22 ♖b4 ♗d5

see following diagram

23 ♖g1!

It is hard to appreciate at first, but this is a brilliant move. 23 ♖a4 failed to 23...♘xc3!
23...♗a8 24 ♖a4 ♕b2 25 ♖b4 ♕a2 26 ♖a4 ♕b2 27 ♖xa7 ♘xc3 28

♘xc3 ♕xc3 29 ♕h5! exd4

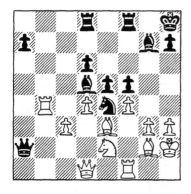

Or 29...♕xe3 30 ♕g5 ♖g8 (30...♗f6
31 ♕h6) 31 ♖xg7!

30 ♖xg7! 1-0

30...♔xg7 is met by 31 ♖c1 ♕xe3 32
♖c7+ and mate. A gem.

Game 65
Wittmann-Miniboeck
Vienna Open 1986

**1 e4 c5 2 ♘c3 ♘c6 3 g3 g6 4 ♗g2
♗g7 5 d3 d6 6 ♘ge2 e5**

This is a perfectly respectable move
here. Black doesn't want to allow
some appalling attack with f4-f5.

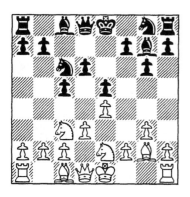

7 h4

I just couldn't resist including this

idea. Wittmann has made something
of a speciality out of it, and there's
more to it than meets the eye. I should
emphasise, this is not the most usual
move here. Most players prefer to castle (see Games 66 and 67).

7...♘f6

Not 7...♘d4?! (wasting time) 8
♘xd4 cxd4 9 ♘d5 ♗e6 10 c4 dxc3 11
bxc3 ♗xd5 12 exd5 ♕a5 13 0-0 ♘e7 14
♕b3 ♕a6 15 ♖b1 and White had a
pleasant initiative on the queenside
(and the bishops!) in Wittmann-
Kraschl, Austrian Team Championship 1996. I suppose if 7...h5 then 8
♘d5, intending to meet 8...♘ge7 with
9 ♗g5.

**8 ♗g5 ♗e6 9 ♘d5 h6 10 ♗xf6 ♗xf6
11 h5**

White already has a clear positional
advantage.

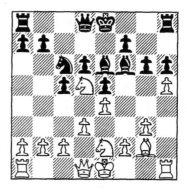

**11...♗g7 12 hxg6 fxg6 13 ♗h3
♗xh3 14 ♖xh3 ♕d7 15 ♖h2 h5 16
♕d2 0-0-0 17 0-0-0 ♗h6 18 f4 ♖df8
19 ♔b1 ♘e7 20 ♘ec3 ♖h7 21 ♖f1
♖hf7 22 ♘xe7+ ♕xe7 23 ♖hf2 ♔b8
24 ♘d5 ♕d7 25 ♖f3 exf4 26 gxf4
g5 27 ♕h2 h4 28 ♖h3 ♗g7 29 f5
♗e5 30 ♕g2 ♗g3 31 ♕f3 ♖g8 32
♕g4 ♕e8 33 ♖hh1 ♕e5 34 ♖f3 a6**

35 f6 ♖h7 36 b3 ♕e8 37 ♖xg3 1-0

Game 66
Spassky-Hort
German Bundesliga 1985/86

1 e4 c5 2 ♘c3 ♘c6 3 g3 g6 4 ♗g2 ♗g7 5 d3 e5 6 ♘ge2 ♘ge7 7 0-0

Boris likes to take things steadier.

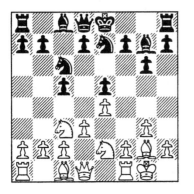

7...d6 8 a3

Game 67 deals with 8 ♗e3.

8...0-0 9 ♖b1 f5

Hort sets a trap.

10 ♗d2

If 10 b4 f4 White can't capture on f4 as the knight on c3 hangs.

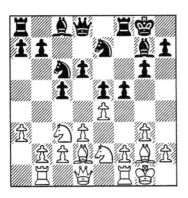

10...a5 11 a4 ♗e6 12 ♘d5 h6 13 c3 ♔h7 14 ♗e3 ♗f7 15 f4 ♘xd5 16

exd5 ♘e7 17 ♕b3 b6 18 ♖be1 ♖a7 19 c4 ♘g8 20 fxe5 ♗xe5 21 d4 ♗g7 22 dxc5 bxc5 23 ♘c3 ♖e7 24 ♘b5 ♖fe8 25 ♗d2 ♗e5 26 g4!?

An amazing move.

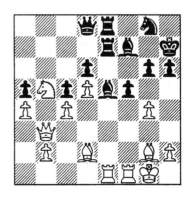

26...♘f6

If 26...fxg4 I'm sure it was Spassky's intention to play 27 ♖xe5! dxe5 and now either 28 d6 or 28 ♕e3!? offers White compensation for the material.

27 gxf5 gxf5 28 ♖xf5 ♗d4+ 29 ♘xd4 ♖xe1+ 30 ♗xe1 ♖xe1+ 31 ♔f2 ♕e7 32 ♖xf6 ♕xf6+ 33 ♔xe1 ♕xd4 34 ♕g3 ♕xc4 35 ♕xd6 ♕c1+ 36 ♔f2 ♕xb2+ 37 ♔g3 ♕g7+ 38 ♔f2 ♕d4+ 39 ♔g3 ♗g7

40 ♕f4?

After 40 ♕c7 a draw would have

been on the cards.

**40...♕xf4+ 41 ♔xf4 ♔f6 42 ♗e4 c4
43 d6 ♗e8 44 ♘d5 ♗xa4 45 ♗xc4
♗c6 46 ♗a2 a4 47 ♗c4 ♗d7 48
♔e3 a3 49 ♔d4 ♗e6 50 d7 ♗xd7 51
♔c3 ♗e6 52 ♗e2 0-1**

A great struggle.

> ## Game 67
> ## Neumark-Goet
> *RLNS 1988*

**1 e4 c5 2 ♘c3 ♘c6 3 g3 g6 4 ♗g2
♗g7 5 d3 e5 6 ♘ge2 ♘ge7 7 0-0
0-0 8 ♗e3**

The most orthodox way of playing
the position.

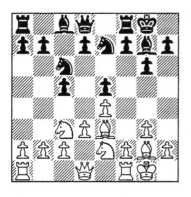

8...d6 9 ♕d2 ♗e6

It is more accurate for Black to play
9...♘d4 first.

10 f4

It would have been better to play 10
♗h6! ♕d7 11 ♗xg7 ♔xg7 12 f4.
White's attack is stronger without the
bishops and Black's centre less secure.

10...♕d7

10...♘d4 is stronger, e.g. 11 ♖ae1
♕d7 12 ♘c1 ♖ad8 13 ♘d1 b6 14 c3
♘dc6 with equality, as in Kholmov-
Tal, USSR Championship 1962.

11 fxe5!

Black cannot capture with the
pawn, so this is strong.

**11...♘xe5 12 ♗h6! f5 13 ♗xg7
♔xg7 14 ♘f4 fxe4 15 ♘xe4 ♗f5 16
♖ae1 ♘7c6 17 c3 ♖ae8 18 b3 b6 19
d4 ♘g4 20 h3 ♘h6 21 ♘g5 ♖xe1 22
♖xe1 ♖e8 23 g4 ♘xg4 24 hxg4
♗xg4 25 ♖xe8 ♕xe8 26 ♗xc6 ♕xc6
27 ♘fe6+ ♗xe6 28 ♘xe6+ ♔g8 29
♕f4 ♕e8 30 ♕f6 1-0**

> ## Game 68
> ## Spassky-Chandler
> *German Bundesliga 1986/87*

**1 e4 c5 2 ♘c3 ♘c6 3 g3 g6 4 ♗g2
♗g7 5 d3 d6 6 ♘ge2 e6**

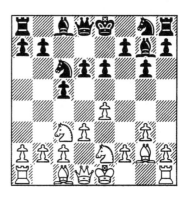

This is another perfectly reasonable response to 6 ♘ge2.

7 0-0 ♘ge7 8 ♖b1

For 8 ♗g5, see Game 69.

8...0-0 9 ♗e3

Threatening d4, when Black has a poor Sicilian (weak pawn on d6).

9...♘d4

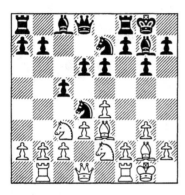

10 b4!

This was the point of ♖b1: the black knight had to jump to d4 and that permitted b2-b4.

10...b6

It is staggering that Black can get away with this.

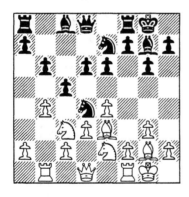

11 e5 ♘d5 12 exd6

12 ♘xd5? exd5 13 ♗xd5 ♗h3 14 ♘xd4 cxd4 15 ♗xd4 dxe5 wins.

12...♘xe2+ 13 ♘xe2 cxb4 14 ♗d2 a5

14...♕xd6? 15 ♗xb4

15 a3 ♖a7

15...bxa3 16 c4 a2 17 ♖a1 ♗xa1 18 ♕xa1 is good for White.

16 axb4 ♘xb4 17 ♗xb4 axb4 18 ♕d2 ♕xd6 19 ♖xb4 ♗d7 20 ♖fb1 b5 21 ♘c3 ♗xc3 22 ♕xc3 ♖c8 23 ♕b3 ♖a4 24 c4 bxc4 25 dxc4 ♖xb4 26 ♕xb4 ♕xb4 27 ♖xb4

The ending should be a draw.

27...♔g7 28 f4 ♔f6 29 ♔f2 e5 30 fxe5+ ♔xe5 31 ♔e3 g5 32 ♖b7 ♗c6 33 ♗xc6 ♖xc6 34 ♖b5+ ♔e6 35 ♔d4 f5 36 g4 ♖d6+ 37 ♔c3 fxg4 38 ♖xg5 ♖a6 39 ♔b4 ♖a2 40 ♖h5 ♖a7 41 c5 ♖f7 42 ♔b5 ♔d7 43 ♖g5 ♖f2 44 ♖g7+ ♔c8 45 ♖xh7 ♖f6 46 ♖h4 ♖f2 47 ♔b6 ♖b2+ 48 ♔c6 ♔b8 49 ♖h8+ ♔a7 50 ♔d6 ♖d2+ 51 ♔c7 ♖f2 52 ♖h7 ♖f8 53 c6 ♖g8 54 ♖e7 g3 55 ♔d6+ ♔b6 56 hxg3 ♖xg3 57 ♖b7+ ♔a6 ½-½

> *Game 69*
> **Spassky-Karpov**
> *Bugojno 1986*

1 e4 c5 2 ♘c3 ♘c6 3 g3 g6 4 ♗g2

♗g7 5 d3 d6 6 ♘ge2 e6 7 0-0 ♘ge7
8 ♗g5

8...0-0

Black wisely resists attacking the bishop: 8...h6 9 ♗e3 ♘d4 10 ♕d2 and it takes time to arrange castling.

9 ♕d2 ♖b8 10 ♗h6 b5 11 ♗xg7 ♔xg7 12 f4

12 a3 ♘d4 would have transposed to Simagin-Taimanov, USSR Championship 1951, where, after 13 ♘xd4 cxd4 14 ♘e2 e5 15 c3 dxc3 16 bxc3 ♗g4 17 f3 ♗e6 18 f4 f6 19 h3 ♘c6 20 ♖ab1 ♕a5 21 ♔h2 ♘d4 Black had created enough counterplay on the queenside.

12...♘d4 13 ♘xd4 cxd4 14 ♘e2 e5

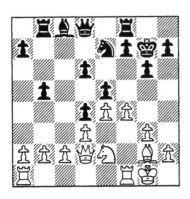

15 c3

15 f5!? f6 (15...gxf5!? 16 ♕g5+ ♘g6 17 ♕xd8 ♖xd8 18 exf5 ♘f8 19 c3 is finely balanced) 16 g4 g5 17 c3 is more double-edged than the game, although I don't think Black should be too afraid.

15...dxc3 16 bxc3 f6 17 ♔h1 a5 18 ♘g1 ♗e6 19 ♘f3 ♕c7 20 ♖ac1 ♖bc8 21 ♕b2 ♖b8 22 ♕d2 ♖bc8 23 ♕b2 ½-½

And here is another beautiful game from Spassky. It's a one-sided encounter; his opponent isn't in the same class, but the former World Champion's strategy is delightful.

Game 70
Spassky-Brochet
French Team Championship 1991

1 e4 c5 2 ♘c3 ♘c6 3 g3 g6 4 ♗g2 ♗g7 5 d3 d6 6 ♘ge2 ♘d4

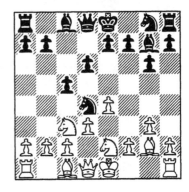

Perhaps this is a little premature here.

7 ♘xd4 cxd4 8 ♘e2 ♗g4 9 f3 ♗d7 10 h4

This looks curious: it doesn't really fit in with the rest of White's strategy in this game.

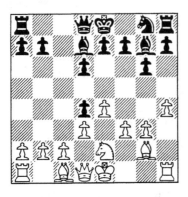

10...♖c8 11 ♗d2 ♛b6 12 ♛b1 e6 13 0-0 ♘e7 14 a4! 0-0 15 b4! f5 16 ♛b3! fxe4 17 fxe4 ♖xf1+ 18 ♖xf1 ♛c6 19 ♗h3 ♛xc2 20 ♗xe6+ ♔h8 21 ♛xc2 ♖xc2 22 ♗xd7 ♖xd2 23 ♖f7 ♖xe2 24 ♖xe7 ♗e5 25 ♗e6 ♗xg3 26 ♖xb7 ♗xh4 27 ♖xa7 g5 28 a5 h5 29 ♖f7 ♖b2 30 a6 1-0

1 e4 c5 2 ♘c3 ♘c6 3 ♘ge2 g6 4 g3 ♗g7 5 ♗g2 e6

Let's see what can happen if Black delays ...d7-d6.

6 d3 ♘ge7 7 h4

Now you know why I was so impressed by Wittmann's idea against ...e7-e5 (Game 65): I've been wheeling out some similar stuff myself. The move doesn't just have shock value. Black already finds himself with a dilemma: he must do something about h4-h5, so should he play his h-pawn forward one square or two?

7...h5

7...h6!? 8 h5!? (8 ♗e3! ♘d4 9 ♛d2) 8...g5 9 f4 gxf4 10 ♗xf4 followed by ♛d2 and 0-0-0 gives both sides chances.

8 ♗g5

A pleasant square for the bishop. Black finds the pin annoying, but has no desire to play ...f7-f6, blocking his own bishop and spoiling his kingside structure.

8...♖b8 9 a3 b5 10 ♖b1

I took some tips from Spassky.

10...d6 11 ♛d2 ♗d7 12 0-0 a5?

Mistake!

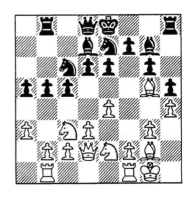

13 a4! bxa4

13...b4 14 ♘b5 and the knight is secure.

14 ♘xa4 ♘e5 15 b3

My plan is simple: to round up the a-pawn.

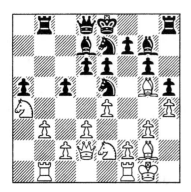

15...f6 16 ♗f4 ♘f7 17 ♘b2 ♘c6 18 ♘c4 ♗c8 19 ♗e3 e5 20 ♖a1 ♖a8 21 ♖a4 ♗e6 22 ♖fa1 ♗xc4 23 dxc4 ♕d7 24 ♕d5 ♖c8 25 ♔h2 g5 26

♗h3 g4 27 ♗g2 ♗h6 28 ♘c3 ♔f8 29 ♕d3 ♕e6 30 ♘d5 ♔g7 31 ♗d2 ♗xd2 32 ♕xd2 ♖b8 33 ♘e3 ♘h6 34 ♘f5+ ♘xf5 35 exf5 ♕d7 36 ♗xc6 ♕xc6 37 ♖xa5

Mission accomplished.

37...♖bd8 38 ♖a7+ ♖d7 39 ♖1a6 ♕c8 40 ♖xd7+?

40 ♕xd6 would have been simpler. I'll blame the clock for that one.

40...♕xd7 41 ♕xd6 ♕xd6 42 ♖xd6 ♖a8 43 ♔g2 e4 44 ♔f1 e3 45 fxe3 ♖a1+ 46 ♔e2 ♖g1 47 b4 cxb4 48 c5 ♖a1 49 ♖d4 ♖a2 50 ♔d3 ♖a3+ 51 ♔e4 ♖c3 52 ♔d5 ♖xc2 53 ♖xb4 ♖d2+ 54 ♖d4 1-0

Summary

It is interesting to see the different interpretations of 6 ♘ge2. Spassky generally plays solidly, but it is also possible to play in a more unorthodox manner – see Games 65 and 71. Pushing the h-pawn is not as silly as it looks. If Black replies to 6 ♘ge2 with 6...♘f6 then he is inviting an attack, but he gains good counterplay on the queenside (Games 62 and 63). The jury is still out on this variation. 6...e5 and 6...e6 are the most solid choices; Karpov's play in Game 69 is exemplary.

1 e4 c5 2 ♘c3 ♘c6 3 g3 g6 4 ♗g2 ♗g7 5 d3 d6
    5...e6 6 ♘ge2 ♘ge7 7 h4 – *Game 71*
6 ♘ge2 ♘f6
    6...e5 *(D)*
        7 h4 – *Game 65*
        7 0-0 ♘ge7
            8 a3 0-0 – *Game 66*
            8 ♗e3 0-0 – *Game 67*
    6...e6 7 0-0 ♘ge7 *(D)*
        8 ♖b1 – *Game 68*
        8 ♗g5 – *Game 69*
    6...♘d4 – *Game 70*
7 0-0 0-0 8 h3 ♖b8
    8...♘d4 – *Game 64*
9 f4 ♗d7 *(D)* 10 ♗e3
    10 g4 – *Game 63*
10...b5 – *Game 62*

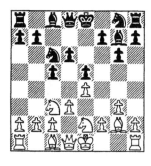

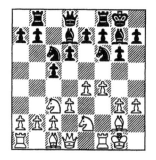

   6...e5   *7...♘ge7*   *9...♗d7*

CHAPTER SEVEN

6 ♘f3 and other Sixth Moves for White

1 e4 c5 2 ♘c3 ♘c6 3 g3 g6 4 ♗g2 ♗g7 5 d3 d6

The modest 6 ♘f3 system has a little more bite to it than it might appear at first sight. White brings out his pieces unpretentiously and keeps his options open. Depending on how Black plays, he might manoeuvre positionally, or perhaps institute a kingside attack. Don't be put off by the move orders in these games, they often come from the Réti opening, but White can arrive at this system just as easily from standard Closed Sicilian paths. In the first three Games (72–74) Black grabs more control in the centre with 6...e5, which at first sight looks powerful, but White's manoeuvres shouldn't be underestimated. 6...e6 (Game 75) is perhaps the most canny move, while 6...♘f6 (which is often reached via a Réti move order) has been the subject of a great many games, as we see in Games 76-80. There are several players who have specialised in this system for White and developed some strong attacking

ideas. In the final game of the chapter we take a look at 6 ♘h3 (I couldn't think where else to put it) and I've included in the notes a couple of other sixth move options for White.

Game 72
Bilek-Barczay
Sousse Interzonal 1967

1 ♘f3 c5 2 g3 g6 3 ♗g2 ♗g7 4 0-0 ♘c6 5 e4 d6 6 d3 e5 7 ♘c3 ♘ge7

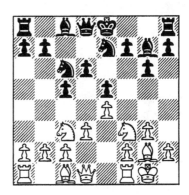

8 ♘d2!

I think that this is the best way for White to handle the position. Before deciding on where to make a pawn break, kingside or queenside, White brings his knight to a better square. 8 ♘h4 is considered in Game 74.

8...♘d4?

The knight only has to retreat a few moves later. 8...♖b8 is more accurate – see the next game.

9 ♘c4 0-0 10 ♘e3 ♖b8 11 ♘cd5 ♘xd5 12 ♘xd5 ♗e6 13 c3 ♘c6 14 a3 a5 15 a4

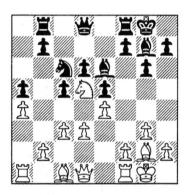

White already has a slight but clear strategic advantage.

15...♘e7 16 ♗g5 f6 17 ♗e3 f5 18 exf5! ♘xf5

18...♗xd5 19 ♗xd5+ ♘xd5 20 ♕b3 wins the piece back and maintains central control.

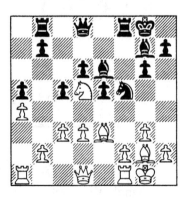

19 ♗d2 ♔h8 20 ♕e2 ♕d7 21 ♕e4 ♘e7 22 ♘xe7 ♕xe7 23 f4 ♗g8 24 fxe5 ♖xf1+ 25 ♖xf1 d5 26 ♕g4 b5 27 ♗g5 ♕xe5 28 ♗f4 ♕e8 29 ♗xb8 ♕xb8 30 ♕d7 d4 31 ♖e1 dxc3 32 bxc3 bxa4 33 ♗d5 ♗xd5 34 ♖e8+ ♕xe8 35 ♕xe8+ ♗g8 36 ♕xa4 ♗xc3 37 ♕d7 ♗d4+ 38 ♔f1 ♗b3 39 ♕d8+ ♔g7 40 ♕xa5 h5 41 ♕b5 ♗e6 42 ♕b7+ ♔f6 43 ♔g2 ♗f5 44 ♕f3 ♔g7 ½-½

Why didn't White play to win this position? Of course, it would have been hard work, but even more so for the defender.

1 e4 c5 2 ♘f3 ♘c6 3 g3 g6 4 ♗g2 ♗g7 5 0-0 e5 6 ♘c3 ♘ge7 7 d3 d6 8 ♘d2 ♖b8

see following diagram

9 a4 a6 10 ♘c4 b5

Ill-judged. Even though Black wins this game quickly, I am not convinced by his plan. He doesn't prevent the knight from arriving at d5, and

White's rook on the a-file is a thorn in his side.

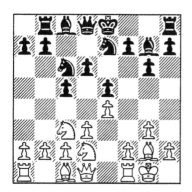

11 ♘e3 0-0 12 axb5 axb5 13 ♘cd5 f5 14 exf5! gxf5 15 f4!

White has no weaknesses in his position, while Black's pawns are overextended.

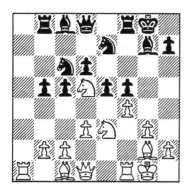

15...♗e6 16 ♖a6 ♕d7 17 ♗d2

17 ♕h5 is more powerful: Black is under severe pressure on both sides of the board. Over the next few moves White drifts a little.

17...♔h8 18 c3 ♘xd5 19 ♘xd5 ♘e7 20 ♘xe7 ♕xe7 21 ♕f3 ♗c8 22 ♖a8?

22 ♖a5 would have kept White very much in the game, although Black is over the worst after 22...♗b7.

22...e4 0-1

Game 74
Shachar-Gofshtein
Israeli Championship 1994

1 e4 c5 2 ♘f3 d6 3 d3 ♘c6 4 g3 g6 5 ♗g2 ♗g7 6 0-0 e5 7 ♘c3 ♘ge7 8 ♘h4

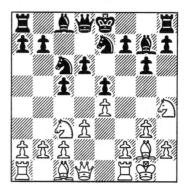

Personally, I prefer 8 ♘d2 to this move, but it does also have its merits. Positions similar to Games 45 and 46 in Chapter 4 are reached.

8...0-0 9 f4 exf4 10 ♗xf4 h6

10...♗e6 is also respectable, though, as usual, the exchange of bishops gives White more chances on the kingside. 11 ♕d2 d5 12 ♗h6 d4 13 ♘e2 ♘e5 14 h3 f6 15 ♗xg7 ♔xg7 16 ♖f2 ♕d6 17 ♖af1 ♖ad8 18 g4 h6 19 ♘f4 and although Black holds a positional advantage, it isn't easy to control White's attack, Hodgson-Eingorn, Sochi 1986.

11 ♗e3 ♘e5 12 h3 b5 13 a3 ♗d7 14 ♘f3

14 ♕d2 is natural and best.

14...♘7c6 15 ♘d5 ♘xf3+ 16 ♕xf3 ♘d4 17 ♕d1 ♗e6 18 c3 ♗xd5 19 exd5 ♘f5 20 ♗f2 a5

White has played carelessly. Black's bishop on g7 is a monster, and if

White waits, then ...b5-b4 will rip open the queenside.

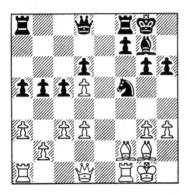

21 g4 ♘h4 22 ♗e4 f5 23 gxf5 gxf5 24 ♕h5 ♕g5+ 25 ♕xg5 hxg5 26 ♗xh4 fxe4 27 ♗g3 exd3 28 ♗xd6 ♖xf1+ 29 ♖xf1 ♗f8 30 ♗xf8 ♖xf8 31 a4

31 ♖xf8+? ♔xf8 32 ♔f2 c4 wins for Black.

31...c4

31...♖xf1+? 32 ♔xf1 bxa4 33 c4 wins for White!

32 axb5 ♖d8 33 ♖f5? d2 34 ♖f1 ♖e8 0-1

---

1 e4 c5 2 ♘f3 g6 3 ♘c3 ♗g7 4 g3 ♘c6 5 ♗g2 d6 6 d3 e6

see following diagram

This is a very standard way to continue.

7 0-0 ♘ge7 8 ♗g5 h6

Black's best response. If 8...0-0 then 9 ♕d2 and ♗h6, and White can claim to have achieved something.

9 ♗e3 ♘d4 10 ♕d2

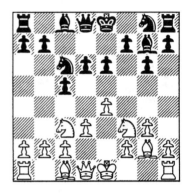

That Black has been prevented from castling for a few moments is a minor inconvenience. White can make very little of it.

10...♕a5

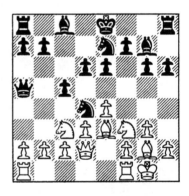

White would like to drop back the knight from c3 and kick Black's knight out of d4 with the pawn, but that is unlikely after this move. The endings are never a problem for Black.

11 ♘e1 ♘ec6

If it comes to it, Black can play ...h6-h5 and then castle.

12 f4 ♗d7 13 ♕f2 f5 14 ♔h1 ♘e7

Black loses the plot around here. 14...0-0 suggests itself.

15 ♘f3 ♘xf3 16 ♗xf3 ♗c6 17 d4 cxd4 18 ♗xd4 e5 19 fxe5 ♗xe5 20

♗xe5 dxe5 21 ♕e3 0-0-0 22 ♖ae1

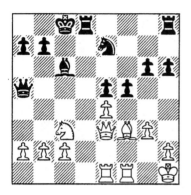

Now Black is struggling: his pawns are weak and his king too open. He does well to grovel into a poor ending. **22...fxe4 23 ♗xe4 ♘f5 24 ♕f3 ♗xe4 25 ♖xe4 h5 26 ♖fe1 ♖he8 27 a3 ♖d4 28 ♖xd4 ♘xd4 29 ♕f7 ♖e6 30 ♖f1 ♕d8 31 ♔g1 ♕e8 32 ♕xe8+ ♖xe8 33 ♘e4 ♘f5 34 ♖f3 ♖d8 35 ♖c3+ ♔b8 36 ♖c5 ♘d4 37 ♘g5 ♖c8 38 ♖xc8+ ♔xc8 39 c3 ♘c6 40 ♔f2 ♔d7 41 ♔e3 ♔e7 42 ♔e4 ♔f6 43 ♘f3 ♔e6 44 a4 a5 45 ♘d2 ♘d8 46 ♘c4 ♘f7 47 ♘xa5 ♘d6+ 48 ♔d3 ♔d5 49 c4+ ♔c5 50 ♘b3+ ♔b4 51 ♘d2 e4+ 52 ♔d4 ♔xa4 53 c5 e3 54 ♔xe3 ♘f5+ 55 ♔f4 h4 56 g4 ♘g7 57 ♔e5 ♔b5 58 ♘e4 ♘e8 59 ♘d6+ ♘xd6 60 cxd6 ♔c6 1-0**

Game 76
Keitlinghaus-Mololkin
Pardubice Open 1994

---

1 e4 c5 2 ♘f3 d6 3 ♘c3 ♘f6 4 g3 ♘c6 5 ♗g2 g6 6 0-0 ♗g7 7 d3 0-0 8 h3

A preparatory move so that the white bishop can sit on e3 without being hassled by ...♘g4. For what it's

worth, let's see how our mentor handled the position: 8 ♗g5 h6 9 ♗d2 e5 10 a3 ♗e6 11 ♖b1 a5 12 a4 d5 13 exd5 ♘xd5 14 ♘xd5 ♗xd5 15 ♗e3 c4 with tremendous complications in Spassky-Tal, Tbilisi Candidates 1965 (Spassky won the game!). 15...c4 is the kind of move which Tal would find hard to resist, but 15...b6 instead would have maintained Black's space advantage, when I prefer his position. Spassky's opening play was, for once, not terribly impressive.

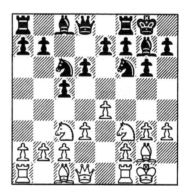

8...♖b8 9 a4!

White can gain good play for his rook on the a-file.

9...a6 10 ♗g5

Tempting Black into playing ...h7-h6. It isn't clear whether he should play this or not. 10 ♗e3 is considered in Games 77-80.

10...b5

I think that Black should call his opponent's bluff and play 10...h6 11 ♗e3 b5 12 axb5 axb5 13 ♕d2 ♔h7. It isn't clear to me that White has gained anything, but he might try 14 e5!? (compare with Game 77). However, I don't think Black stands worse here.

11 axb5 axb5 12 ♕d2 b4 13 ♘d5 e6

If 13...♘xd5 14 exd5 then White can hope to put pressure on e7.

14 ♘xf6+ ♗xf6 15 ♗xf6 ♕xf6 16 c3

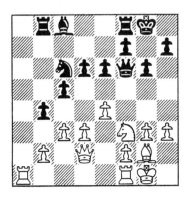

White has the more pleasant position. He intends d3-d4; Black prevents it, but eventually finds that his pawn structure is simply too rigid to do anything with.

16...e5 17 ♘e1 ♕e7 18 ♘c2 bxc3 19 bxc3 ♖b2 20 ♕c1 ♖b3 21 ♘e3 ♗e6 22 f4 f6 23 f5 ♗f7 24 h4 ♕d8 25 fxg6 hxg6 26 ♘g4 ♗e8 27 ♖a2 ♘b8 28 ♖af2 ♘d7 29 ♗h3 ♖b7 30 ♘e3 ♘b6 31 ♗e6+ ♗f7 32 ♖xf6 ♗xe6 33 ♖xf8+ ♕xf8 34 ♖xf8+ ♔xf8 35 c4 ♘d7 36 ♘d5 ♔f7 37 ♕h6 ♘f8 38 h5 ♗xd5 39 exd5 ♖e7 40 g4 ♔g8 41 ♕g5 ♖f7 42 ♔g2 ♔h7 43 ♕d8 gxh5 44 gxh5 ♘d7 45 ♕c7 ♔h6 46 ♕xd6+ ♔xh5 47 ♕e6 ♖g7+ 48 ♔f3 ♔g5 49 d6 ♖h7 50 ♔e4 ♖g7 51 ♔d5 e4 52 dxe4 ♔f4 53 ♕f5+ 1-0

Game 77
Sibilio-Gikas
Lugano Open 1989

1 ♘f3 ♘f6 2 g3 g6 3 ♗g2 ♗g7 4 0-0 0-0 5 d3 d6 6 e4 c5 7 ♘c3 ♘c6

8 h3 ♖b8 9 a4 a6 10 ♗e3

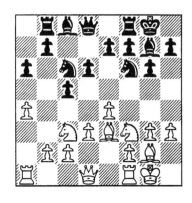

10...b5

This allows White the option of opening up the position. The more conservative 10...♗d7 is dealt with in Game 79 and 10...e5 in Game 80.

11 axb5 axb5 12 e5!?

This radically changes the character of the game. The more sedate 12 ♕d2 is considered in Game 78.

12...♘e8

Black ought to capture: 12...dxe5 13 ♗xc5 when I prefer White, but don't let that sway you! The position is just complicated, and in any case, Black must try this. In the game he is simply worse.

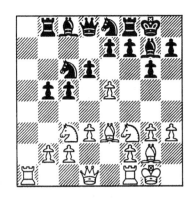

13 exd6 exd6 14 d4! c4 15 d5 ♘b4

16 ♘d4 ♘c7 17 ♕d2 ♖e8 18 ♗g5 f6
19 ♗f4 g5 20 ♗e3 ♖e5 21 ♘cxb5
♘cxd5 22 ♘c6 ♘xc6 23 ♗xd5+
♔h8 24 ♗xc6 ♗xh3 25 ♖fd1 ♕c8
26 ♕xd6 ♗g4 27 ♖d4 ♖exb5 28
♗xb5 ♗f3 29 ♕d7 ♕f8 30 ♗c6 1-0

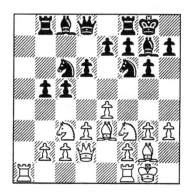

Game 78
D.Ledger-Roberts
British Championship 1993

1 ♘f3 ♘f6 2 g3 g6 3 ♗g2 ♗g7 4
0-0 0-0 5 d3 d6 6 e4 c5 7 ♘c3 ♘c6
8 h3 ♖b8 9 a4 a6 10 ♗e3 b5 11
axb5 axb5 12 ♕d2

12 e5!? was considered in Game 77.

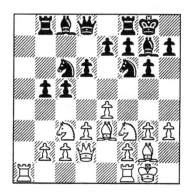

12...b4 13 ♘d5

This has been seen a few times, and
looks promising, but 13 ♘e2 and 13
♘d1 are good alternatives.

13...♘xd5 14 exd5 ♘e5

14...♘d4 initiates interesting complications with 15 ♘xd4 cxd4 16 ♗h6.
Now after the exchange of bishops
White can get good play by attacking
the pawns on e7, d4 and b4, so Black
usually decides to complicate with
16...♗xh6 (McDonald, a fierce attacking player, must have had bad vibes
about this move and chose instead

16...b3 17 ♗xg7 ♔xg7 18 ♕f4 bxc2 19
♕xd4+ ♔g8 20 ♖fc1 ♕b6 21 ♕xb6
♖xb6 22 ♖xc2, although he was a clear
pawn down and eventually lost in
Norwood-McDonald, British Championship 1990) 17 ♕xh6 b3 and now
instead of 18 c4 as in Herzog-Weis,
Germany 1992, I think White could
have won by playing 18 ♖a4! bxc2
(18...♕b6? 19 c3) 19 ♖xd4 e5 20 ♖h4
♖e8 21 ♕xh7+ ♔f8 22 ♕h6+ ♔e7 23
♕g5+ ♔d7 24 ♕c1!? with a winning
position.

**15 ♘xe5 ♗xe5 16 d4 ♗xd4 17
♗xd4 cxd4 18 ♕xd4**

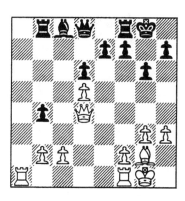

White stands better. He has a space
advantage and can play on the weak
pawns on b4 and e7.

**18...♗f5 19 ♖fc1 ♕b6 20 ♕xb6
♖xb6 21 g4 ♗c8 22 ♖a7 ♗b7 23
♖e1 ♖e8 24 ♖e3 ♔f8 25 ♗e4 h6 26
h4 ♖c8 27 ♔f1 ♖c4 28 f3 f5 29
gxf5 gxf5 30 ♗xf5 ♖xh4 31 ♗e6
♖b5 32 ♖e4 ♖xe4 33 fxe4 ♔g7 34
♔f2 ♖b6 35 ♔e3 ♔f6 36 ♔f4 ♖b5
37 ♗d7 e5+ 38 ♔g4 ♖b6 39 ♔h5 b3
40 c3 ♗xd5 41 exd5 e4 42 ♗e6
♔e5 43 ♔g4 ♖b8 44 ♔g3 ♖f8 45
♖f7 ♖g8+ 46 ♔f2 ♖g5 47 ♖f8 ♖h5
48 ♔e3 ♖g5 49 ♖g8 ♖h5 50 ♖b8**

♖g5 51 ♖g8 ♖h5 52 ♖g2 ♖h1 53 ♖f2 1-0

Game 79
Martin del Campo-Verduga
Bayamo 1990

1 e4 c5 2 ♘f3 d6 3 g3 ♘f6 4 ♘c3 g6 5 ♗g2 ♘c6 6 0-0 ♗g7 7 d3 ♖b8 8 a4 a6 9 h3 0-0 10 ♗e3 ♗d7

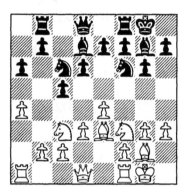

Black had an inkling that White wanted to play e4-e5, so hangs back for a moment with ...b7-b5.

11 ♕d2 ♖e8

Although it is quite common for Black to try to preserve his dark-squared bishop in this way, in this case I think it is a mistake. The course of the game bears out my feeling: it is too risky for Black to allow the bishop around his king, not to mention the knight on g5.

12 ♗h6 ♗h8 13 ♘g5! b5 14 axb5 axb5 15 f4 c4 16 f5 b4 17 ♘e2 b3 18 d4 bxc2 19 ♕xc2 ♘b4 20 ♕c3 ♕c8 21 b3!

see following diagram

Now the f7 square becomes the target!

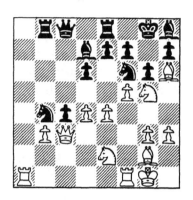

21...gxf5 22 bxc4 fxe4 23 ♖ab1 ♘c6 24 ♖xb8 ♘xb8 25 g4 ♗e6 26 ♕e3 ♗g7 27 ♘xe6 ♕xe6 28 ♕g5 ♘h5 29 ♕xh5 ♗xh6 30 g5 ♗g7 31 ♗xe4 h6 32 gxh6 ♗f6 33 ♖f4 ♔h8 34 d5 ♕e5 35 ♕xf7 ♕g5+ 36 ♔f2 ♕g8 37 ♖xf6 ♘d7 38 ♕xg8+ ♔xg8 39 ♖g6+ ♔f7 40 ♘g3 ♘f6 41 ♖g7+ ♔f8 42 ♗f5 ♖b8 43 ♗e6 1-0

Game 80
Urban-Steinmacher
Baden Baden Open 1991

1 ♘f3 ♘f6 2 g3 g6 3 ♗g2 ♗g7 4 0-0 0-0 5 d3 c5 6 e4 ♘c6 7 ♘c3 ♖b8 8 a4 d6 9 h3 a6 10 ♗e3 e5!

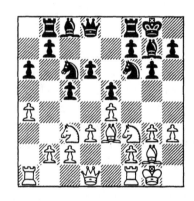

A good move. Black prevents White

from playing e4-e5 and clamps down on the centre.

11 ♕d2 b5 12 axb5 axb5 13 ♗g5

Mr Urban obviously wasn't satisfied with his play in this game and three years later tried something else: 13 ♘h2 b4 14 ♘e2 ♘d4 15 ♘xd4 cxd4 16 ♗g5 ♕b6 17 b3 ♕c5 18 f4 ♘h5 19 ♗h4 h6 20 f5 g5 21 f6 ♘xf6 0-1 Urban-Stocek, Budapest 1994. Back to the drawing board.

13...♗e6 14 ♘h2 ♕d7 15 f4

If White is to make anything of the position then he must try this move. For a pawn he gets some attack.

15...exf4 16 gxf4 ♗xh3 17 f5 ♗xg2 18 ♔xg2 b4

Not 18...♘e5 19 ♗xf6 ♗xf6 20 ♘d5 ♗h8 21 ♘f3 and with a bit of luck, mate on the h-file.

19 ♗xf6 bxc3 20 ♕xc3 ♗xf6 21 ♕xf6 ♘e5 22 b3 ♖a8 23 ♕h4 ♕d8 24 f6 h5 25 ♕g5 ♔h7 26 ♖ae1 ♖h8 27 ♘f3 ♕e8 28 ♘h4 ♕e6 29 ♘f5 ♘g4 30 ♖h1 ♔g8 31 ♖a1 ♖xa1 32 ♖xa1 ♔h7 33 ♕xg4 ♕xf6 34 ♖h1 d5 35 ♘e3 ½-½

Game 81
Spassky-Petrosian
World Championship, Moscow 1966

1 e4 c5 2 ♘c3 ♘c6 3 g3 g6 4 ♗g2 ♗g7 5 d3 d6 6 ♘h3

This will often transpose to other systems, for instance, after 6...e5 7 f4 we are into Chapter 4, but it does have independent significance. While we are dealing with strange sixth moves I should mention the following: 6 h4 h5 7 ♘h3 e6 8 0-0 ♘ge7 9 ♗g5 with a reasonable position in Kislov-

Horvath, Budapest 1989; and 6 ♘d5 e6 7 ♘e3 ♘ge7 8 f4 0-0 9 ♘f3 d5 10 0-0 (10 e5!?) 10...dxe4 11 dxe4 b6 12 e5 ♗a6 13 c4 (13 ♖e1) 13...♕xd1 14 ♖xd1 ♖ad8 15 b3 ♘f5 with equal chances in Jovic-Bernard, Dortmund 1989.

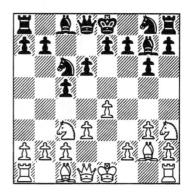

6...♘f6

If I were White, the aggressive 6...h5 would concern me.

7 0-0 ♗g4 8 f3 ♗xh3 9 ♗xh3 0-0 10 ♗e3 ♘e8 11 ♕d2 ♘c7 12 ♖ae1 b6 13 ♘d1 d5 14 ♕e2 e6 15 f4 f5

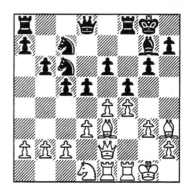

The position is approximately equal, but that doesn't mean it is drawish. What I like about Spassky's play here is his patience: he doesn't wreck his position with a rash kingside attack, but waits while the position opens for his bishops.

16 &c1 Rf7 17 &g2 Wd7 18 ♘f2 Rd8 19 c3 b5 20 exd5 exd5 21 &d2 c4 22 Wf3 ♘e7 23 dxc4 bxc4

23...dxc4 would have been met by 24 &e3!

24 b3! ♘c8 25 bxc4 dxc4 26 &c1 Wa4 27 Rd1! Rdf8

If 27...Rxd1?! 28 Rxd1 or 27...Rfd7?! 28 Rxd7 Rxd7 29 Re1.

28 &e3!

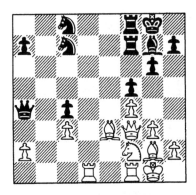

28...♘b6

Perhaps 28...Wxa2?! 29 &c5 Re8 30 Wc6 with the idea of 31 &d5.

29 &c5

An interesting alternative was 29 ♘h3!? h6 30 Rd6.

29...Rc8 30 &b4 ♘a6

30...a5? would have been met by 31 &c5.

31 &d6 Wa5 32 g4 Wxc3 33 We2! Wf6 34 Rfe1! Rd7 35 &e7! Rxe7

Not 35...Wf7? 36 Rxd7 ♘xd7 37 &b7!

36 Wxe7 Wxe7 37 Rxe7 ♘c5 38 gxf5

see following diagram

38...c3!

38...gxf5 would have been met by

39 &h3!, when Black's king begins to feel the draught.

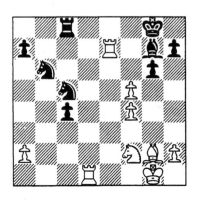

39 fxg6 hxg6 40 Re2

40 Rxa7 &d4! 41 Rxd4 c2 42 Rd1 ♘d3! offers Black good counterplay.

40...Rc7 41 ♘e4 ♘e6! 42 ♘xc3!

The sealed move.

42...♘d4!

Not 42...♘xf4 43 Re8+ &f7 44 ♘b5!

43 Re5! &xe5 44 fxe5 Rxc3 45 Rxd4 &f7 46 Rd6 Rc5 47 Rf6+ &g7 48 &e4 Rxe5 49 Rxg6+ &f7 50 &c2

It would have been better to play 50 Rg4! and only then 51 &c2.

50...Re1+ 51 &f2 Ra1 52 Rc6 Rxa2 53 h4 ♘d5 54 &f3 Ra3+ 55 &e4 Rc3 ½-½

Summary

White's system in Games 76-80 shouldn't be taken lightly. Game 77, in particular, is worth a second look. Perhaps Black's best defensive idea is seen in Game 80. However, Game 75 showed that it is difficult to make progress against 6...e6.

1 e4 c5 2 ♘c3 ♘c6 3 g3 g6 4 ♗g2 ♗g7 5 d3 d6

6 ♘f3
> 6 ♘h3 – *Game 81*

6...e5
> 6...e6 7 0-0 ♘ge7 – *Game 75*
> 6...♘f6 7 0-0 0-0 8 h3 ♖b8 9 a4 a6
>> 10 ♗g5 – *Game 76*
>> 10 ♗e3 *(D)*
>>> 10...b5 11 axb5 axb5 *(D)*
>>>> 12 e5 – *Game 77*
>>>> 12 ♕d2 – *Game 80*
>>> 10...♗d7 – *Game 78*
>>> 10...e5 – *Game 79*

7 0-0 ♘ge7 8 ♘d2 *(D)*
> 8 ♘h4 – *Game 74*

8...♖b8
> 8...♘d4 – *Game 72*

9 ♘cd5 – *Game 73*

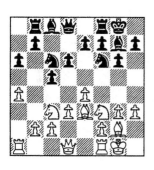

10 ♗e3

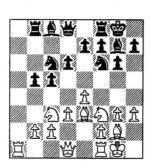

11...axb5

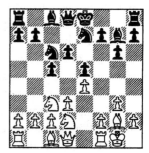

8 ♘d2

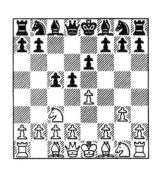

CHAPTER EIGHT

Black plays ...e7-e6 and ...d7-d5

So far I have only considered systems in which Black fianchettoes his king's bishop. But what happens if he attempts to cut across White's standard plan of development by an advance in the centre? After 1 e4 c5 2 ♘c3 e6, White may play either 3 ♘f3 or 3 ♘ge2 followed by 4 d4, transposing back into a standard Open Sicilian, but we are playing the Closed to avoid all that theoretical nonsense, right? For that reason I am only considering the Closed Sicilian move 3 g3 here. Play is generally much quieter than in the earlier chapters. It really all depends on one's style. Black can be fairly sure that he won't be checkmated if he plays solidly, but White might be able to count on a slight advantage if he understands what he is doing. In Games 82 and 83 White plays an early d2-d4 and the position becomes quite tactical – immediately contradicting what I wrote above. Spassky's game against Kasparov is definitely worth studying, but perhaps the most promising way for White to play is shown in Game 86.

1 e4 c5 2 ♘c3 e6 3 g3 d5 4 exd5 exd5 5 d4!?

In this chapter I'm mainly going to be examining 5 ♗g2 at this point. However 5 d4 is a tricky move that might be worth trying out if well-prepared beforehand.

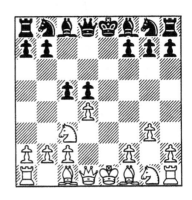

5...cxd4

Most people play this, but it isn't

necessarily the best. For instance, 5...♘c6 6 dxc5 d4 7 ♘e4 ♗xc5 8 ♘xc5 ♕a5+ 9 ♗d2 ♕xc5 10 ♗g2 is assessed by Gary Lane as slightly better for White because of the bishops, and that looks about right; but 5...♘f6 is more sensible, e.g. 6 ♗g2 cxd4 7 ♘ce2 (for 7 ♕xd4 ♘c6 8 ♕a4 – see the next game) 7...♗b4+ 8 ♗d2 ♗xd2+ 9 ♕xd2 ♘c6 10 ♘xd4 ♘xd4 11 ♕xd4 0-0 12 0-0-0 ♗f5 with good counter-chances for Black on the queenside in Rossetto-Bronstein, Buenos Aires 1989.

6 ♕xd4 ♘f6 7 ♗g5

7 ♗g2 transposes to the next game.

7...♗e7 8 ♗b5+

Also interesting is 8 0-0-0!? ♘c6 9 ♕a4 ♗e6 10 ♗g2 0-0 11 ♘ge2 ♕b6 (11...♘g4!?) 12 ♗e3 ♗c5 13 ♗xc5 ♕xc5 14 ♘f4 with chances for both sides in Kupreichik-Morawietz, Germany 1996.

8...♘c6 9 ♗xf6 ♗xf6 10 ♕c5

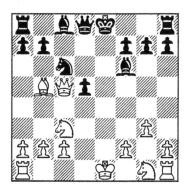

This is exactly the same as a Goring Gambit reversed, with the exception that White has a pawn on g3 rather than g2 – which doesn't help. The following sequence is just about forced for Black if he wishes to avoid any problems and with best play the resulting endgame should be equal.

10...♗xc3+ 11 bxc3 ♕e7+ 12 ♕xe7+ ♔xe7 13 0-0-0 ♗e6 14 ♘e2 ♖hd8

14...♔d6 is a little risky: 15 ♖he1 ♔c5 16 c4 dxc4 17 ♗xc6 bxc6 (17...♔xc6! should still hold after 18 ♘d4+ ♔c7 19 ♘xe6+ fxe6 20 ♖xe6 ♖he8) 18 ♘f4 with a powerful initiative for White in Lane-Nunn, England 1980.

15 ♖he1 ♖d6 16 ♗xc6?!

16 ♘f4! is more comfortable for White to play than Black.

16...♖xc6 17 ♖d4 ♖ac8 18 ♖a4 a6 19 ♖b4 ♖8c7 20 ♔d2 d4 21 ♖xd4 ♗xa2 22 ♘f4+ ♔f6 23 ♘h5+ ♔g6 24 ♘f4+ ♔h6 25 ♖e3 g6 26 h4 ♔g7 27 g4 h6 28 h5 g5 29 ♘d5 ♗xd5 30 ♖xd5 ♖f6 31 f3 ♖cc6 32 ♖d4 ♖b6 33 ♖b4 a5 34 ♖xb6 ♖xb6 35 ♖e5 ♖d6+ 36 ♔c1 ♖f6 37 ♖e3 ♖f4 38 ♔b2 ♔f6 39 ♔b3 b5 40 ♔b2 a4 41 ♔a3 ♔g7 42 ♔b2 ♔f8 43 ♔a3 f6 44 ♔b2 ♔f7 45 ♔a3 ♔g8 46 ♔b2 ♔f8 47 ♔a3 ♔f7 48 ♔b2 f5 49 ♖d3 ♔e6 50 ♖e3+ ♔d5 51 ♖d3+ ♔c5 52 ♖e3 fxg4 53 fxg4 ♖xg4 54 ♖e6 ½–½

Game 83
Bartsch-Clemens
German Bundesliga 1982/83

1 e4 c5 2 ♘c3 e6 3 g3 d5 4 ♗g2

It is more accurate for White to capture on d5 first as here Black has the option to play 4...dxe4, giving him a comfortable position: ...♘c6, ...♗e7, ...♘f6 and so on. However, 4...d4 isn't that great. White gets a favourable reversed King's Indian.

4...♘f6 5 exd5 exd5 6 d4

6 ♘ge2 or 6 d3 are more usual.

6...cxd4 7 ♕xd4 ♘c6 8 ♕a4!?

That's the new idea. 8 ♕d1 is too passive. After 8...d4 9 ♘ce2 ♗c5 10 ♘f3 ♗f5 11 0-0 0-0 12 ♘f4 Black had a space advantage, and no difficulties (the pawn on c2 is also weak) in Suttles-Tal, Hastings 1973/74.

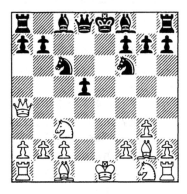

8...d4

Simple development also wasn't bad: 8...♗e7 9 ♘ge2 ♗d7! tests White's idea. If 10 ♕b3 here, then 10...♘a5 is embarrassing.

9 ♘ce2 ♗d7 10 ♕b3 ♗b4+ 11 c3 ♗a5 12 ♘f3 dxc3 13 ♘xc3

Instead of this I would suggest 13 bxc3 0-0 14 0-0 ♗b6 15 ♖d1 or 13 0-0!? with play for a pawn.

13...♕e7+ 14 ♗e3 ♗e6 15 ♕a4 ♘d5 16 0-0 ♗xc3 17 bxc3

Why Black now takes on c3 is beyond me.

17...♘xc3

17...♘xe3 18 fxe3 0-0 is very good for Black.

18 ♕c2 ♘d5 19 ♗c5 ♕c7 20 ♖ac1 a6 21 ♕b2 ♖g8 22 ♘d4 ♘xd4 23 ♗xd4 ♕d7 24 ♖fe1 g5 25 ♖cd1 ♖c8 26 ♗f6 ♔f8 27 ♖xd5 ♗xd5 28 ♕a3+ 1-0

1 e4 c5 2 ♘c3 e6 3 g3 d5 4 exd5 exd5 5 ♗g2 d4

More normal is 5....♘f6, as in Games 85-90. The pawn advance is generally frowned upon by established theory because of ...

6 ♕e2+!

This check is rather awkward.

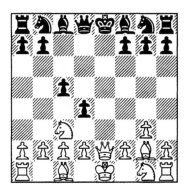

6...♗e7!

Not 6...♗e6? 7 ♗xb7 or 6...♕e7 7 ♘d5 ♕xe2+ 8 ♘xe2 with a great lead in development.

7 ♘d5 ♘c6 8 d3 ♗e6 9 ♘f4 ♗d7 10 g4!?

Radical, but if White is content to draw then 10 ♘d5 ♗e6 11 ♘f4 ♗d7 12 ♘d5 was agreed drawn by repetition in Davies-Beim, Tel Aviv 1992.

10...♘f6 11 g5 ♘g4 12 ♘d5 ♘ge5 13 ♗f4 ♘g6 14 ♗c7 ♕c8 15 h4 ♗e6 16 ♗g3 ♗d8 17 h5 ♘ge7 18 h6 ♘xd5 19 hxg7 ♖g8 20 ♗xd5 ♖xg7 21 ♘f3 ♕d7 22 ♗xe6

After 22 ♗e4!? or 22 ♗b3!? the position still looks favourable to White.

22...♕xe6 23 ♕xe6+ fxe6 24 ♔f1
♔d7 25 ♖h6 ♗e7 26 ♖e1 ♖f8 27
♔g2 ♖gf7 28 ♘e5+ ½-½

I don't think that the assessment of
this line has changed; Black must suffer for a while if he plays 5...d4.

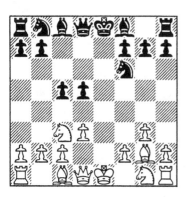

Game 85
Casper-Vaiser
Berlin 1982

1 e4 c5 2 ♘c3 e6 3 g3 d5 4 exd5
exd5 5 ♗g2 ♘f6 6 d3

For 6 ♘ge2 see Games 88-90.

6...d4

In Game 87 Black delays this move
in favour of 6...♗e7.

7 ♘e4 ♘xe4 8 ♗xe4

8 dxe4 is the subject of the next
game. It is impossible to say which is
better; it is purely a matter of taste. 8
dxe4 unbalances the position a little
more, while 8 ♗xe4 is extremely safe:
Black has no point in White's position
which he can attack.

8...♘d7!

If the knight isn't played over to the
kingside, then Black may run into difficulties.

9 ♘e2 ♘f6 10 ♗g2 ♗d6 11 0-0 0-0

12 h3 ♖b8 13 ♗f4 b5 14 ♗xd6
♕xd6 15 ♘f4 ♖e8 16 ♘h5 ♘d5 17
♕f3 ♗b7 18 ♕g4 ♕g6 19 ♖fe1 ♔f8
20 ♕h4 h6 21 ♗xd5 ♗xd5 22 ♘f4
♕d6 23 ♘xd5 ♕xd5 24 ♕f4 ♖bc8
25 b3

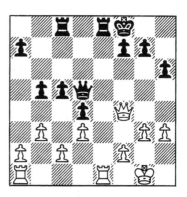

A typical scenario for this variation.
Black has managed to quell White's
slight initiative, and the one open file
ensures that further liquidation is
about to occur. Yawn. Vaiser battles
on but he never had any serious winning chances.

25...c4 26 bxc4 bxc4 27 dxc4 ♕xc4
28 a3 ♕c3 29 ♕d6+ ♔g8 30 ♖xe8+
♖xe8 31 ♖d1 ♖e4 32 ♕b8+ ♔h7 33
♕b3 ♖e2 34 ♕xc3 dxc3 35 ♖d7 a5
36 ♖xf7 ♖xc2 37 ♖c7 ♖c1+ 38 ♔g2
♔g6 39 ♖c5 a4 40 ♔f3 ♔f6 41 ♔e2
c2 42 ♔d3 ♖a1 43 ♖xc2 ♖xa3+ 44
♔e4 ♖b3 45 ♖c6+ ♔f7 46 ♖c7+
♔g6 47 ♖c6+ ♔h7 48 ♖a6 a3 49 h4
♖b4+ 50 ♔f3 ♖b3+ 51 ♔e4 ½-½

Game 86
Donev-Felsberger
Austrian Team Championship 1995

1 e4 c5 2 ♘c3 e6 3 g3 d5 4 exd5
exd5 5 ♗g2 ♘f6 6 d3 d4 7 ♘e4

②xe4 8 dxe4

Objectively, this might be no better than 8 ♗xe4, but it is certainly more interesting.

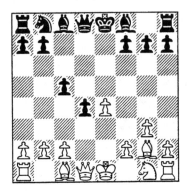

8...♗e7 9 ②e2

Playing the knight to d5 straightaway is the correct plan. 9 f4 and ②f3 have also been tried, but Black's queenside pawn majority is more dangerous in that case.

9...0-0 10 0-0 ②c6 11 ②f4 ♖e8 12 ②d5

A beautiful square for the beast. It is now much harder for Black to advance the queenside pawns.

12...♗d6

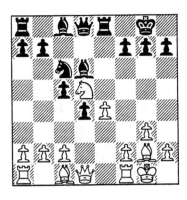

13 c4

This is the most sound move, ce-

menting the knight and also blocking Black's pawns.

13 f4!? is fairly crude, when 13...♖b8 14 c4 ♗f8 15 e5 ♗e6 16 ♗e4 led to a powerful attack for White in Lommen-Ottens, Porz 1991. I would have put a stop to the pawns immediately with 13...f5.

13...dxc3

Black removes one of the knight's supports, but in so doing gives away his protected passed pawn and, more to the point, gives White use of the d-file. Alternatively, 13...②e7 14 ♗g5! ♕d7 (not 14...f6 15 ♗xf6 gxf6 16 ②xf6+ ♔g7 17 ②xe8+ ♕xe8 18 f4 and the pawn storm is ultimately irresistible) 15 ♗xe7 ♗xe7 16 f4 b6 17 ♕d3 ♗b7 18 ♖ae1 with a strong initiative.

14 bxc3 ♖b8 15 ♕c2 ♗e6 16 ♖d1 f6 17 ♗f4 ♗xf4 18 ②xf4 ♕e7 19 ②xe6

White plays in classical style, securing a large and permanent positional advantage. It was also possible to start hacking with 19 e5!?, threatening ②xe6 and ♗d5, e.g. 19...♗c4 20 e6 ♖bd8 21 ♗e4 with a juicy attack.

19...♕xe6 20 ♖d5 ♕e7 21 ♖ad1 ♖bd8 22 ♕b3 ②a5 23 ♕b5 b6 24 ♖d7 a6 25 ♕a4

25 ♖xe7? would have spoilt everything: 25...♖xd1+ 26 ♗f1 axb5 27 ♖xe8+ ♔f7 28 ♖b8 ②c4 and Black is back in the game. The key to the position is to keep the knight trapped on the edge.

25...♖xd7 26 ♖xd7 ♕e5 27 ♖d5 ♕e7 28 f4 ♖d8 29 e5 ♖xd5 30 ♗xd5+ ♔f8 31 ♕e4! g6 32 g4

Korchnoi claims that 32 e6! ♕d6 33 f5 is the most powerful continuation.

32...fxe5 33 ♕xe5 ♕xe5 34 fxe5
♔e7 35 ♔f2 ♔d7 36 ♔e3 ♘c6 37
♔e4 ♘e7

37...b5 38 e6+ ♔d6 39 ♗xc6 ♔xc6
40 ♔e5 a5 41 ♔f6 b4 42 e7 wins.
38 ♗b7!

Forcing a crucial weakness on the queenside.

38...a5

The game is reminiscent of the famous endgame Fischer-Taimanov from their Candidates match in 1971.
**39 a4! ♔c7 40 ♗d5 g5 41 ♗c4 ♔d7
42 ♗f7 ♔c7 43 ♗e8! ♔d8 44 ♗b5
♔c7 45 h3 h6 46 c4**

Zugzwang.

46...♔d8 47 e6! ♘c8

Or 47...♔c7 48 ♔e5.

48 ♔e5

48 ♔d5 ♔e7 49 ♗d7 ♘d6 50 ♗c6
♘c8 51 ♗b5 ♘d6 52 ♗d7 Zugzwang.
**48...♔e7 49 ♗d7 ♘d6 50 ♔d5! ♘b7
51 ♔c6 ♘d6 52 ♔xb6 ♘xc4+ 53
♔xc5 1-0**

Game 87
Murey-Ungure
Cappelle la Grande Open 1995

1 e4 c5 2 ♘c3 e6 3 g3 d5 4 exd5

exd5 5 ♗g2 ♘f6 6 d3 ♗e7 7 ♘ge2
d4 8 ♘e4 0-0

8...♘xe4 would be fairly dull if
White recaptured with the bishop: 9
♗xe4 ♘d7 10 0-0 0-0 11 ♗g2 ♘f6 12
♗g5 h6 13 ♗xf6 ♗xf6 14 ♘f4 ♗e5 15
♕f3 ♖b8 16 ♖fe1 ♖e8 17 ♖e2 ♕d6 18
♖ae1 ♗d7 19 ♘d5 b6 when White is
minutely better, but if Black is sensible, and he was, then a draw is in the
bag, as in Taimanov-Polugayevsky,
USSR Championship 1965. However,
9 dxe4 isn't bad, as we have seen.
**9 ♘xf6+ ♗xf6 10 0-0 ♘c6 11 ♘f4
♗e5**

11...♘e5 transposes to Chigorin-
Tarrasch, Ostend 1907 (hot theory!),
which continued 12 ♘d5 ♗g4 13 f3
♗e6 14 ♘xf6+ ♕xf6 15 f4 ♘c6 16
♕h5 with a clear advantage to White,
according to *ECO*.
12 ♖e1 ♗d6 13 ♕h5

The difference between this game
and the one in the note above is that
Black's king is less well protected: the
manoeuvre ...♘d7-f6 is important to
Black's defence, as we see in the next
game.

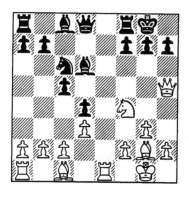

**13...♘e7 14 ♗d2 ♖b8 15 a4 a5 16
♖e2 ♗d7 17 b3 b6 18 ♖ae1 ♗c6 19**

♗xc6 ♘xc6 20 ♘d5 ♘b4 21 ♗g5 f6
22 ♗xf6 gxf6 23 ♘e7+ ♔h8 24
♘g6+ ♔g7 25 ♘xf8 ♕xf8 26 ♕g4+
♔h6 27 ♕h3+ ♔g6 28 ♖e4 h5 29 g4
h4 30 ♕f3 ♕h6 31 ♕f5+ ♔g7 32
♕d7+ ♔g8 33 ♕xd6 ♖f8 34 ♖e8
♘xc2 35 ♕d5+ 1-0

Game 88
Spassky-Kasparov
Bugojno 1982

**1 e4 c5 2 ♘c3 e6 3 g3 d5 4 exd5
exd5 5 ♗g2 ♘f6 6 ♘ge2 d4 7 ♘e4
♘xe4 8 ♗xe4 ♘d7 9 0-0 ♘f6 10
♗g2 ♗d6**

Kasparov has carried out the standard manoeuvre, ...♘d7-f6, and looks set to completely equalise. (He actually assesses the position after 11 d3 0-0 12 ♗f4 ♖e8 as slightly better for Black.) But Spassky has a different idea in mind.

11 c3!

One of the points behind this move is that after 11...dxc3 White recaptures with the d-pawn – see Game 90.

11...d3!?

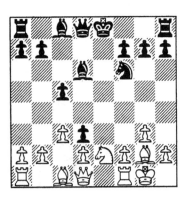

Mixing it. Kasparov judges the position after 11...0-0 12 cxd4 cxd4 13 d3

♖e8 to be equal. See the next game to find out whether this is true!

12 ♘f4 0-0

12...♗xf4 13 ♕a4+ ♗d7 14 ♖e1+ ♔f8 15 ♕xf4 is good for White, as the bishop can always emerge after b2-b3.

13 ♘xd3 ♗xg3 14 fxg3!

Not 14 hxg3 ♕xd3 15 ♕f3 ♗f5!

14...♕xd3 15 ♕f3 ♕xf3

15...♖d8 16 ♕xd3 ♖xd3 17 ♖e1 followed by ♗f1 should untangle and then the bishops have some fun.

16 ♗xf3 ♗h3 17 ♗xb7

17 ♖d1 ♘g4 was played in an obscure game in Germany, but as Kasparov points out, the logical move is to exchange bishops with 17...♗g4!, solving Black's problems.

17...♖ae8

After 17...♗xf1 18 ♗xa8 ♗d3 19 ♗f3 ♖e8 20 b3 White untangles, remaining a pawn up – Kasparov.

18 ♗g2 ♗xg2 19 ♔xg2 ♖e2+ 20 ♖f2 ♖fe8 21 b3

21 ♖xe2 isn't much of an improvement: 21...♖xe2+ 22 ♔f3 ♖xh2 23 b3 ♘d7 24 d4 cxd4 25 cxd4 f5 26 a4 ♔f7 27 b4 ♘f6 28 ♗e3 ♖b2 29 d5 ♖xb4 30 ♗xa7 ♘xd5 31 a5 and eventually drawn in Dudek-Pfrommer, Germany 1996.

21...♖xf2+ 22 ♔xf2 ♘g4+ 23 ♔g2 f5

Not 23...♖e1? 24 ♗b2 ♖e2+ 25 ♔f3 ♖xd2 26 ♗a3 ♘xh2+ 27 ♔e4 with a clear advantage (Kasparov).

24 h3 ♘e5 25 d4 cxd4 26 cxd4 ♘d3 27 ♗g5 h6 28 ♖d1 hxg5 29 ♖xd3 ♖e2+ 30 ♔f3 ♖xa2 31 d5 ♔f7 32 d6 ♔e8 ½–½

A likely finish being: 33 ♖e3 ♔d7 34 ♖e7 ♔d6 35 ♖g7 ♖b2 36 ♖g5 ♔e6

37 ♔f4 ♖f2 38 ♔e3 ♖b2. Equal. These notes were based on Kasparov's illuminating comments in *Informator 33*.

1 e4 c5 2 ♘c3 e6 3 ♘ge2 ♘f6 4 g3 d5 5 exd5 exd5 6 ♗g2 d4 7 ♘e4 ♘xe4 8 ♗xe4 ♘d7 9 0-0 ♘f6 10 ♗g2 ♗d6 11 c3 0-0

Varying from Kasparov's 11...d3.

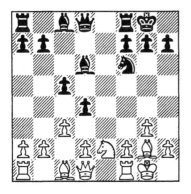

12 cxd4 cxd4 13 d3 ♖e8

This is the position that Kasparov assessed as equal. Let's see.

14 ♘f4

This knight is White's problem. If it were on c4, then everything would be fine, but at the moment it is on a bad circuit, and rather gets in the way. 14 ♘xd4 is obviously critical; but Black has 14...♗xg3 15 hxg3 ♕xd4, when he is very active. Note also that 14 ♗f4? wouldn't be too bright: 14...♗g4 15 f3 ♗h5 and there is a gaping whole for Black to fill on e3.

14...♕b6!

Putting pressure on b2 and protecting b7 enabling the bishop to move.

15 ♕b3! ♕a5 16 ♕c2 ♗f5 17 ♗d2 ♗b4 18 ♗xb4 ♕xb4 19 a3 ♕b5 20 ♕d2 h6 21 h4 ♖ac8 22 ♖fc1

'Equal' is the correct assessment, though Black now overplays his hand. 22...b6 23 ♖xc8 ♖xc8 24 ♖c1 ♖c5 25 b4 ♖xc1+ 26 ♕xc1 ♕e5 27 ♕d2 ♔f8 28 ♗f3 g5 29 hxg5 hxg5 30 ♘e2 ♗g4 31 ♗xg4 ♘xg4 32 ♕b2 ♕b8 33 ♕xd4 ½-½

1 e4 c5 2 ♘c3 e6 3 g3 d5 4 exd5 exd5 5 ♗g2 ♘f6 6 ♘ge2 d4 7 ♘e4 ♘xe4 8 ♗xe4 ♘d7 9 0-0 ♘f6 10 ♗g2 ♗d6 11 c3 dxc3?

A poor move. Black underestimates White's position.

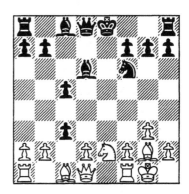

12 dxc3 0-0 13 ♕c2

The pawn on c5 is ugly: there is nothing to stop the bishop on g2 raking across the board, and the bishop on d6 is misplaced as it stands, without support on the open file.

13...♖b8? 14 ♖d1 ♕e7 15 ♖xd6 ♕xd6 16 ♗f4 ♕e7 17 ♗xb8 ♗g4 18 ♗xa7 1-0

Summary

In Games 82 and 83 an early d2-d4 was interesting, but I suspect not enough for the advantage if Black plays accurately. Game 86 was the most dynamic way for White to play – at least the pawn structure becomes unbalanced. Spassky's idea was interesting, but against accurate play should be fine for Black, as Games 88 and 89 both showed. In conclusion, 2...e6 3 g3 d5 remains a solid and viable option for Black.

1 e4 c5 2 ♘c3 e6 3 g3

3...d5 4 exd5
> 4 ♗g2 ♘f6 5 exd5 exd5 – see *Games 85-90*

4...exd5 5 ♗g2
> 5 d4 cxd4 6 ♕xd4 ♘f6 *(D)*
>> 7 ♗g5 – *Game 82*
>> 7 ♗g2 – *Game 83*

5...♘f6
> 5...d4 – *Game 84*

6 d3
> 6 ♘ge2 d4 7 ♘e4 ♘xe4 8 ♗xe4 ♘d7 9 0-0 ♘f6 10 ♗g2 ♗d6 11 c3 *(D)*
>> 11...d3 – *Game 88*
>> 11...0-0 – *Game 89*
>> 11...dxc3 – *Game 90*

6...d4
> 6...♗e7 – *Game 87*

7 ♘e4 ♘xe4 *(D)* 8 ♗xe4
> 8 dxe4 – *Game 86*

8...♘d7 – *Game 85*

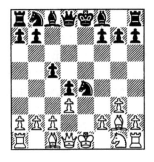

6...♘f6	*11 c3*	*7...♘xe4*

CHAPTER NINE

1 e4 c5 2 g3

Strictly speaking, this final chapter doesn't really fall into the category of the 'Closed Sicilian', which is normally classed as all positions arising out of 1 e4 c5 2 ♘c3 ♘c6 3 g3. I've decided to include a chapter on 2 g3 as in certain cases White can achieve a much improved version of the kind of Closed Sicilian positions which I examined in the first four chapters.

You might recall that in many games White experienced difficulties on the long diagonal: the pawn on b2 was sometimes vulnerable; the knight on c3 could be attacked by the b-pawn; and it was often difficult to expel the knight on d4. So on the face of it, leaving the knight on b1 and playing the pawn to c3 makes good sense. This system, often named 'The Clamp' as White intends squashing Black on all sides of the board, has a good reputation. As with the usual Closed Sicilian with ♘c3, White can play the system in many different ways (the same applies to Black as well), so an understanding of typical

positions is often more important than 'variations' – there aren't any.

Theoretical opinion has not yet crystallised on this system. However, getting into the system is often the problem. Many players (myself included) like to begin with 1 g3 g6 2 ♗g2 ♗g7 3 e4 and so on. The reason being that after 1 e4 c5 2 g3, Black may play the logical move 2...d5!, cutting across White's plans completely. I'm not saying that this is good for Black, the position is very complicated, but it prevents White setting up his 'Clamp'. (See Games 91–93.) Alternatively, White can play 1 e4 c5 2 d3, hoping that Black makes the standard moves. ...g7-g6, ...♗g7 etc., and doesn't look at what is going on in front of him. If Black is alert, and capable of playing other systems, then 2...♘c6 3 g3 d5! 4 ♘d2 will transpose to some kind of reversed King's Indian, though that might not be to everyone's taste.

Games 94–103 feature the Clamp in all its glory.

1 e4 c5 2 g3 d5

Black takes advantage of the fact that White has omitted ♘c3 and breaks in the centre. As the long diagonal is slightly vulnerable, this is a sound and potentially dangerous move for White to meet. He must already compromise.

3 exd5 ♕xd5 4 ♘f3

The only decent move. 4 ♕f3 ♕xf3 5 ♘xf3 ♘c6 promises White nothing and in fact I prefer Black as he has a space advantage.

4...♗g4 5 ♗g2 ♕e6+

If it weren't for this check, then White could castle and perhaps take advantage of the queen on d5.

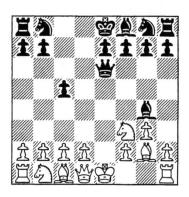

6 ♔f1

It's a trade off. White would rather not have his king on f1, blocking in the rook on h1, but Black is also a little behind in development as the queen blocks the e-pawn. White is forced to move his king since 6 ♕e2 ♕xe2+ 7 ♔xe2 ♘c6 gives Black a

pleasant endgame.

6...♗h3

This is the old move, originally recommended by theory. In principle one would like to exchange off the bishop on g2, but here Black is taking liberties. He is already lagging in development, and this gives White a chance. 6...♘c6 is the subject of Games 92 and 93.

7 b4!?

This shocking move is White's best chance of upsetting Black. Instead 7 d4 doesn't achieve the desired effect, e.g. 7...cxd4 8 ♘xd4 ♕d7 9 ♘c3 ♘c6 10 ♘xc6 ♕xc6 11 ♕d5 ♕xd5 12 ♘xd5 ♗xg2+ 13 ♔xg2 0-0-0 should be equal once Black develops on the kingside, as in Pachman-Taimanov, Buenos Aires 1960. 7 ♘c3 ♘c6 8 d3 ♕d7 9 ♗e3 ♗xg2+ 10 ♔xg2 e6 is also level

7...cxb4 8 a3

White knocks out one of Black's centre pawns so that he can roll forward with his own. The pawn sacrifice also opens up files and diagonals for the attack.

8...b3

8...♘c6 9 axb4 ♘xb4 10 ♘a3 ♕d7 11 d4 ♗xg2+ 12 ♔xg2 e6 13 c4 is a quite typical position in which White has a tremendous initiative, as in Korolev-Panjushkin, Correspondence 1978.

9 ♘c3

Rapid development is crucial.

9...♘f6 10 ♖b1 ♗xg2+

Or 10...g6 11 ♖xb3 (Korolev-Rusakov, Correspondence 1978) and now Lepeshkin analyses 11...b6!? 12 ♘b5 ♘a6 13 ♖e3 ♕d7 14 ♕e2 ♗h6 15 ♖d3 ♕e6 16 ♕xe6 ♗xe6 17 ♘fd4 as being better for White.

11 ♔xg2 ♕c6 12 ♖xb3 e6 13 d4 ♗e7 14 d5!

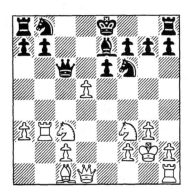

14...♕c8

If 14...exd5 15 ♖e1 gives White an irresistible attack and 14...♘xd5 likewise: 15 ♘xd5 ♕xd5 16 ♕xd5 exd5 17 ♖e1.

15 ♕e2 0-0 16 dxe6 fxe6 17 ♖e1 ♗c5 18 ♕xe6+ ♕xe6 19 ♖xe6 b6 20 ♘e4 ♘bd7 21 ♗b2 ♘xe4 22 ♖xe4 ♘f6 23 ♖e2 ♖ae8 24 ♖xe8 ♖xe8 25 ♘e5 ♖c8 26 ♖d3! ♗e7 27 c4 ♔f8 28 ♔f3 ♔e8 29 g4 ♖c5 30 g5 ♘g8 31 h4 h6 32 ♔g4 hxg5 33 hxg5 b5 34 ♖h3 bxc4 35 ♖h8 c3 36 ♖xg8+ ♗f8 37 ♘g6 1-0

6...♗h3 has been discredited by 7 b4! Black has to be very foolish or very brave to go into this sacrifice.

Game 92
Hort-Ribli
Baden Baden 1992

---

1 e4 c5 2 g3 d5 3 exd5 ♕xd5 4 ♘f3 ♗g4 5 ♗g2 ♕e6+ 6 ♔f1 ♘c6!

This is stronger than 6...♗h3. Black thinks about developing the rest of his pieces, and it is also useful to maintain the pin on the knight.

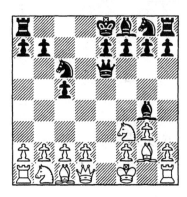

7 h3

It is best to flick this move in. White prepares to break the pin and rules out ...♗h3.

7...♗h5 8 ♘c3

8 d3 is considered in the next game

8...♘f6

This is the most popular move here, but I don't think it is the most accurate. After 8...♕d7 9 d3 e6 10 a4 ♘f6 11 a5 ♖d8! 12 g4 ♗g6 13 ♘h4 ♗e7 14 ♘xg6 hxg6 15 h4 a6 16 ♗e3 ♕c7 17 g5 ♘h5 the game was already swinging in Black's direction in Short-Sveshnikov, European Club Cup 1992.

9 d3 ♕d7 10 g4 ♗g6 11 ♘h4

White grabs the two bishops, but at the cost of compromising his kingside pawn structure. 11 ♗f4!? e6 12 g5 ♘g8 13 ♕e1 ♘ge7 14 h4 ♗h5 15 ♘e5 ♘xe5 16 ♗xe5 ♘c6 17 a4 was better for White in Speelman-Sunye Neto, Graz 1981, and still hasn't been improved upon.

11...e6!

This is the structure that Black should aim for. It is important to cover a few of the light squares.

12 ♗e3 ♗e7

13 ♘xg6

13 g5 is worth considering in this position, e.g. 13...♗h5 (13...♘h5 is met by 14 ♗f3, but 13...♘d5!? is possible) 14 ♕e1 ♘g8 (not 14...♘d5? 15 ♘xd5 exd5 16 ♗xc5) 15 ♘e4 ♘d4 16 ♕c3 ♖c8 17 b4 b6 18 bxc5 e5 19 ♗xd4 exd4 20 ♕b3 (perhaps 20 ♕d2!? ♗xc5 21 ♖e1, and if 21...♘e7? 22 ♘f6+ gxf6 23 gxf6) 20...♗xc5 21 ♖e1 ♘e7 22 ♘g3 ♗g6 23 ♘xg6 hxg6 24 h4 ♖d8 25 ♗e4 ♔f8 26 ♔g2 ♗d6 27 ♖e2 ♖c8 and Black was fine in Shaw-Wells, Oakham 1994.

13...hxg6 14 h4

For the moment Hort is careful not to lunge forward with the g-pawn. That would cede the f5 and h5 squares to Black. White would have a promising position if he could find a safe place for his king – he has a superb bishop on g2, and the makings of a pawn storm on the kingside – but that isn't easy. The position of the king also means that the rooks don't connect.

14...♘d4!

A powerful square for the knight: it hits c2 and restricts the movement of White's queen.

15 a4 ♖d8!

As one might expect from Ribli, his strategy is careful and sensible: he clears his pieces from the long diagonal out of the line of the bishop on g2. White can make little progress on the queenside.

16 ♖h3 ♔f8

A curious situation: both kings have been displaced, though this is rather common for this line. Black is right not to castle. In that case he would face the pawn storm.

17 ♔g1 b6 18 ♖c1 ♔g8 19 b3 ♖h7 20 ♔h1 ♖h8 21 g5

Hort can think of no other way to proceed. This does give him a little more room to manoeuvre, but it also gives Black some squares as well.

21...♘e8 22 ♕g4 ♘d6! 23 ♘e4 ♕c8 24 ♘xd6 ♗xd6 25 ♗e4 ♘f5 26 ♔g2 ♗e5 27 ♖ch1 ♖h5 28 ♗f3 ♗d4 29 ♕e4 ♖h8 30 ♗f4 ♕d7 ½–½

Neither side can make much progress. If White breaks with 31 h5, then 31...gxh5 32 ♗xh5 g6 33 ♗g4 ♖xh3 34 ♖xh3 ♔g7 and Black remains solid.

Game 93
Flower-Aseev
London Lloyds Bank Masters 1994

1 e4 c5 2 g3 d5 3 exd5 ♕xd5 4 ♘f3 ♗g4 5 ♗g2 ♕e6+ 6 ♔f1 ♘c6 7 h3 ♗h5 8 d3 ♕d7!

As we saw in the previous game, it is best to delay developing the knight to f6.

9 ♘a3

9 g4 ♗g6 10 ♘h4 e6 11 ♘a3 ♗e7 12 ♘xg6 hxg6 13 ♘c4 ♘f6 14 a4 ♘d5 15 ♗d2 g5 16 a5 ♖d8 was similarly good

for Black in King-Sveshnikov, Neu Isenburg 1992. I thrashed around on the queenside, but eventually the weaknesses in my kingside told. Delaying ...♘f6 enables Black to 'clear up' the situation on the kingside by playing ...♗e7, forcing the capture. Now you know why I prefer to enter the 'Clamp' system via the move order 1 g3 g6 2 ♗g2 ♗g7 3 e4.

9...e6 10 ♘c4 f6

Another reason for delaying ...♘f6. Black has managed to organise the bishop's escape. White now has little to compensate for his poor king position.

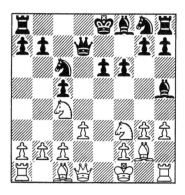

11 ♗e3 ♖d8!

Usually the best square for the rook in this line. White was threatening to break out with g3-g4 and d3-d4.

12 g4 ♗f7 13 a4 b6 14 ♕e2 ♘ge7 15 ♗f4 ♘d5 16 ♗g3 ♗e7 17 h4 0-0 18 h5 h6 19 ♘h4 ♘d4 20 ♕d1 e5 21 g5

Ill-judged, but I don't trust White's position anyway: his king is badly placed and Black is tremendously powerful in the centre.

21...fxg5 22 ♘xe5 ♕e6 23 ♗h3 gxh4 24 ♗xe6 ♗xe6 25 ♔g1 hxg3

26 fxg3 ♘e3 27 ♕d2 ♗g5 0-1

Game 94
Strikovic-Kurajica
Ibercaja Open 1994

1 e4 c5 2 d3 g6 3 g3 ♗g7 4 ♗g2 e6 5 f4 ♘e7 6 ♘f3 0-0 7 0-0 ♘bc6 8 c3

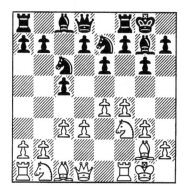

This is one of the basic starting positions of the 'Clamp'. I have found it difficult to organise these Clamp games into a sensible structure. First because of the vast number of games played with the system; and second because there aren't neat lines and established variations to give guidance. Therefore, I have grouped the games according to similar early middlegame plans rather than specific variations. For instance, Games 94-96 feature an early ...d7-d5 from Black; in Games 97-99 Black plays ...e7-e5; and 100-103, others. The difficulties I've had ordering these games reflects one of Black's problems. He does have a wide choice of plans, and to a certain extent may choose how he wishes to position his pawns in the centre; but which is the best? As a White player, I have used the Clamp on several occasions and found that my opponents were often racked by indecision. For the sake of comparison, 8 ♘c3 would be a 'normal' Closed Sicilian.

8...b6

Here's a good example of the indecision I mentioned above: 8...♖b8 9 ♗e3 b6 (if he had wanted to keep playing for ...b7-b5, then 9...d6 was the move) 10 ♘a3 ♗b7 11 ♗f2 d6 12 ♕d2 ♗a6 (another change of mind) 13 ♘c2 e5 (and another!) 14 ♖fe1 exf4 15 gxf4 ♕c7 16 d4 ♖fe8 17 ♖ad1 ♖bd8 18 d5 ♘a5 19 b3 ♗c8 20 ♘e3 ♘b7 21 ♗h4 with an enormous position for White in King-Gunawan, London 1994.

9 ♘a3

As c3 has been taken from the knight, this is probably the best square for it, eyeing c4 and b5. Very often the knight drops back to c2, and then over to e3, in the long-term.

9...♗a6 10 ♖e1 d5

10...d6 is a more patient approach, although the game Shchekachev-Khalifman, St Petersburg Open 1994, showed that even the strongest players in the world aren't entirely at ease on the black side of the position: 11 ♗e3 ♖c8 12 ♗f2 ♕d7 13 ♘c2 ♗b7 14 ♕e2 ♖fe8 15 ♖ad1 a6 16 d4 cxd4 17 ♘fxd4 ♕c7 and White stands more comfortably (this was a good choice of opening against Khalifman who is usually well-versed in the main lines of openings).

11 e5

In general, this kind of pawn structure favours White as he has good chances to build an attack on the king-

side in the long-term. The plan is usually g3-g4 and f4-f5. Obviously, it takes a lot of organising, but the space advantage helps.

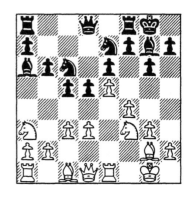

11...d4?!

Black was worried that White was going to play d3-d4 himself (possibly), but this is an over-reaction. Now White can use the e4 square for a bishop or, better, a knight.

12 c4 ♕d7 13 ♘g5! ♘f5 14 ♘c2 ♗b7 15 ♕e2 ♖ae8 16 ♘e4!

White is ready to push with g3-g4, or break with b2-b4 on the queenside. Black has to break himself before he gets squashed, but White still holds the trumps.

16...f6 17 exf6 ♗xf6 18 ♘xf6+ ♖xf6 19 a3 e5 20 ♗d5+ ♖fe6 21 b4! b5 22 bxc5 bxc4 23 ♗xc4 ♔g7 24 ♗xe6 ♖xe6 25 ♖b1 ♗a8 26 ♕f2 ♕d5 27 ♖e4 ♕xc5 28 g4 ♘d6 29 f5 ♘xe4 30 dxe4 ♖e8 31 ♗h6+ ♔g8 32 fxg6 ♘d8 33 ♕f6 ♕c7 34 ♖f1 1-0

Game 95
Kharlov-Sherbakov
Russian Championship, Elista 1994

1 e4 c5 2 d3 g6 3 g3 ♗g7 4 ♗g2

♘c6 5 f4 e6 6 ♘f3 ♘ge7 7 0-0 0-0
8 c3 b6 9 ♗e3

Often they will transpose, but
White can choose to leave the knight
on b1 for a while if he wishes and
perhaps develop it to d2 or, if the centre clears, c3 after all.

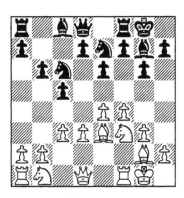

9...♗a6 10 ♘a3

10 ♗f2 ♕c7 (10...e5!? 11 fxe5 ♘xe5
12 ♘xe5 ♗xe5 13 ♖e1 ♗g7 14 d4 ♘c6
15 e5 ♖c8 16 ♘d2 d5 17 a3 cxd4 18
cxd4 f6 was fine for Black in Maki-
Sadler, Tyniste 1995) 11 ♖e1 ♖ae8 12
♘a3 f5 13 d4 (13 e5! looks stronger to
me: 13...d6 14 ♘g5 ♘d8 15 exd6 ♕xd6
16 ♕b3 ♘ec6 17 ♘b5 ♕d7 18 a4)
13...fxe4 14 ♖xe4 c4 worked out well
for Black in Mikac-Zagrebelny, Ljubljana Open 1994.

10...d5 11 e5 f6

Black is wise to play this before it is
too late. Thereafter his position is less
cramped.

12 exf6 ♗xf6 13 ♖e1

13 ♗f2 e5 14 fxe5 ♘xe5 15 ♘xe5
♗xe5 16 ♖e1 ♕d6 17 d4 ♗g7 18 ♗e3
♖ad8 19 ♕a4 was better for White in
Arkhipov-Nevostruev, Vladivostock
1995, but Black isn't obliged to play
...e6-e5.

13...♕d7 14 ♗f2 ♘f5 15 g4 ♘g7 16
♘c2 ♗e7 17 ♗g3 ♖f7 18 ♕d2 ♖af8
19 ♖f1 ♗d6 20 ♘e5 ♘xe5 21 fxe5
♗e7 22 ♖xf7 ♖xf7 23 ♘e1 d4 24 c4
♗b7 25 ♗xb7 ♕xb7 26 ♕g2 ♕xg2+
27 ♔xg2

White is slightly better due to the
poor position of Black's knight on g7,
but it is very hard to making anything
of it.

**27...♘e8 28 ♘f3 a5 29 a3 ♘c7 30
b4 cxb4 31 ♘xd4 bxa3 32 ♘c6 ♗c5
33 d4 ♗f8 34 ♗e1 b5 35 ♗xa5
bxc4 36 ♘d8 ♖d7 37 ♗xc7 ♖xc7 38
♘xe6 ♖a7 39 d5 ♗b4 40 d6 a2 41
d7 ½-½**

Black's opening play was sound and
sensible.

Game 96
Gavrikov-Ivanchuk
USSR Championship, Lvov 1987

**1 e4 e6 2 d3 c5 3 g3 ♘c6 4 ♗g2 g6
5 f4 ♗g7 6 ♘f3 ♘ge7 7 0-0 0-0 8
c3 d5**

Black doesn't mess around and
plays the pawn to d5 straightaway. At
least it is a clear decision.

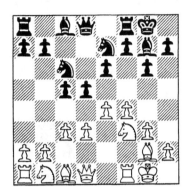

9 e5

It is also possible to wait for a bit before making this push. I like to gain some space on the queenside: 9 a4 b6 10 ♘a3 dxe4 (Black couldn't stand the tension!) 11 dxe4 ♗a6 12 ♘b5 ♕xd1 13 ♖xd1 ♖ad8 14 ♗e3, when my space advantage gave me the better prospects in King-Hausner, Bundesliga 1992.

9...b6

If Black plays ...b7-b5, he might find that the c5 square becomes weak, e.g. 9...b5 10 d4! cxd4 11 cxd4 ♕b6 12 ♗e3 ♗a6 13 ♘c3! ♖fc8 14 ♗f2 ♖c7 15 g4 b4 16 ♘a4 ♕a5 17 ♖e1 ♖ac8 18 ♘c5! (see what I mean) 18...♗f8 19 ♘xa6 ♕xa6 20 ♗f1 ♕b6 21 ♗d3 b3 22 a3 ♘a5 23 ♖e2 ♘c4 24 f5 exf5 25 gxf5 ♘xf5 26 ♗xf5 gxf5 27 ♗h4 with a strong attack in Strikovic-Rodriguez Aguilera, Seville 1994. An excellent example of White's strategy.

10 ♖e1

Also effective was 10 a4!? ♗b7 11 ♘a3 ♘a5?! 12 b4 cxb4 13 cxb4 ♘ac6 14 ♘c2 ♕d7 15 b5 ♘a5 16 ♘cd4 with a dominating position in Prie-Bacrot, Nice 1994.

10...♕d7 11 ♗e3 ♗b7 12 ♗f2 ♖fd8 13 ♘bd2 ♕c7 14 ♖c1 ♘b8 15 ♕e2

♘d7 16 g4 ♖f8 17 ♗g3 ♖ae8 18 d4 ♕c8 19 h3 ♗a6 20 ♕e3 ♗b5 21 ♘b3 ♕c7 22 ♘h4 ♗h6 23 ♘d2 ♕b7 24 ♘hf3 ♕a6 25 ♗h4 ♘c6 26 a3 ♖c8 27 ♗g5 ♗xg5 28 ♘xg5 cxd4 29 cxd4 ♘e7 30 ♕f2 ♖xc1 31 ♖xc1 ♖c8 32 ♕e1 ♖xc1 33 ♕xc1 ♕c8 34 ♕xc8+ ♘xc8 35 f5 gxf5 36 gxf5 ♘f8 37 fxe6 fxe6 38 h4 h6 39 ♘h3 ♘e7 40 ♔f2 ♘f5 41 ♘f3 ♘g6 ½-½

Ivanchuk played with great care, but even he found himself under pressure.

Now we come to games where Black plays his pawn to e5. Note my move order in the next game!

1 g3 c5 2 ♗g2 ♘c6 3 e4 e5 4 d3 g6 5 f4 ♗g7 6 ♘f3 d6 7 0-0 ♘ge7 8 c3 0-0 9 ♘a3

I've reached this position on a couple of occasions. Black must play with great care.

9...b6?

This is an outright blunder. King-Stohl, Bundesliga 1994, continued: 9...d5 10 ♕e1! (Black finds himself in a reversed King's Indian – which favours White) 10...d4 (or 10...exf4 11 gxf4 and White's queen is ready to leap to h4) 11 c4 gave me the better chances, but 11 cxd4 cxd4 12 ♘c4 may have been even stronger). 9...♔h8 10 f5! gxf5 11 ♘h4 fxe4 12 dxe4 ♗e6 13 ♘f5 ♗xf5 14 exf5 f6 15 ♕h5 gave White a strong attack in King-Fossan, Gausdal 1994. However, 9...exf4 is a solid reaction. I've had some blitz games with Joe Gallagher that went 10 gxf4 (10 ♗xf4 is more solid) 10...f5 11 ♕b3+ ♔h8 12 ♘g5 ♘a5!? 13 ♘f7+ ♔g8 and now White can take a draw if he wants to, or play this ending: 14 ♘xd8+ ♘xb3 15 axb3 ♖xd8 which I reckon is better for White and Joe thinks is better for Black. The truth is probably somewhere in between.

10 f5!

If you have already gone through the earlier chapters then this positional pawn sacrifice ought to be familiar.

10...gxf5 11 ♘h4 fxe4 12 dxe4 ♗a6?

Black had to try 12...♗e6 13 ♘f5 ♕d7, but anyway White has great compensation after 14 ♕h5 (14 ♘xg7 ♔xg7 15 ♕h5 also isn't bad).

13 ♖f2 ♕c7 14 ♘c2 ♗c4 15 ♘e3 ♗e6

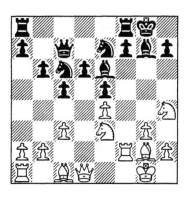

White has gained so much time, that the attack is now irresistible.

16 ♘d5 ♕d7 17 ♘f6+ ♗xf6 18 ♖xf6 ♔h8 19 ♘f5 ♘g8 20 ♗g5 ♖ad8 21 ♕h5 ♘ce7 22 ♘xe7 ♕xe7 23 ♖af1 ♖de8 24 ♗h3 ♗xh3 25 ♖xf7 ♖xf7 26 ♖xf7 ♕xf7 27 ♕xf7 ♖e6 28 ♔f2 ♖g6 29 ♗d8 a6 30 ♔e3 b5 31 ♕f8

♗g4 32 ♗e7 1-0

Black only plays ...e6-e5 later in the game here, but it doesn't look particularly convincing. His structure is just too flimsy.

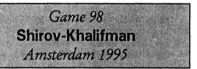

Game 98
Shirov-Khalifman
Amsterdam 1995

1 e4 e6 2 d3 c5 3 g3 ♘c6 4 ♗g2 g6 5 c3 ♗g7 6 ♗e3 d6 7 f4 ♘ge7 8 ♘f3 0-0 9 0-0 b6 10 ♘a3 ♗a6 11 ♖e1 ♕d7

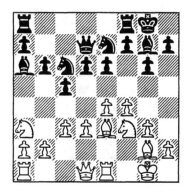

The game which turned Shirov on to this variation was 11...♖c8 12 d4 cxd4 13 ♘xd4 ♘xd4 14 ♗xd4 e5 15 ♗e3 ♕d7 16 ♕b3 exf4 17 ♗xf4 ♖c5 18 ♖ad1 ♗e5 19 ♗xe5 ♖xe5 20 ♘c2 ♗b5 21 ♕a3 ♘c8 22 ♖d4 ♖fe8 23 ♕b3 ♔g7 24 ♘b4 ♘e7 25 ♕d1 ♖d8 26 c4 ♗c6 27 ♕d2 ♘c8 28 ♘d3 ♖e7 29 b4 ♖de8 30 c5 ♕c7 31 cxd6 ♘xd6 32 e5 ♗xg2 33 exd6 1-0 Kaidanov-Shirov, Moscow GMA 1989. A convincing victory. When White manages to achieve d3-d4 in these positions and exchanges the dark-squared bishops, then the combination of weakened kingside and weak pawn on d6 makes life awkward for Black. Like the chap who bought the razor company, Shirov was so impressed he thought he would try the system out himself.

12 ♘c2 e5 13 d4 cxd4 14 cxd4 exd4

This gives the centre to White. Instead, what about 14...exf4 15 gxf4 (15 ♗xf4 is stronger, when White has the slightly better position.) 15...d5 16 e5 ♘f5 with a decent blockade?

15 ♘fxd4 ♖ac8 16 ♕d2 ♘xd4 17 ♘xd4 ♗b7 18 ♖ad1 ♖fd8 19 ♗f2 ♕e8 20 b3 ♕d7 21 a4 a6 22 ♘e2 b5 23 ♗b6 ♖e8 24 a5 ♕e6 25 ♘d4 ♕d7 26 ♖e3 f5 27 ♗h3 d5 28 e5 ♗f8 29 ♗g2 ♗a8 30 ♖d3 ♔h8 31 ♘c2 ♗g7 32 ♘b4 ♗b7 33 ♘xd5 ♘xd5 34 ♗xd5 ♗xd5 35 ♖xd5 ♕e6 36 ♕d3 g5 37 ♖d6 ♕e7 38 ♗d8 ♕f7 39 ♖d7 ♕e6 40 ♗xg5 1-0

1 e4 c5 2 g3 ♘c6 3 ♗g2 g6 4 d3 ♗g7 5 f4 d6 6 ♘f3 e6 7 0-0 ♘ge7 8 c3 0-0 9 ♗e3 b6 10 ♗f2

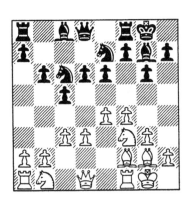

This idea of retreating the bishop

back to f2 before developing the knight on b1 is a popular way of playing the Clamp. One of the advantages is that it is useful for the bishop to be out of range of the knight if White pushes on with e4-e5 after ...d6-d5. However, Black should box clever and meet 10 ♗f2 with ...

10...e5

This is mildly irritating for White as the f4 pawn doesn't have the same support as in the previous game for example.

11 ♘a3

Instead 11 d4? is a blunder: 11...exd4 12 cxd4 ♗g4 13 ♕d2 ♗xf3 14 ♗xf3 ♘xd4 Wagener-Borge, Yerevan Olympiad 1996. 11 f5 is worth a second glance, but obviously isn't as effective with the bishop on f2: 11...gxf5 12 ♘h4 fxe4 13 dxe4 ♗e6 14 ♘f5 d5 15 ♕g4 ♘xf5 16 exf5 ♗c8 17 ♗e3 e4 18 ♗h6 ♕f6 19 ♗g5 ♕e5 20 ♘d2 h5 21 ♕xh5 ♗xf5 22 ♗f6 ♗g6 23 ♗xe5 ♗xh5 24 ♗xg7 ♔xg7 25 ♖f5 ♗g6 26 ♖xd5 f5 27 ♘c4, as in Brandner-Petrone, European Junior Championship, Arnhem 1989.

11...h6

11...exf4 is a more severe test, although according to these games White passes after 12 gxf4 and now:

a) 12...d5 13 ♗h4 f6 14 ♘e5 (an extraordinary move, just to give his queen a decent square) 14...♗e6 (or 14...fxe5 15 exd5 ♕d7 16 dxc6 ♘xc6) 15 ♘xc6 ♘xc6 16 ♕f3 ♘e7 17 ♖ae1 ♗f7 18 f5, as in Yandemirov-Poluljahov, Cheliabinsk 1991.

b) 12...♗h6 13 f5 ♔h8 14 ♗g3 f6 15 ♘b5 gxf5 16 ♘h4 f4 17 ♕h5 fxg3 18 ♕xh6 gxh2+ 19 ♔h1 ♗a6 20 ♖xf6 with a winning attack in De Jong-Damljanovic, Wijk aan Zee 1990.

Alternatively, 11...♖b8 12 ♘c2 exf4 13 gxf4 d5 14 ♗h4 ♕d7 15 ♖e1 ♗b7 16 ♘e3 ♖be8 17 ♕d2 d4 18 ♘c4 ♘c8 19 f5 dxc3 20 bxc3 f6 with a powerful attack. Strikovic-Cabrilo, Yugoslav Team Championship 1993. A common theme in these ♗f2 lines is moving the bishop out to h4, looking at f6 and also pinning the knight.

Finally, 11...♗b7 12 f5 gxf5 13 ♘h4 fxe4 14 dxe4 f5 and now 15 ♘c4 led to random complications in King-Espig, Bundesliga 1995, but 15 ♘xf5 ♘xf5 16 exf5 ♖xf5 17 ♕d3 is simple and strong. White has excellent compensation for the pawn.

12 ♘h4

12 f5!? gxf5 13 ♘h4 isn't Balashov's style, but is worth considering.

12...exf4 13 gxf4 ♖b8 14 ♗g3 f5

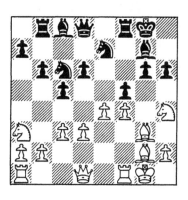

Black is persuaded to play ...f7-f5, blocking White's pawn, but Balashov has realised that because Black has played ...h7-h6, the pawn on g6 has been severely weakened. That's why the knight is sitting on h4. His subtle strategy almost pays off.

15 ♘c2 ♕e8 16 ♘e3 ♕f7 17 ♗f3

♗e6 18 ♕e2 ♖bd8 19 ♕g2

Black's position is about to crack, so Magerramov decides to do it on his terms. He gives up a pawn and survives into an ending.

19...d5 20 ♘xg6 ♕xg6 21 exd5 ♘xd5 22 ♘xd5 ♕f7 23 ♘xb6 axb6 24 ♗xc6 ♖xd3 25 a3 ♖fd8 26 ♖ae1 ♖8d6 27 ♖e2 ♔h7 28 ♖fe1 ♗c4 29 ♗e8 ♕f6 30 ♖e7 ♗d5 31 ♗h4 ♕xe7 32 ♗xe7 ♗xg2 33 ♗xd6 ♗e4 34 ♗c7 ♖d2 35 ♗xb6 ♖g2+ 36 ♔f1 ♖xb2 37 ♗xc5 ♗xc3 38 ♖d1 ♖xh2 39 ♖d7+ ♔h8 40 ♗b4 ♗xb4 41 axb4 h5 42 ♗g6 h4 43 ♖h7+ ♔g8 44 ♖h5 ♖b2 ½-½

In the following game Black hangs back in the centre, retaining a degree of flexibility with his pieces and waiting for White to make the first break. In my experience playing the white side of these positions, I have always found this to be the most difficult strategy to deal with. Should one be advancing on the kingside, or is it best to gain more space in the centre with d3-d4? In these games White mainly advances with d3-d4, though it is also possible to sit tight and then advance on the kingside (Game 103).

> ### Game 100
> ### Minasian-Cao
> *Yerevan Olympiad 1996*

1 e4 c5 2 g3 ♘c6 3 ♗g2 g6 4 d3 ♗g7 5 f4 e6 6 ♘f3 ♘ge7 7 0-0 0-0 8 c3 d6 9 ♗e3 b6 10 ♖e1

Or 10 ♗f2 ♗a6 (10...♕d7 11 ♖e1 h6 12 d4 cxd4 13 cxd4 ♗b7 14 ♘c3 ♔h7 15 h4 ♖ae8 16 ♗h3 f5 17 h5 gxh5 18 d5 exd5 19 exf5 ♘xf5 20 ♖xe8 ♕xe8

21 ♗xf5+ ♖xf5 22 ♕c2 should win for White, as in Makarichev-Dolmatov, USSR Championship 1979) 11 ♖e1 ♕d7 12 ♘a3 ♖ac8 13 d4 cxd4 14 cxd4 (after this Black gets good counterplay on the queenside; 14 ♘xd4! would have been better) 14...d5 15 e5 ♘a5 16 b3 ♖c3 17 ♖e3 ♖xe3 18 ♗xe3 ♖c8, when White is too busy defending on the queenside to develop an attack; Cherniaev-Gallagher, Hastings 1993.

10...♗b7 11 d4

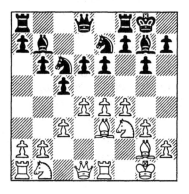

The advantage of playing d3-d4 with the knight still on b1 is that after an exchange of pawns on d4, White may play the knight to its best square, c3. Another example is 11 ♗f2 ♕c7 12 d4 f5? 13 exf5 exf5 14 dxc5 dxc5 15 ♘g5 ♘d8 16 ♗xb7 ♕xb7 17 ♕b3+ with a winning position, as in Braga-Bischoff, Yerevan Olympiad 1996.

11...♕c7 12 ♘a3 ♖ad8 13 ♗f2 h6 14 ♖b1 e5 15 d5 ♘b8 16 c4 ♘c8

The plan White chooses looks powerful at first glance, but Black survives. Perhaps 17 f5 could be considered instead. When the kingside closes, White can play on both wings. Black would then have had a miserable defence ahead of him.

17 h4 ♕e7 18 h5 ♘d7 19 ♘h4 ♕f6 20 hxg6 exf4 21 gxf7+ ♖xf7 22 ♘f5 ♘e7 23 ♗h3 ♘xf5 24 exf5 fxg3 25 ♗xg3 ♘e5 26 ♕h5 ♕g5 27 ♕xg5 hxg5 28 f6 ♖xf6 29 ♗xe5 dxe5 30 ♖e4 ♖f4 31 ♖be1 ♔f8 32 ♘b5 ♗f6 33 ♘xa7 ♖a8 34 ♘c6 ♖xa2 35 ♘xe5 ♔g7 36 ♖xf4 gxf4 37 ♘d3 ♗a6 38 ♘xf4 ♗d4+ 39 ♔h1 ♗xc4 40 d6 ♗b5 41 ♘e6+ ♔f6 42 ♘xd4 cxd4 43 d7 ♗xd7 44 ♗xd7 ♖xb2 45 ♖e6+ ♔g5 46 ♖d6 ♖b4 47 ♔g2 ♔f4 48 ♔f2 ♖b2+ 49 ♔e1 ♔e5 50 ♖h6 d3 51 ♖h4 ♖e2+ 52 ♔d1 ♖e4 53 ♖h6 ♔d4 54 ♖d6+ ♔c5 55 ♖c6+ ♔d4 56 ♖xb6 ♔e3 57 ♗f5 ♖f4 58 ♖e6+ ♔d4 59 ♗g6 ♖f1+ 60 ♔d2 ♖f2+ 61 ♔c1 ♖f1+ 62 ♔b2 ♖g1 63 ♗h5 ♖g2+ 64 ♔b3 ♖g5 65 ♗d1 ♖b5+ 66 ♔a2 ♖e5 67 ♖d6+ ♔c3 68 ♖c6+ ♔d2 69 ♗g4 ♖g5 70 ♖c4 ♖a5+ 71 ♔b3 ♖b5+ 72 ♔a3 ♔e3 73 ♔a2 ♔d2 74 ♖c7 ♔e1 75 ♖e7+ ♔f2 76 ♔a3 ♖g5 77 ♗e6 ½–½

In the next game, unusually for the 'Clamp', White plays an e4-e5 pawn sacrifice similar to that in Chapter 1. The most notable difference is that White can't play his knight to e4. However, White does manage to capture the pawn on c5 and establish a strong pawn chain which is very much as we saw earlier. It just shows that it is worth taking into account lots of different variations as the ideas can often be transferred between them

Game 101
Nadyrhanov-Imanaliev
Bishkek Zonal 1993

1 e4 c5 2 g3 ♘c6 3 ♗g2 g6 4 d3

♗g7 5 f4 e6 6 ♘f3 ♘ge7 7 0-0 0-0 8 c3 d6 9 ♗e3 ♖b8 10 ♗f2 b6 11 ♘a3

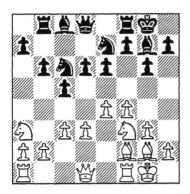

11...b5

Once again we see evidence of indecision. Black has option paralysis. He can't just follow variations by rote.

12 e5 a6

12...dxe5 13 fxe5 ♘xe5 14 ♘xe5 ♗xe5 15 ♗xc5 followed by d3-d4 is more comfortable for White to play than Black, although with hindsight this is stronger than the game continuation.

13 ♖e1 h6 14 ♕e2 ♗b7 15 ♘c2 dxe5 16 fxe5 ♕c7 17 a4 g5

17...b4!? might have been better. In the game the open a-file is decisive.

18 axb5 axb5 19 ♗xc5 ♘xe5 20 d4 ♘xf3+ 21 ♗xf3 ♗xf3 22 ♕xf3 ♕b7 23 ♕xb7 ♖xb7 24 ♘b4 ♖c8 25 ♖a6 ♗f8 26 ♔f2 ♘f5 27 ♗xf8 ♔xf8 28 ♖e5 ♖c4 29 d5 ♖c5 30 ♖c6 ♖xc6 31 dxc6 ♖b6 32 ♖xf5 1-0

In the last two games Black lashes out with ...f7-f5, which is an understandable reaction: He isn't exactly sure where his play is coming from, and this looks like a constructive way of putting pressure on White's centre.

The move isn't quite as effective as in the earlier chapters as White has the crucial d4 square covered.

> ## Game 102
> ## Parker-Hennigan
> *British Championship 1995*

1 f4 g6 2 ♘f3 ♗g7 3 g3 c5 4 ♗g2 ♘c6 5 e4 e6 6 0-0 ♘ge7 7 d3 0-0 8 c3 d6 9 ♗e3 f5 10 ♘bd2 ♖b8 11 a4

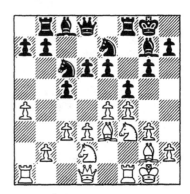

I don't like a2-a4 in this position. First and foremost, I don't think that Black was actually threatening ...b7-b5, at least not if White develops his queen, e.g. 11 ♕e2 b5 12 e5! (an echo of the previous game), when the c5 pawn becomes vulnerable. It is also possible to play the queen to c2, but I prefer it on e2 keeping an eye on the e-file – see the next game.

11...b6 12 d4 fxe4

12...cxd4 13 ♘xd4 ♘xd4 14 cxd4 (not 14 ♗xd4 e5!) 14...fxe4 15 ♘xe4 ♘d5 16 ♗f2 is better for White if he plays on e6 with ♖e1, ♕b3, ♘g5, and so on.

13 ♘xe4 ♘f5 14 ♗f2 d5 15 ♘eg5 h6

Eventually Black pays for having

weakened his kingside pawns.

16 ♘h3 cxd4 17 cxd4 ♗d7 18 ♖e1 ♖c8 19 ♖c1 ♘b4 20 ♖xc8 ♕xc8 21 g4 ♘e7 22 ♘e5 ♗xe5 23 fxe5 ♘c2 24 ♖f1 ♗xa4 25 ♕d2 ♔g7 26 ♗h4 ♘g8 27 ♘f4 g5 28 ♘h5+ ♔h8 29 ♗f2 ♕c4 30 ♖c1 a5 31 ♗f1 ♕b4 32 ♖xc2 ♗xc2 33 ♕xc2 ♕e7 34 ♗e3 ♕h7 35 ♗d3 ♕f7 36 ♗e2 ♕h7 37 ♕xh7+ ♔xh7 38 ♗d3+ ♔h8 39 ♗d2 ♘e7 40 ♗c3 ♘c6 41 ♘f6 ♖f7 42 ♗b5 ♖c7 43 ♔f2 ♘b4 44 ♔e3 ♘a2 45 ♔d3 ♘xc3 46 bxc3 ♖a7 47 c4 dxc4+ 48 ♗xc4 ♖e7 49 ♗b5 ♔g7 50 ♗d7 b5 51 ♗xb5 ♖b7 52 ♘e8+ ♔f8 53 ♘d6 ♖b8 54 ♔c4 ♔e7 55 d5 ♖f8 56 ♘e4 exd5+ 57 ♔xd5 ♖b8 58 ♘d6 ♔f8 59 ♔c6 ♔e7 60 ♔d5 ♔f8 61 ♔e6 ♖a8 62 ♔f6 ♖d8 63 ♘f5 ♖b8 64 e6 ♖b6 65 ♗d7 1-0

To finish, appropriately enough, a win from the great champion of the Closed Sicilian. It is interesting to see that he plays the Clamp in his own style, more in keeping with the traditional Closed Sicilian strategy rather than the games we have been looking at so far with the system.

Game 103
Spassky-Hoffmann
Lugano Open 1982

---

1 e4 c5 2 d3

Note Spassky's move order – see my comments on this in the introduction to the chapter.

2...e6 3 g3 ♘c6 4 ♗g2 g6 5 f4 ♘ge7 6 ♘f3 ♗g7 7 0-0 0-0 8 c3 d6 9 ♘a3 b6

Black pushed the b-pawn to b5 in Damljanovic-Jukic, Cetinje 1990, but

White got the better position: 9...♖b8 10 ♘c2 b5 11 a3 a5 12 ♗d2 b4 13 axb4 axb4 14 ♘e3 ♗d7 15 g4 bxc3 16 bxc3 f5 17 gxf5 exf5 18 ♘c4 fxe4 19 dxe4 ♗e6 20 ♕e2 h6 21 ♖a6 and White has uncomfortable pressure. We can see how important it is to have the pawn on c3, preventing Black's knight from arriving on d4.

10 ♘c2 ♗b7

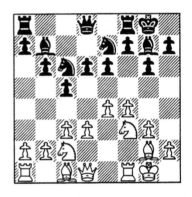

11 ♕e2

Sharply played. It has not escaped Spassky's attention that Black's e6 square is weakened as the bishop has moved to b7. The significance of this becomes apparent later on, although I'm sure that Spassky just played ♕e2 on intuition.

11...♕d7 12 ♗d2 ♖ac8 13 ♖ae1 ♖fe8 14 ♗c1 ♖cd8 15 g4! f5 16 ♘g5 h6

If 16...fxe4 17 ♕xe4 e5 18 fxe5 ♗xe5 19 ♘f7 gives White a ferocious attack.

17 exf5 exf5 18 ♘e6 ♖b8 19 g5 h5 20 ♘xg7 ♔xg7 21 ♕e6 ♖bd8 22 ♕f6+ ♔g8 23 c4 ♖f8 24 ♗d5+ ♔h7 25 ♗f7 ♗a8 26 ♘e3 ♖g8 27 ♘d5 ♘xd5 28 cxd5 ♖g7 29 dxc6 ♕xc6 30 ♗xg6+ 1-0

Summary

The Clamp has an excellent reputation. I might add that in my own games, my opponents have experienced great difficulty in finding a constructive plan. This variation is not always to the taste of Sicilian players who are not used to waiting before getting down to hand-to-hand fighting. The problem is, how to reach it. 1 e4 c5 2 g3 d5! has its drawbacks (if Black plays accurately – see Game 93 in particular); otherwise, 2 d3 is a bit lame, and 1 g3 can lead anywhere; likewise 1 f4. If you want to try the Clamp, it is a case of weighing up which is the lesser evil.

1 e4 c5 2 g3 ♘c6
> 2...d5 3 exd5 ♕xd5 4 ♘f3 ♗g4 5 ♗g2 ♕e6+ 6 ♔f1 *(D)*
>> 6...♗h3 – *Game 91*
>> 6...♘c6 7 h3 ♗h5
>>> 8 ♘c3 – *Game 92*; 8 d3 – *Game 93*

3 ♗g2 g6 4 d3 ♗g7 5 f4 e6
> 5...e5 – *Game 97*

6 ♘f3 ♘ge7 7 0-0 0-0 8 c3 *(D)* b6
> 8...d5 – *Game 96*
> 8...d6
>> 9 ♗e3
>>> 9...b6 *(D)*
>>>> 10 ♘a3 – *Game 98*; 10 ♗f2 – *Game 99*;
>>>> 10 ♖e1 – *Game 100*
>>> 9...♖b8 – *Game 101*
>>> 9...f5 – *Game 102*
>> 9 ♘a3 – *Game 103*

9 ♘a3
> 9 ♗e3 – *Game 94*

9...♗a6 – *Game 95*

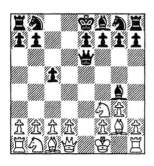

6 ♔f1

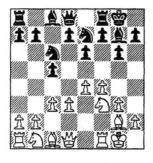

8 c3

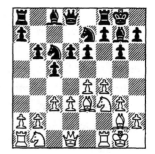

9...b6

INDEX OF GAMES

CPSIA information can be obtained
at www.ICGtesting.com
Printed in the USA
BVHW042307270221
600953BV00004B/50